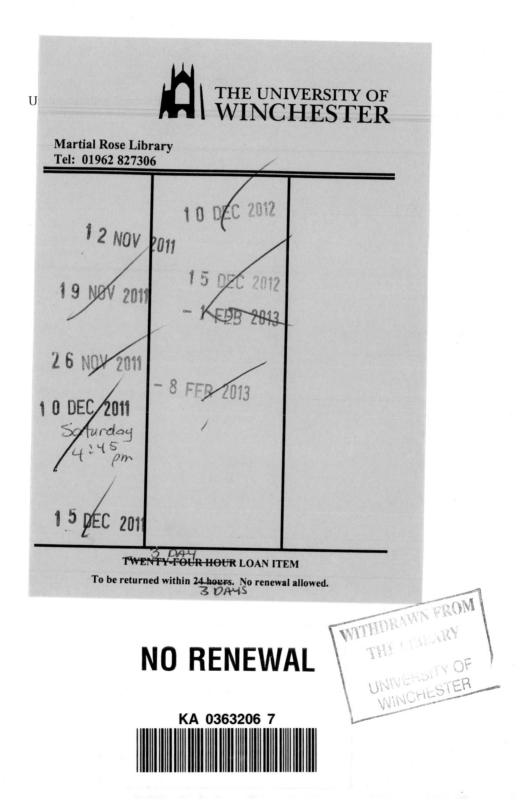

For my students, especially Abby, Helen, Katy and Rhonda, and in memory of Jane

Understanding Inequalities

Stratification and Difference

LUCINDA PLATT

polity

The right of Lucinda Platt to be identified as Author of this Work has been asserted in accordance with the UK Copyright, Designs and Patents Act 1988.

First published in 2011 by Polity Press

Polity Press
65 Bridge Street
Cambridge CB2 1UR, UK

Polity Press
350 Main Street
Malden, MA 02148, USA

ISBN-13: 978-0-7456-4175-1
ISBN-13: 978-0-7456-4176-8 (pb)

A catalogue record for this book is available from the British Library.

Typeset in 9.5 on 12 pt Utopia
by Servis Filmsetting Ltd, Stockport, Cheshire
Printed and bound in Great Britain by MPG Books Group Limited, Bodmin, Cornwall

The publisher has used its best endeavours to ensure that the URLs for external websites referred to in this book are correct and active at the time of going to press. However, the publisher has no responsibility for the websites and can make no guarantee that a site will remain live or that the content is or will remain appropriate.

Every effort has been made to trace all copyright holders, but if any have been inadvertently overlooked the publisher will be pleased to include any necessary credits in any subsequent reprint or edition.

For further information on Polity, visit our website: www.politybooks.com

Contents

Figures, Tables and Boxes

Tables

Acknowledgements

I would like to thank Emma Longstaff of Polity, who originally encouraged me to start thinking about this book, and Jonathan Skerrett, who saw it through to completion with remarkable patience and with helpful and constructive comments. It has been a pleasure to work with him. I have drawn on the contributions of many scholars, and I am grateful to all those who allowed me to reproduce illustrations from their work or from our joint work. Much of this book draws on ideas developed through teaching in the Sociology Department at the University of Essex, and I worked on it while at the Institute of Social and Economic Research, also at the University of Essex. Essex is a stimulating and supportive workplace, and I learnt much on issues of inequality and difference from colleagues in both departments. I also learnt much about stratification and mobility from attendance at the meetings of the Research Committee 28 of the International Sociological Association. David Colclough provided detailed and invaluable comments on two chapters, as well as consistent encouragement. My thinking about inequality gained much from the work of and conversation with Stephen Jenkins, from whom I have learnt a huge amount. I am grateful for the comments of three reviewers who took the trouble to comment in detail on the book, one of whom additionally sent helpful comments on the revised version. As a result of their suggestions and comments, I believe the book is much stronger – and more readable. The manuscript was substantially advanced while I was visiting the Melbourne Institute during autumn 2009 and was completed while taking up a Marie Curie Fellowship at the Institute of Economic Analysis (IAE), Barcelona, during 2010. I am grateful to the directors of both institutes, Mark Wooden and Clara Ponsati, for their hospitality and for providing such excellent working environments. Since much of this book started life in the seminar room, it is dedicated to the students with whom I shared so many happy and stimulating exchanges. In particular, it is for Jane Brown, whose tragic loss following her early death in December 2010 is keenly felt.

1 Introduction

1.1 The importance of inequality

Inequality and its counterpart, equality, are words of many meanings. Inequality is deployed in diverse settings by a range of actors. It is both assumed as a fact of everyday life and denounced as an offence to a civilized society. Inequality and the discussions and debates associated with it are rediscovered and rehearsed anew over time and in changing contexts. Many of these debates have been central concerns since the early days of sociological investigation, but are reworked for the purposes of and to meet the needs required by policy makers, politicians, academics, campaigners, and individuals seeking to make sense of their lives. They are underpinned by normative perspectives on human motivation and the way that society functions, perspectives which themselves are subject to re-creation as different discourses come to dominate and shape people's thinking (Foucault [1969] 1972).

In political and popular discourse, inequality emerges as lack of opportunity, as the counterpart to effort and achievement, as simply differences between people, as well as an expression of the disadvantage suffered by vulnerable groups in society. In this last use (in)equalities can even become synonymous with the definitions of groups themselves or the more general promotion of equalities. For example, the body responsible for overseeing the implementation of anti-discrimination law in the UK, the Equalities and Human Rights Commission, refers to protected groups in the language of equalities groups.

Inequalities can be distinguished in terms of whether they are inequalities of opportunity, inequalities of outcome, inequalities of access or inequalities in entitlement, and are also differentiated as to whether they are just or unjust, avoidable or unavoidable, 'natural' or artificially sustained. At the same time these uses often merge or overlap, creating apparent contradictions or confusions, or resulting in slippages that allow for different understandings of inequality to operate side by side. One person's equality is another's inequality.

This introduction sets out to describe some of these uses of the terms equality and inequality, to disentangle them in relation to the underlying concepts and literatures from which they derive, and to help reveal how they are reworked in practice. In particular it highlights how commitment to equality may operate alongside the acceptance of wide inequalities between individuals or groups of people. Separating the more technical usage of commonplace words from the general currency is something with which sociologists have continually to engage, and this often requires some compromise between the two to facilitate communication outside the academy. This is, for example, a particular conundrum for researchers on 'race' and ethnicity: how to reveal the inequalities faced by marginalized groups without acceding to the language of race, which is obsolete and theoretically discredited (Banton 1998).

The first part of this chapter is, then, concerned with concepts and definitions. Providing an account of the conceptual and definitional issues in discussing inequality leads to an outline of how terms for inequality/inequalities are used in this book and how they apply across social groups. The second part considers more directly the coverage of the book: what is included and what is excluded, which groups are considered as subject to inequalities and on what basis. It asks: What are the major inequalities that affect people's lives, and how do they vary with circumstances? It also treats the question of the extent to which individual bases of inequality can be considered separately and how far the experience of inequality always has to be considered in a multifaceted or intersectional context. Finally the introduction outlines the structure of the book and the key features that appear across chapters as well as those that are distinctive within chapters.

Inequality in policy and research

Inequality is a longstanding subject of sociological concern. It is implicit in research on stratification as well as on poverty, wealth and the varying aspects of social position. These concerns and bodies of sociological research often reappear in new forms in the mouths of politicians and others who help to frame the ways we think about our society. Discussions of inequality and cognate issues such as poverty have arguably come to much greater prominence in political debate in recent decades and have developed corresponding commonsense meanings that have their own logics and contradictions. Overall, there appears to be a widespread acknowledgement of the value of equality and its promotion within policy and society. But that support for equality can be found on close inspection to be bounded.

We have, for example, seen 'equality of opportunity' strongly endorsed as *social mobility* has moved into the political limelight. Social mobility has for decades proved a major component of the sociology of stratification and the subject of some of the pioneering works of British sociology, from Glass's (1954) study onwards. It is also an area of sociological analysis that has been considered worthy of extended contention and critique (Crompton 1998) and subject to the promotion of alternative analytical approaches. However, despite a range of rigorous studies in recent years, class analysis and investigations of social mobility have ceased to be regarded as so central to much contemporary British sociology, though they remain a thriving area in the international arena. The fact that it is now such a key concern of both left and right suggests that this is a good moment to reconsider both the implications of a commitment to a particular concept of equality implied by social mobility and the contribution to our understanding that sociological analyses have to offer. Social mobility and an open society, though widely regarded as 'good things', raise a number of problems for the realization of a just society and demand scrutiny of what might be regarded as fair outcomes for individuals. These problems typically remain unacknowledged at the level of political debate.

We also see increasing attention paid to inequality as *difference* in all its facets in the policy arena. Intersectionality, developed, refined and debated within feminist theory, is now a core term for policy organizations such as the Equality and Human

Rights Commission, where attempts to mainstream it, to pin it down and to operationalize it in relation to an extended set of inequality 'domains' are accompanied by a revival of debates in the sociological and policy literature on its proper usage and its shifting application. Furthermore, inequality in everyday lives is picked up in policy concerns with work–life balance, which have begun to appropriate insights from research and analysis into the domestic division of labour that challenged the earlier tendency of sociology to focus on the 'public sphere'. Political anxieties about 'new' immigration struggle to incorporate some of the shifts in the recognition and understanding of 'others' beyond the (post)colonial context. Who is different, who is unequal, and to what extent explicit inequalities or differentiated opportunities are justified are questions raised by highlighting the experience of marginalized and continually redefined outsiders. Moreover, such debates show how much internal inclusion and emphasis on local equalities is predicated on a process of boundary setting, albeit the boundaries of who is included and who excluded remain somewhat indistinct and have been subject to continual reworking since the earliest immigration legislation. New boundaries and new inequalities also come to the fore in the recent emphasis on religious inequality and difference – an emphasis which both stimulates and feeds on the expansion of sociological investigation into religious minorities and on the intersection of religious affiliation with more traditional interpretations of ethnic difference.

In these – and other – ways, (in)equality is very much in the mainstream of political debate. Yet in its very prominence there is a risk that concepts, and the differences between uses of equality, become blurred. It often appears that the contradictions between promotion of equality and simultaneous implementation of measures that perpetuate inequalities are not fully recognized. For example, we can observe the consensus that has developed among politicians from both sides of the political spectrum in espousing social mobility, fairness and the fact that children should not be constrained in their opportunities by accidents of birth. This occurs at the same time as an increase in economic inequality. It also coincides with an increasing tendency for sanctions against those who do not engage in paid work to be built into the changing form of the UK's (and other countries') welfare states, with punitive and derogatory language referring to the 'workshy' and limited support for those not in employment. These are tendencies which have been found as much under 'left' as under 'right' governments. On the one hand, equality of opportunity is regarded as fundamental and in accordance with the right of everyone to 'get on', presupposing that there must be some who do not make it; on the other hand, the belief in human motivation does not extend to those who cannot for whatever reason achieve; instead they are considered to require external inducements – or penalties – and to lack the motivation that is part of the argument for justifying inequalities in the first place.

Moreover, such contradictions are not limited to politicians but extend across the population. Studies have highlighted the contradictions and paradoxes of individuals' responses to inequality and the fact that, in recent decades, a decline in egalitarianism has taken place at the same time as widening economic inequality (Orton and Rowlingson 2007). Among the public there is, for example, an intolerance of large income gaps at the same time that there is a widespread popular belief that economic inequalities are justified and that those who do better 'deserve' it (Bamfield and Horton 2009; Park et al. 2010). Large inequalities of socio-economic position are not only tolerated but even endorsed, and merit is seen as underpinning inequalities, even when the arbitrary nature of some rewards, such as inheritances, is acknowledged. Such contradictions have been explained in terms of psychological adaptation in the tendency to rationalize others' success, but also to locate oneself in relation to others in such a way as to minimize the conflict between attitudes and personal reality. Runciman's ([1966] 1972) influential discussion of relative deprivation illustrated the power of 'reference groups' in rationalizing inequalities and incongruities in position. More recently, others have discussed the tendency of individuals to underplay both the random and structural features of society which benefit some while harming others. For example, Sayer points to the lay morality that tends towards the belief that rewards stem from actions which merit them and that 'even the unlucky may prefer to avoid the pain of resentment' by assuming that wealth is earned or entitled. At the same time, 'belief in a just world motivates actors to both be moral and to blame the unfortunate and disregard injustice, by attributing disadvantage to personal failure' (2005, p. 957).

To grasp the implications and compromises of these political and social formulations of the meanings of injustice and inequality, and to gain the ability to challenge or resist the dominant ways of talking about them, requires us to pay attention to the logic and illogic in which inequality is understood and used. It involves breaking down some of the inherent contradictions in concepts relating to equality and inequality. This introduction aims to elucidate distinctions between equality and fairness, the internally contradictory notion of equal opportunity, the distinction between entitlement and desert, and the distinction and interconnection between concepts of inequality and difference. One central issue is the consideration of inequality within society (or within groups) compared with inequality between social groups. While the implications are apparently rather different if a focus is on overall inequality rather than on inequalities between groups within a society – who themselves may have very different outcomes – the two are not in fact neatly separable. Differences between groups imply general social inequality, and the greater the inequality the more serious the potential inequalities faced by specific groups: an attempt to contrast the two approaches may be somewhat misleading (Hills et al. 2010).

Moreover, a further distinction can be found in relation to whether we focus on groups defined by their (potential) inequality – such as disabled people – or whether we focus on unequal circumstances – such as poverty – which are suffered more by some groups than others. Both ways of looking at intergroup inequalities are pertinent to describing and understanding them, and this book aims to balance these two approaches, treating, for example, class as a social grouping – albeit one often considered in economic terms – but income as an experience, which may differ across social groups. The two approaches are explicitly brought together in chapter 8, where disability and health inequalities are discussed side by side. Disability tends to be conceived of as defining a group facing inequalities and health inequalities as operating across social groups. But the distinction is partly broken down by drawing attention to the overlap between ill health and disability – in measurement even if not in theory.

Before moving on to these conceptual issues in more detail, and the implications for the coverage and structure of the book as a whole, it is worth emphasizing briefly why inequalities matter and what they mean to individuals. There are increasingly strong arguments, led in large part by the body of work developed by Richard Wilkinson, that (economic) inequality is bad for societies and bad for individuals, regardless of where they are placed in the social hierarchy. In *The Spirit Level* (2009), Wilkinson and Kate Pickett enumerated the ills of inequality. These were all at society level. As they graphically summarized: 'Across whole populations, rates of mental illness are five times higher in the most unequal compared to the least unequal societies. Similarly, in more unequal societies, people are five times as likely to be imprisoned, six times as likely to be clinically obese, and murder rates may be many times higher' (Wilkinson and Pickett 2009, p. 176). The authors highlight the fact that inequality brings social costs. It is bad for human societies and, in general, those who live in unequal states.

At the individual level, inequalities on the basis of social class can mean, quite simply, having fewer years of life to live. Inequalities on the basis of disability can mean reduced opportunities for achieving educational qualifications and all that that implies across the life course. Inequalities on the basis of ethnicity can increase chances of being unemployed, or of being in poorly paid work, and can result in higher chances of being the victim of violence. Gender inequalities can mean lower lifetime incomes for women and greater possibilities of being poor in old age. The inequalities faced by disabled people, ethnic minorities, women, and those from lower social classes can involve daily humiliations of being patronized, insulted, demeaned or denigrated. While some perpetrators may be relatively unaware of the damage they are doing in these cases, such persistent 'low-level' discrimination can effect psychological or emotional damage and impact on self-perception, aspirations and overall engagement with society (Reay 2005). The impacts can be internalized as shame (Sayer 2005; Skeggs 1997) as well as resentment, anger and lack of self-worth. Inequalities mean some people having fewer or no choices to live their lives in ways that others take for granted. They can limit mobility, work, income, social opportunities, access to justice, health and happiness. They matter.

This recognition that inequalities are of fundamental importance to both the welfare of societies and the well-being of individuals is the rationale for revealing, analysing and attempting to understand them. An investigation of inequalities is not an academic exercise but is fundamental to grasping how people live, how they relate to and are treated by others, and how those relationships are maintained or altered. The chapter now goes on to consider issues of what is 'fair' – a term often considered synonymous with 'equal', but which can also be used to justify and maintain inequalities of income, class or social position – before moving on to address the relationship between common ideas of fairness and wider inequalities of social or economic position. I then tease out questions of inequality between, as opposed to inequality within, what I here term 'social groups'. The concluding chapter returns to a consideration of 'social groups'.

1.2 Equality and inequality: concepts and definitions

What is fair?

Despite widespread approval of opportunity, mobility and versions of equality, these concepts are not straightforward: they are subject to intense sociological debate and are beset by questions of value and worth. If people should receive their 'desert', how are we to judge what they deserve? In fact discussions of opportunity and mobility are riven by contests over what such concepts actually mean, and over the nature of competition and reward as well as which inequalities we should care about and which are 'natural'. Are inequalities which arise simply because of the way a society structures its opportunities and rewards acceptable – or even desirable? After all, in democratic nations, those structures can presumably be said to command popular support.

General commitments to 'fairness' among politicians and the public in fact disguise the extent to which there is little agreement as to what fairness might consist in – not to mention how it might be achieved. And they hedge issues of whether an unequal society is really undesirable or is instead not only unavoidable but positively to be welcomed – leading to the apparent contradictions noted above. An emphasis on 'fairness' can encompass egalitarianism or highly differentiated outcomes in wealth, health and other resources. The meaning of 'fairness', and the ways it interpenetrates inequality and equality, is influenced both by normative perspectives on how the world and those who populate it function and by the organizing principles of societies. Attitudes hinge on considerations of what it is that brings economic stability, welfare, prosperity and comfort to citizens and what is desirable in a 'good society'. In this light, is inequality necessary or does it impede the effective functioning of societies and states? Even if inequality is undesirable in some ways, is intervention even more undesirable in terms of introducing distortions into 'natural' processes?

Views on fairness thus link to views on wider social processes, which can often seem inevitable to those caught up in them, and views of human motivation and capacity, which, by contrast, lead to assumptions that all those who wish to succeed are in a position to do so (Bamfield and Horton 2009). This dualism between an acceptance of deterministic 'structures' and an acknowledgement of individual agency has been a source of debate and struggle within sociology and the ongoing 'structure–agency' divide. To what extent are individuals products of the structures within which they operate or to what extent are they able to engage with the world – and prosper or fail in it according to their own actions and choices?

Following criticisms that an overriding emphasis on social structure denies the ways in which individuals can and do act and understand those actions, substantial attention has been paid within sociological theory to the question of how individual agency can be acknowledged without dismissing the constraints that clearly restrict people's lives. For example, Giddens's structuration theory argued for a way of integrating an acknowledgement of the power and relevance of both social structures *and* individual agency, by suggesting that it is 'in and through their activities [that] agents reproduce the conditions that make these activities possible' (Giddens 1984). In repetition of action, over time structures come into being that themselves shape action, but these actions are undertaken self-consciously or 'reflexively'. Nevertheless, the notion of reflexivity and the self-consciousness of individual actions has itself been substantially critiqued. The model can be seen as excessively individualized, and its implication that actors have the capacity both to reflect on and to make choices about individual acts underplays the role of situational and relational factors in influencing what people do and when they do it. People do not act in a vacuum, nor do they necessarily act consistently in line with considered perspectives, but respond differently to different sets of circumstances not necessarily in reliable ways.

Perceptions of possibilities are themselves shaped by context and influenced by those by whom they are surrounded. Such perceptions, even if not 'realistic' in terms of actual opportunities, may be influential nevertheless on subsequent behaviour, expectations and views on fairness and injustice.

The recognition of the limits on agency is important in modifying the assumptions that equality of opportunity will necessarily result in fair outcomes. Opportunities are conditioned by circumstances and histories, and finding a starting point from which to consider opportunities as equal can lead to a vanishing point. On the other hand, allowing a role for agency (including recognizing the ways that agency operates relationally and situationally) avoids a deterministic perspective, whereby inequalities become unavoidable and irremediable. Lives are not fully predictable, and differences across individuals and variations in otherwise similar sets of circumstances may lead to widely different futures.

Opportunity as equality

Equality of opportunity is the freedom to pursue success, achievement or individual goals unimpeded by artificial constraints. Any resulting inequalities that remain in society are then considered both natural and fair. Equality of opportunity does not imply equality in society. Indeed, the implication is that, because human beings are different and have different talents, interests and preferences, there will be substantial overall inequality. By contrast, those concerned with inequality of outcome evaluate fairness by the extent to which there are disparities in outcomes, be they in income, education or health. These are themselves revealing of the way that society is organized and of its systems of reward and allocation.

Equality of opportunity is often used to refer specifically to social mobility – equal chances for those from different backgrounds of ending up in either high or low social positions (Neckerman and Torche 2007). I discuss the debates around social mobility further in chapter 2. But it can in theory apply to any situation where the assumption is that differences in circumstances at birth (or at various crucial points in life) should not affect the possibilities for realizing one's potential. This is demonstrated by the use of the term in an employment-related context. For example, we may consider whether opportunities for promotion or retention are equivalent across otherwise similar people with different backgrounds. If none are obstructed, even if not all can be promoted, we may be confident that we have equality of opportunity. Equally, we might look at the extent to which those who are best qualified do actually succeed. This perspective accords primacy to the potential of human agency as long as it is enabled by the removal of obstacles. All those who are potentially eligible for promotion can take their chance. There should be a level playing field, but, once given that, everyone should be left to themselves. This does assume, however, that all those 'eligible' will encounter the same expectations, have similar information and respond equally well to the conditions placed on them, over and above their ability to fulfil the higher-level post.

Since we can rarely actually determine whether people have equality of opportunity, it has to be inferred. Typically, in the case of measuring social mobility, its *absence* is inferred simply on the basis that those with different social backgrounds have systematically different outcomes. Given the assumption that abilities and talents will be evenly distributed across the population, any resulting association between social background and outcomes is interpreted as problematic – as evidence of lack of opportunity. The fact that, if there is no association between background and outcomes, there may still be large disparities between the successful and the non-successful is not regarded as of concern, since these disparities are understood to represent individual differences in talent, motivation and hard work, or in preferences for particular types of lifestyle or behaviour, and therefore worthy of differential success or reward. Indeed, some would argue that large inequalities of outcome encourage social mobility, since they provide motivation for success. Moreover, in order to establish that there is social mobility, it is necessary that people come from different backgrounds in the first place, or opportunities to rise and fall would not be available.

Those concerned to emphasize equality of outcome would, by contrast, be interested in correcting the disadvantage and attempting to get rid of the biggest disparities in social position, regardless of the cumulative series of actions that may have led to them. Indeed, they would see that correction of disadvantage as a precondition for enabling mobility. Rather than allowing those at the bottom of the social or income or class hierarchy to rise (and those at the top to fall), an alternative would be to reduce the difference between the top and the bottom of the heap, thus removing the salience of the gap between them. While this might seem a logical alternative towards achieving more equal chances across society, it is often resisted, as allowing insufficiently for genuine differences between individuals. Nevertheless, despite the emphasis in political discourse on mobility and opportunity as the means to a just society, it has often been merged with a case for addressing current inequalities – at least making some impact on the situation of those right at the bottom of the distribution, who lack mobility or who have fallen the furthest. This is justified in terms of enabling future opportunity, even if an explicit egalitarian agenda is eschewed (Acheson 1998; DWP 2005). By such means it becomes possible to avoid some of the more difficult implications of a 'strong' version of equal opportunity, which contains no commitment to addressing contemporary inequalities *per se*.

By merging consideration of outcomes with attention to opportunity – or the realization of potential – it is possible to dodge the insight that equality of opportunity makes sense only in the context of inequality of outcomes. As a result, the implication that inequality is being sanctioned in one form as it is being discredited in another is glossed over. We can see the interconnectedness of opportunity and inequality more clearly if we turn to some of the defences of inequality as being desirable, unproblematic or necessary in its own right (Hayek 1945; Marshall et al. 1997; Nozick 1974; Rawls 1971). Box 1.1 summarizes the reasons as to why inequality is regarded by some as not only defensible but also a state to be aspired to. It clearly illustrates how individual opportunity and societal inequalities are closely linked in these positions.

These arguments are both persuasive and accord to a substantial degree with common perceptions of the way the world works, at least in the West. However, it is worth elaborating some of the critiques of these claims, as they can demonstrate the fundamental complexities not only in describing and accounting for inequalities but also in responding to them. Crucially, the opposition of these positions and their critics shows that inequality is multifaceted and that reducing inequalities in one area may create others: some claims for equality are balanced against others. These are topics that are a particular feature of the discussion in chapter 3, but recur throughout the book.

Box 1.1   Defences of inequality

- It enables people to achieve their potential, to know what they have is their entitlement.
- It values freedom, which is often considered to be an essential or fundamental value: once allowed certain freedoms, people are able to fulfil their own trajectories and to be rewarded or suffer according to their deserts.
- It values equality of opportunity, and the outcomes can take care of themselves.
- It is intuitively sensible at the individual level: each person knows that there are differences in talent and in application – therefore these should be somehow differentially rewarded.
- It creates incentives: people will feel motivated to aim for the top as long as they believe that any position is potentially open to them.
- A gap between those better off and those worse off is not a problem as long as those at the bottom do not fall further behind.
- Fundamental freedoms are only achieved if inequality is allowed.
- The market will not operate successfully unless inequality is at least a potential outcome. The regulation of talent or of gifts – 'innate', 'inherited' or transferred (income or personal) – is more dangerous and damaging than allowing such talents to get themselves where they will.

Box 1.1 demonstrates the variety of positions that have been used to defend inequality (of outcome). And, as the link between *equality* of opportunity and *inequality* of outcome immediately shows, the defences of inequality are defences of inequality in some domains but not in others. Making these points more emphatically, Marshall and his colleagues stated that

> What we find in most non-philosophical efforts to justify inequality is a combination of arguments from desert, merit, entitlement, equality of opportunity, and functionality, without any clear recognition that these may involve disparate, and in some cases incompatible, assumptions. On the one hand, there is nothing wrong with people climbing the social ladder as long as it is through their own efforts, while on the other they are entitled to pass on their advantage to their children. Unequal outcomes are justified both on the grounds that they are needed to give people incentives, and so contribute to social justice by helping the poor, and because they give individuals what they deserve. Clearly, conceptions of justice that validate some forms of inequality may invalidate others. (Marshall et al. 1997, pp. 12–13)

Equality of what?

The issue of the choice between different forms of equality is one that Sen has cogently elaborated.

> If a claim that inequality in some significant space is right (or good, or acceptable, or tolerable) is to be defended by reason (not by, say, shooting the dissenters), the argument takes the form of showing this inequality to be a consequence of *equality* in some other – more centrally important – space. Given the broad agreement on the need to have equality in the 'base', and also the connection of that broad agreement

> with this deep need of impartiality between individuals . . ., the crucial arguments
> have to be about the reasonableness of the 'bases' chosen. (1992, p. 21)

For Sen therefore, the argument should not be about inequality or equality in themselves, but about where (at what level) we demand that there should be equality and
where we consider it to be peripheral or inequality to be tolerable. The difference of
opinion between those who tolerate distributional inequality and those who do not
becomes, therefore, one not about whether equality or inequality is a good thing but
about where we insist that equality should be enacted and where we are happy to
restrict it.

We can find, for example, that the emphasis on freedom that is at the heart of lib-
ertarian views and is seen as the non-negotiable element, the fundamental 'equality',
is disputed by those who regard distributional justice as more important. Supporters
of greater social equality, such as Tawney, acknowledged that freedom needs to be
restricted in the pursuit of equality. Freedom itself, though, is contextually specific.
And the question of course becomes: whose freedom?

There is, additionally, the question of whether equality of opportunity actually
represents fairness. Given differences in people's dispositions and skills, why should
we reward some and not others? Is leaving people to their own devices or possibilities
just and fair? It may be good for society to reward particular talents more than others,
but it is not necessarily fair or just. This point has been made by a number of commentators in different ways. Sen points to the fact that individuals are diverse and
that therefore providing some notional level playing field misses the point. He suc-
cinctly states that 'equal consideration for all may demand very unequal treatment in
favour of the disadvantaged' (1992, p. 1). His solution is to argue for – and attempt to
measure – the 'capability' to achieve various essential functionings (Sen 1983, 1992).
This avoids both conflating outcomes with opportunities and treating adaptation
to sub-optimal conditions as preference for less. Adam Swift made the point more
explicitly when he asked:

> in what sense are the more able the more deserving? Imagine the parent of two
> children: one unusually gifted, the other who finds learning difficult. Does society
> give them justice when it gives them radically different amounts of resources over
> their lifetimes? Some contributors to this debate seem particularly concerned about
> the clever children of poor parents. What about the well-being of not-so-talented
> children, whatever their social origins? (2003, p. 209)

We can compare also Miller's comment

> If we try to take seriously the idea that people can only deserve things when they
> are fully responsible for what they achieve – in the sense that the outcome was not
> affected by the contingencies which impinge unequally on different people – we
> find that the scope of desert shrinks to vanishing point. We can never say, in a real
> sense, that a person deserves rewards and benefits for what they have done, because
> it is always reasonable to assume that their performance was affected by factors for
> which they were not responsible. (Miller 1997, p. 91)

The influential philosopher John Rawls used the image of the 'veil of ignorance'
to engage people in how they might wish a society to be organized should they not
know which life chances they had been dealt in the handing out of different risks and

abilities. Making decisions from behind such a veil would be fair in that it would not predispose them to favour their own circumstances (not knowing what they were), but would instead force them to consider the disadvantage they might face. The outcomes, he then argues, would be just – justice as fairness would be achieved. Although Rawls defends inequalities of reward or position as being functional for society, this is conditional on being for the benefit of the *least advantaged* members of society. While he does not reject the principle of equality of opportunity, his argument is that it is possible to achieve it 'fairly' only in a society structured under such terms. In this way he attempts to argue the case of combining adherence to inequality with consideration for disadvantage. However, the device of the 'veil of ignorance' does not fully take account of how people have reached the position in which they are imagining themselves, which will tend to bring back questions of merit and worth. Life experiences are cumulative, and to realize Rawlsian justice from any particular position requires addressing all the different life stages at the same time. I may favour having support for pensioners if I imagine I could end up as a poor pensioner, but that also implies going through various cognitive stages to envisage how I ended up as a poor pensioner. And are all pensioners equally worthy of the same amount of support? Or should there be differentiation between, say, a wealthy adult who has spent all their money and someone who has never earned more than a small amount in their life? Or should we assume that the fairness will have applied to the unskilled worker throughout their life to reward them more highly so that they cannot be poor as a pensioner? Is it the current situation or the history that is relevant to a consideration of what is just, given that Rawls allows for inequalities under his conditions? Are all life events to be treated as equivalently accidental? How a society is structured will also influence the chances of certain accidents or life events occurring over the course of time and the risks associated with them.

From an egalitarian perspective, large disparities (in income, in educational qualifications, in mortality), whether or not they differ by social group, are considered problematic, in that they indicate an unjust society and fail to recognize how people's behaviours, activities and rewards are constrained by social structures; that it is not logical to reward individuals for skills over which they may have no control; that the existence of large disparities – for example, in income – may make some social groups at greater risk of inequalities of opportunity, and that it is often regarded as the responsibility of the state to intervene to check such inequalities by changes in the way society works.

Limits to equality

An emphasis on fairness, then, can lead to sanctioning some level of inequality, though at what point it actually becomes 'fair' is obscure. Even how to recognize different levels of inequality, for example, or how to distinguish improvements in equality (Temkin 1993) is a difficult question. Support for (particular forms of) inequality or equality depends substantially on particular perspectives on the world that prioritize certain elements of society as fundamental or unassailable. Moreover, Fish (1994) has also pointed out the way in which the language of fairness and freedom (and of rights) can be manipulated or adapted to conditions, depending on its apparent content, when its aim is actually the reverse. By 'speaking in code', people can take words such as equality and fairness and use them to argue for the sustaining of an 'unfair' and systematically disadvantaging status quo.

Nevertheless, despite these differentiated perspectives, a position which stresses the importance of equality of opportunity within a system of differentiated rewards is largely considered more defensible in popular and political discourse, and tends to accord more closely both with individuals' willingness to regard themselves (and others) as having rights to their own achievements – the right to not be thwarted in their aspirations – and with a belief in some level of inequality (in income, pay, quali-fications, and so on) as being justified. We do not like to think that we are not masters of our own destiny, to some degree, and an emphasis on the value of social mobility speaks to such concerns.

The consequences of such endorsements of inequality and the prioritization of equality of opportunity over equality of outcome can be substantial. It can be dam-aging for individuals whose destiny is (as for most of us) not only not fully under their control but beset by constraints which make either the possibilities of achieve-ment or the rewards from their achievements incommensurate with those of more favoured individuals. At the extreme, as Wilkinson and Pickett (above, p. 5) claim, acceptance of large inequalities as justifiable in some societies can have dramatic consequences for well-being across the social spectrum. Moreover, it is important to recognize the extent to which such 'opportunities' can be illusory and that sup-porting them can in fact reinforce the status quo. In particular, espousing equality of opportunity may deny the very different starting points and constraints that dif-ferent groups in society face in realizing their potential. Belief in a 'moral world' can result in discounting the role of luck in people's success and failure (Sayer 2005). It also risks both normalizing systematic differences between groups who hold differ-ent positions in the social hierarchy and attributing the marginalized positions of minorities to their own failings. It is to the issue of inequalities between social groups that the next section turns.

1.3 Inequalities across groups

It is widely held that there are many characteristics which are – or should be – irrelevant to the opportunity to flourish in society. Such irrelevant factors are often deemed to be those with which people are born, such as their sex, ethnicity or social group (even though these may change in content and in meaning over time), but may also cover factors which arise or are subject to fluctuation, such as health status, income or area of residence. At the level of trying to disentangle what is fair from what is unfair, the inference is clear: any systematic group inequalities are unfair and therefore unjustified. And to that extent they demand a response.

At the same time, however, marked differences in experience, life chances and outcomes across these 'irrelevant factors' persist and are even justified, in academic literature as well as in popular attitudes, with reference to preferences, competence or inevitability. For example, and as subsequent chapters show, women's greater vulnerability to poverty is often seen through the lens of the 'choice' to have children, while minority group labour market segmentation is often attributed to occupa-tional or residential preferences (Battu and Zenou 2010). The low employment rates of particular groups of disabled people or those with chronic health problems are frequently regarded as a fact of life, while systematic differences in educational outcomes across social classes or ethnic groups might merit greater reaction if there were not at some level a willingness to regard them as justified (Burgess and Greaves 2009; Reay 2005; Saunders 1995).

When exploring inequalities across social groups and what they mean in terms of life chances and differential opportunities and expectations, there are three important considerations. First is the effective description of such inequalities, so that their extent and nature is clear. The scale of inequalities is important in considering whether and how far they are (in)tolerable, whatever the underlying causes or contributory factors. An employment gap of 3 per cent, for example, may reasonably be considered less serious than an employment gap of 30 per cent. It also enables reflection on how group inequalities are a product of, or relate to, inequalities within society as a whole. For instance, in a country where income polarization is low, even disadvantaged groups are less likely to be seriously poor than those in a country where income polarization is high.

The second consideration is the separation of 'group' differences from other characteristics associated with the group in order to define the extent to which relevant factors (age, qualifications, etc.) might be shaping the inequalities. For example, in the labour market, an employment gap might be due partly to differences in qualifications between two groups. This is not to say that 'explicable' inequalities are not thereby a cause for concern. For instance, if disabled people are more likely to be in low-paid work because of lower educational qualifications, it does not mean that they are not disadvantaged. But such a discussion gives a purchase on the extent to which general patterns of reward and penalty, of equality and inequality, operate across groups. If, to continue with the example, qualifications are equally rewarded across the groups, and it is the lack of qualifications that is causing the gap, a search for long-term solutions to employment gaps might best be focused on the processes leading to educational disadvantage. Additional 'deficits' over and above such explanatory factors, moreover, indicate the significance of the category or social group for being considered as a social division (Anthias 2001; Payne 2006).

The third important task is to explore the points at which processes – for example, of social mobility, educational success, health, and accumulation of income – operate differently across different social groups and to examine the ways in which intersections between different social groups – or sets of characteristics – reveal different patterns from straightforward single majority–minority comparisons and inequalities. Identifying differences in the ways inequalities emerge or are transmitted both questions the assumed naturalness of those processes and can modify the thrust of existing accounts (Platt 2005a). For example, if the gap between the school performance of poor children and those who are not poor varies by ethnic group, this can challenge notions of how low income (or not having low income) influences educational performance. And the different stories emerging from an exploration of intersections of inequalities can similarly refine our understanding of unequal outcomes, as well as the meanings and boundaries and salience of the intersecting groups themselves. For instance, if we find that women from lower social classes have more in common with men from lower social classes than they do with women from higher social classes (in terms of, say, lifetime income, pension entitlement, and so on), this may lead us to reconfigure our representation of gender inequalities in terms of gender-class inequalities – at least as far as income is concerned.

It is worth noting at this point, and partly given these considerations, that I use the term 'social group' in a loose sense throughout to designate particular subpopulations who share a particular characteristic, be it ethnic group, disability status, area of residence, sex or type of housing. It is not intended to imply a comprehensive and theoretically robust notion of coherent and clearly bounded groups. In fact, the intention is quite the opposite, as I note when moving on to the final section of this chapter, where I consider the book's coverage and themes. In the conclusion I return to the term and discuss its use further. Here, it suffices to say that it is designed to be general: to designate groups that have some social meaning and where it makes sense from an inequalities perspective to group them in this way.

First, then, it is necessary to provide a straightforward description and enumeration of inequalities as they face different social groups or are experienced across them. This needs to be comprehensible and up to date in order to make sense of the experience of groups and to be able to map from one element covered in a chapter (such as class) to a related discussion (such as income) in another. While there is a widespread acknowledgement of the key inequalities that individuals face, enumerating them at a sufficient level of specificity and accuracy is an essential first step towards being able to analyse and theorize. Perceptions or impressions of inequality, while of sociological interest in their own right, are not a sufficient basis on which to extrapolate how society functions. Indeed, I would go further, and say that they can properly be understood only if the empirical regularities which they do or do not reflect are also grasped. Therefore each chapter provides a detailed description of the extent of *absolute* inequality across the topic(s) considered.

In order to make a case for 'unjustified' inequalities, much analysis attempts to exclude from consideration all potentially relevant characteristics before determining that there are inequalities between groups. While, as I have noted, what is justified or unjustified is highly contested, it can nevertheless be illuminating to reveal the extent to which there are differences between 'otherwise similar' individuals who differ only in their social group. This then makes it possible to engage in a debate about what are irrelevant or relevant factors, as well as to demonstrate the routes through which inequalities emerge. For example, if one group is on average older, and older people tend have more health problems, then an apparent health inequality may be put down to age differences. This health difference would then disappear if we controlled for health across the groups, or held it constant, effectively comparing only those of the same age with each other. Thus an absolute inequality would disappear on the basis of an 'other things being equal' principle. The inequality, of course, would still exist, but one argument would be that we would not have to be concerned about it in relation to that group because it had been 'explained' by age (though we might still be concerned about the health of older people in general). If, however, on holding age constant, we still found that there was a difference in health between the groups, albeit a smaller one, then this could be interpreted as a demonstration of inequality that can be attributed to social group membership *per se* – or, further, to characteristics, unaccounted for, that are associated with both group membership and health inequality. Identifying such differences that emerge between groups might also justify the allocation of individuals to particular groups or categories in the first place. This would be a *relative* inequality, relative to those who were otherwise similar but from a different group.

In pay, for example, many would expect that high educational qualifications should lead to higher pay and that this should be regarded as relevant to economic outcomes and therefore 'fair'. It then becomes possible to infer the existence of *relative* inequality from whether those with the same education but of, say, a different sex have different pay. Such a measure gives a powerful illustration of *relative* disadvantage and how the accepted workings of society, even in the unequal ways they distribute rewards, do not apply to all groups. Where there is suitable evidence, and it is appropriate, the chapters below therefore include assessment of relative disadvantage alongside the description of absolute inequalities.

There are, however, two caveats to this approach. First, we might be concerned not only with the structural factors within society that systematically disadvantage particular groups relative to similar others but also with those that shape outcomes at all levels. Then the differences in education, which partly 'explained' the pay gap, would themselves need to come under scrutiny. If, for example, social class background leads to differences in qualifications, and thereby to lower pay, we should be asking why.

The second caveat is that an insistence on comparability – Do those with the same qualifications but from different social groups fare equally or not? – may risk neglecting the extent to which groups are so different, in so many dimensions, that a comparison of 'like with like' is to all intents meaningless. For example, if most women with children interrupt their career and leave the labour market at some point, then to institute a comparison between men and women with children and their later life outcomes based only on those who have uninterrupted careers is not going to be very meaningful (Hakim 1995). We may well find that they have very similar outcomes, but that would not tell us much about gendered employment experiences.

On the other hand, there are those who would dispute the implication that *relative differences* tell us anything about structural inequalities by maintaining that any remaining differences between apparently similar people are necessarily the result of actual and relevant differences between them. The existence of relative inequalities is taken to represent factors that it is hard to measure, such as imagination, intelligence or motivation, and which, it is argued, differ systematically across the groups being compared. Such arguments have been made for both social class differences in mobility and ethnic group differences in employment. According to such arguments, rather than inequalities between groups telling us something about the way society disadvantages those with particular characteristics, relative inequalities would be telling us about important differences between the groups themselves that we simply cannot see. While many would consider such arguments implausible or problematic, it is nevertheless important to be aware of them.

Intersectionality

Linked to the discussion of relative differences or 'group' effects is the question of whether the inequalities 'story' changes as we look across groups and, in particular, at their intersections. As I have noted, looking at the ways in which outcomes differ at particular intersections can challenge naturalized expectations of the development of inequalities, such as how education and outcomes are linked; how ethnicity and education are linked; how gender and income are linked. The chapters therefore appropriate the concept of intersectionality from feminist analysis (though it is increasingly being 'mainstreamed' in research and adopted for policy domains such as the equalities agenda) to reveal and tackle the complex nature of inequalities and how they vary across, and themselves reshape, social groups at their intersection.

According to Davis, '"Intersectionality" refers to the interaction between gender, race, and other categories of difference in individual lives, social practices, institutional arrangements, and cultural ideologies and the outcomes of these interactions in terms of power' (Davis 2008, p. 68). The brief discussion here cannot address the full complexity of debates and theories developed within the feminist literature on intersectionality (Phoenix and Pattynama 2006). Nor can it acknowledge all the ways in which intersections are realized and shape our understandings of the world. Nevertheless, as Davis (2008) has pointed out, intersectionality can provide a basic shorthand term which encompasses a multitude of ways of looking at the relationship between categories that mark forms of difference in people's lives. An intersectional approach encourages a focus which does not prioritize one particular category for analytical attention but acts as a shifting lens by which gender is brought into relief by a focus on class, and ethnicity by a focus on health. Such a shifting lens can prove vital to the effective analysis of inequalities. It enables the point of investigation to be switched from a category implied as the basis of inequalities to other factors that may be more pertinent.

An intersectional perspective also encourages an approach to inequalities which recognizes how they have been historically located and formed over time (Bottero and Irwin 2003) and needs to pay attention to the ways in which categories shift their meaning or become obsolete. Thus it is important to bring a contingent approach to the categories and inequalities illustrated here and to realize that they may not represent what is most salient for describing or understanding inequalities in the future. It has often been noted that an intersectional perspective requires that interactions between categories of difference – or difference itself – need to be understood relationally (Irwin 2005): different intersections are salient by virtue of the relations by which they are brought into being (Irwin 2003). It is also important to consider the ways in which agents act to create or maintain barriers which result in inequalities for those at the intersection of particular categories.

This, of course, leads to the very vexed question of what it is that intersects. What are the categories, or social groups? Who determines them? And what do they mean? The division of society into groups has been criticized as naturalizing divisions and regarding as fixed and permanent what are fluid, flexible and dynamic and relational categories or entities brought into being as they are enacted or spoken. It is by and large recognized, for example, that ethnicity is fluid and contingent (Fenton 2010), and similar claims have been made for gender (Butler 1990). Groups, such as the social groups addressed in this book, do not have prior significance as, *by definition*, the source of attachments, loyalties and social meaning. Rather, they come into being as a result of political processes that relate to particular circumstances of time and place (Carter and Fenton 2009). This also emphasizes the role of others in constructing one's own group and group membership. Even outside individual relations and the situated meanings and constructions of particular identities, being a woman, from an ethnic minority, disabled, young or old has wider implications.

At a pragmatic level, to expose inequalities and to enable an analysis which reveals the systematic disadvantage suffered through membership of a group or allocation to a particular category or intersection of categories requires that such categories are defined, named and relatively well bounded. Thus this book describes inequality across social groups, recognizing that these are not necessarily fixed or stable categories but that temporarily to 'fix' them is necessary to the process of identifying differences in material well-being that can be associated with them (McCall 2005). Moreover, the actual categories employed are largely those which are possible given the sources employed in the description of inequalities. Those for whom inequality is counted and counts are subject to the pre-existing ways in which society is divided, regardless of theoretical positions which would suggest a rather different allocation of individuals to groups. This necessitates some consideration of the measurement of groups or categories and its implications. Each chapter, as I discuss below, pays attention to the question of measurement. Furthermore, the consideration of groups as the basis of inequalities or as social groupings across which inequality is played out does not presuppose that there is recognition of the group by individuals so allocated or that they identify with it. This issue of identification, or its absence, is one which leads to the coverage of the book – not only what it includes but also, importantly, what is excluded.

1.4 Coverage and key themes

What is in and what is left out

This book has an ambitious remit. It sets out to outline inequalities across nine different strands or domains. It presents contemporary evidence on the extent and nature of the inequalities in these areas while enlarging on specific sociological debates that are of particular relevance or have an enduring contribution to make to the topic. It sets out to provide an impression of the scale of inequalities and the existence of relative inequalities and to highlight key points of intersection. It attempts to explain and justify the social groups across which inequalities are measured and to draw some inferences about how particular inequalities come about and are maintained.

There are, needless to say, a number of areas that might nevertheless be considered relevant to a study of inequality which are not given full treatment. The chief exclusions relate to issues of identity and identification and the attitudes of individuals themselves to inequality. Social identity is an important area of sociological inquiry. There has been increasing attention paid to questions of identity and identification either as constitutive of groups or as expanding our understanding of them. For some analysts, ethnic groups, for example, can only exist as identities. That is, the research perspective presupposes the identification of individuals with an ethnic category for it to be valid. It is sometimes argued that only 'owned' categories are ethical and do not violate the individual's right to self-determination. Those who focus on class consciousness may also stress that class boundaries are those that are felt through class membership – or at least that they are coterminous with 'objective' measures of class (Devine 1992). Similarly, much of the disability literature envisages a conscious subject who defines themselves as disabled (by society) through their interactions with the world and the constraints it places upon them. Important issues of recognition and of the power of categories and those doing the categorizing are raised by an attention to subjectivity and identification – or its neglect. Attention to what are acceptable and unacceptable categories is, moreover, crucial to avoid further disempowering those who are subject to material and social inequalities (Aspinall 2002).

Nevertheless, there are still many who would maintain that the existence of inequalities across subgroups of the population is worthy of attention, even if those concerned do not directly identify with the categories to which they are being allocated. In relation to class, Savage and his colleagues argued that 'sociologists should not assume that there is any necessary significance in how respondents define their class identity' (2001, p. 875). And, as Runciman pointed out, 'whatever theoretical or terminological framework is used by the academic investigator, his subjects will not necessarily think in terms of it; but the framework will not be right or wrong solely for that reason' ([1966] 1972, p. 50).

So, while research on how individuals think about their identities is valuable and brings many insights to bear on the lived experience of inequalities (for example, the shame and pain, defensiveness or pride, contempt or arrogance associated with feeling higher or lower in the social scale on any dimension, or with being the victim or the perpetrator of inequalities), such research is largely beyond the scope of this book. This is both for practical reasons of space and for theoretical and pragmatic reasons relating to the purpose of identifying inequalities.

The other main exclusion is also in terms of subjective views – views about inequality itself. Attitudes to inequality are of interest in their own right, and perhaps particularly of interest among those trying to build a consensus or explore changing mores or patterns of belief over time; but they are not the same as the material life chances that people actually experience. People's views on economic inequality are typically found to be a long way from any objective reality – whether they are among the better off or the worse off (Bamfield and Horton 2009; Orton and Rowlingson 2007). Indeed, when the views of the majority are projected onto minorities, they can even be a source of inequality and exclusion in their own right. For example, the erroneous belief that migrants and minorities have privileged access to social housing can contribute to the exclusion of such groups. Perceptions of social structure and social stratification do not, then, lie within the scope of this book. This is not to say that people's views of their place in the hierarchy do not matter. Indeed, Wilkinson and Pickett (2009) have been at pains to argue that it is the continual awareness of inequality and distance that drives the negative impacts of inequality that can be observed across a wide range of indicators. However, to develop the connection between the perception of social and economic location and the evidence for all the social groups would require another book. This one could not claim to do justice to the subject. While perceptions and expressed experience of inequality do not, therefore, form a core focus, the book does use illustrative epigraphs taken from some of the wealth of literature on people's situated experience of inequality to provide touchstones for subsequent discussions or demotic accounts of technical issues of definition and measurement.

Finally, the book's coverage relates to the UK. There are occasional international comparisons where these are considered particularly interesting or illuminate the argument more effectively than a single-country focus, but these do not form a key feature.

Key themes

Having discussed what is not included in this text, it is now worth drawing out what is covered in each chapter and some key themes that recur throughout, even if they are not developed in each and every chapter.

The book explores inequalities across nine separate areas. The first three are the traditional domains of stratification research and teaching: class, gender and ethnicity. These three areas, alongside disability, which is combined with the chapter on health, represent groups to which individuals are allocated, frequently from birth, and which are regarded as relatively stable – even if not fixed and unchanging. Lower social classes, women, ethnic minorities and disabled people are groups which are compared with a normalized majority and face inequalities across a range of domains. These domains of unequal experience are the subject of most of the remaining chapters. Thus inequalities in education, in income, in housing, in health, are outlined, and how they are experienced across inequalities groups or at their intersections is analysed. Yet, even within these areas, their potential for stratifying the experience of those who are in a common position (poor people, those in social housing) in their own right is touched upon. In between the two, the chapter on youth and age relates to issues of the life course. Like women or disabled people, young and old face inequalities by virtue of – or associated with – their youth and age. Yet these are also life stages that everyone can expect to pass through.

Across these distinct inequalities and inequality domains, each chapter has a number of common components. There is a focus on the measurement and definition of the group under consideration, there is a contemporary account of inequalities in a particular domain or domains that are salient for the group, and there is a more detailed focus on a particular aspect of the group inequalities, typically at the intersection of groups. For example, in chapter 4 it is the intersection of ethnicity, sex and class in educational outcomes that is the particular focus.

The stress on measurement is regarded as crucial for understanding what the description of inequalities means. I have discussed how groups are constructed through the allocation of individuals to particular categories. The nature of those categories and the process of allocation are crucial to a meaningful interpretation of regularities and contradictions. Moreover, measurement of outcomes that are unequal also frequently deserves some clarification. For example, what do we mean when we say women do more housework than men? Or that minority groups are more likely to live in poor quality housing? Who are the women and the minority groups that are being referred to and what is captured by 'housework' or 'poor housing'? It requires some grasp of the issues of measurement involved to be able properly to read and interpret the evidence, not only in this book but also more widely.

In addition, there are a number of cross-cutting themes that are considered central to an effective understanding of how inequalities are distributed and how they can be interpreted. These themes comprise time and temporality, heterogeneity within groups, and choice or agency and constraint. Time and temporality is important for understanding changes over historical time, differences in experience of those born at different periods, and how inequalities emerge or develop over individual life courses. Though these issues are covered in chapter 5, they also emerge as significant to understanding differences at various points in other chapters.

As I have noted, the subpopulations or social groups that are considered here are loose collections of those identified on the basis of a common characteristic. But they are necessarily very varied. There is a range of ways in which social groups defined in terms of one characteristic are diverse if we look at other characteristics. Heterogeneity is thus another cross-cutting theme of the book. It is explicitly considered in chapter 3, which explores the differences between women and men relative to the differences among women, and again in chapter 8, where different forms of disability are considered; but it occurs throughout as a complicating factor in any discussion of group-based inequalities.

The question of preferences and constraints picks up on the questions of agency raised earlier. The agency of individuals needs to be acknowledged in order to avoid a purely deterministic view of inequalities. But agency may also imply the exercise of choice. At what point are perceived inequalities expressions of the choice of individuals with different sets of preferences, or to what extent can they be understood as constrained by circumstances, so that the possibilities for action and choice are limited to certain pathways? The question of choices and constraints is relevant to many discussions in this book, such as those relating to women and caring or to disability and employment. It is picked up most explicitly, however, in the discussion of choice and constraint in housing in chapter 9.

Overview

As well as providing sections on definition and measurement, picking up on the key themes that permeate the whole book, and stressing the interconnections or intersections between different forms or bases of inequality, each chapter offers some overview of the area. However, given the fact that a single chapter cannot do justice to the whole domain, each one explores a specific topic or source of debate at slightly greater length.

Following a description of class schemes and class distribution, chapter 2 focuses on the debates surrounding political aspirations towards creating a meritocracy. This is not only highly topical, it is also likely to remain a key consideration for unequal societies struggling to compensate for high levels of inequality. It demonstrates the ways in which concepts can fundamentally shift their meaning when translated into the language of political imperatives. The discussion also picks up on some of the central concerns about the incomparability of certain aspirations to fairness with 'equality'.

Chapter 3 gives an overview of women's labour market inequalities. It links this to caring responsibilities and the 'double burden', providing a detailed discussion of inequalities in domestic work. The final section treats questions of heterogeneity among women and addresses the longstanding question of whether the achievement of greater equality for some comes at the expense of those who are less powerful. Chapter 4 provides a detailed discussion of the problems involved in defining ethnicity and explores the experience of minority ethnic groups. It investigates ethnic minorities' labour market experience in some detail, including occupational mobility. Chapter 5 gives an overview of life-course issues and trajectories before honing in on the particular topic of women's inequalities in old age.

Chapter 6 addresses the data on educational achievement. It concentrates on school performance, with a focus on debates about the underachievement of boys. It also addresses the complicated patterns of achievement revealed by an analysis of ethnic group and sex differences. The chapter further introduces the notion of credentialism and treats the differential impact of the expansion of higher education. Chapter 7 looks at income and wealth. Even though economic inequalities are seen as being fundamental to class and class stratification, class and income are not synonymous. Nor is class typically assessed solely in terms of income and spending capacity. Instead there are many markers of class that may outlive relocation to a different class position. By contrast, income and direct command over resources is a relatively simple concept, though one that has received relatively less attention from sociologists. The chapter highlights the ways in which particular areas of research remain unspoken and begins to uncover the intersection of gender, ethnicity and poverty.

Chapter 8 treats disability and health together. While this may at first sight seem a surprising combination of two discrete topics, the chapter makes the case that it is an appropriate one. Although theoretically they are distinct, in terms of measurement the dividing line between ill health and disability is ambiguous in many contexts. Indeed, disability is typically measured – for the purposes of law as well as analysis – as chronic ill health, albeit a chronic health condition that limits daily activities. Moreover, it is not clear that, outside of arguments about group consciousness, discussed above, the distinction can be conceptually maintained. Most disabled people have been non-disabled for the majority of their lives, and some cease to be disabled. Older people are more likely to be disabled and face different issues from younger disabled people (Priestley 2003). Disability is therefore not a fixed state, and many people who are officially recognized as disabled do not recognize themselves as such. On the other hand, illness may continue indefinitely and be profoundly disabling. The distinction that is made is in exploring how disabled people as a group experience inequalities and in looking more generally at health inequalities across groups.

Chapter 9 explores the role of geography and housing as powerful structural constraints in perpetuating inequality. At the same time, the unequal distribution of housing and concentration of residence across social groups is a form of inequality. The specific topic treated in this chapter is residualization in social housing and the poorer relative outcomes associated with living in social housing. Chapter 10 briefly concludes by reflecting on the cumulative story presented from the various preceding chapters.

Each chapter is designed to be read separately. However, there is considerable complementarity between them, especially given the ways in which they draw out intersections from different perspectives. Thus, for example, the chapter on income draws out the unequal position of ethnic minority women, which is related in part to family structure and preference arguments as well as to questions of the invisibility of the private sphere, complementing the chapters on gender and ethnicity. The chapter on education draws out class differences that relate to the discussion of opportunity and mobility in the chapter on class. It also highlights ethnic differences in educational outcomes, which are implicit in some of the discussion of the labour market in the chapter on ethnicity. The intention is to minimize duplication and maximize the potential for making connections between different domains and types of inequality.

Each chapter concludes with some questions for reflection, which are intended to enable review of the key issues covered and to take forward points and questions raised in the course of discussion. Each also ends with some suggestions for further reading which provide greater detail on some of the topics covered in the text.

Questions for reflection

1 What is inequality?
2 Why does it matter?
3 How do equality and fairness differ?
4 Does justice presuppose equality?
5 Does inequality matter if people aren't aware of it?
6 Do all defences of inequality assume some equality in some space, as Sen would argue?

Further reading

In terms of general reading on inequalities, Wilkinson and Pickett (2009) give a persuasive account of the impact of economic inequality across societies, including on the way it relegates particular groups to the margins. Bradley's (1995) account of fractured identities offers a wealth of insights on inequalities. Payne's (2006) edited volume gives a full take on the social divisions in society, with contributions by some of the leading writers on the different topics. In relation to conceptual issues, Callinicos (2000) provides a short and accessible but wide-ranging account of positions on equality from a Marxist perspective. Neckerman and Torche's (2007) review article presents a useful overview of the bases of inequality from a predominantly US perspective. And Franklin (1997) provides an edited volume comprising a range of perspectives on equality and critiques of its uses.

2 Class

Despite the fact that people inherit rather than deserve their natal class, they may feel class pride or shame and care a great deal about how they are positioned with respect to class and how others treat them. They are likely to be concerned about class in terms of recognition of their worth, and want to be respected or respectable. But recognition and valuation are in part conditional on what people do, how they behave and live, so 'class concern' is also about having access to the ways and practices that are valued, and class of course renders this highly unequal. The inequalities in resources and opportunities themselves have little or nothing to do with the moral worth or merit of individuals but they have a major impact on the possibility of achieving valued ways of life that bring recognition and self-respect.

(Sayer 2005)

I'm just trying to move up in society, to *become* those people that have just lived with [privilege] all their lives and it's normal for them. For me, it's not normal, but it will become normal for my children. [I tell myself] 'look at what they have, you could have that too. So you should work harder to get that.'

(Lehmann 2009)

I knew this would come up. A jumped up working-class who has now entered the middle class. I hate to say it, I can't escape it, but I think we have become more middle-class from humble origins. We're the class that grew up with working-class parents keen on education, who pushed us and we all went to grammar schools and college and university and came out and suddenly found that we didn't belong to where we came from.

(Savage et al. 2001)

The first quotation above is from a discussion by Sayer (2005) on moral worth, class and recognition, which explicitly addresses the strong emotions that felt class position can elicit, particularly shame and its counterpoint pride, and how these can be rooted in unequal access to valued sources of recognition. The emotions associated with discussions of class have been pointed out by a number of writers concentrating on the range of feelings associated with class and contrasts in class position, such as shame, defensiveness and pride, as well as contempt, disgust and resentment (Hebson 2009; Lawler 2005; Reay 2005; Sayer 2005). At the same time it has been argued that how people feel about class is not necessarily a meaningful or appropriate way of ascertaining class position in terms of socio-economic location (Savage et al. 2001), in part because of the reluctance to speak about it and to place oneself in a class which is itself, somewhat paradoxically perhaps, bound up with the emotional response to class. Nevertheless, the powerful and subtle ways in which people live, demonstrate and speak about class, and the ways in which it permeates social intercourse, is one manner by which the continuing salience of class has been demonstrated. Whether or not people have class consciousness in terms of group solidarity associated with their class position (Devine 1992; Goldthorpe and Marshall 1992), they can nevertheless recognize and act on class signals in others' behaviour, speech, dress, and so on. The UK remains a classed society (Cannadine 1998). These behavioural and relational aspects of class are one of the ways in which class can be distinguished from income, although it has been argued that a range of similar emotions are associated with experiencing or responding specifically to poverty (Lister 2004). Moreover, as Sayer points out, class distinctions and the emotions they provoke can be the more painful because they are felt as individual failings, even as they stem from unequal possibilities of achieving recognition and respect.

The salience of class remains in its ability not just to define social relations but also, perhaps more importantly, to shape outcomes. It reflects 'origins' that may be redefined over time, as the aspirations in the second (Lehmann 2009) and third (Savage et al. 2001) quotations above indicate, but may at the same time continue to affect the experience and self-representation of the upwardly mobile (Skeggs 1997). Social mobility, movement from the class in family of origin to a different class in own adult life, defies the constraints of class origins. At the same time, mobility is often regarded as articulating with class background, the background that provides the reference point for the experience – or absence – of mobility. Achievement of upward mobility can only be recognized if the experience of class is perceived as contingent, as the latter two opening quotations show. Those who are the subject of Lehmann's article are on their way up, with all the pride, discomfort and defiance that that brings, but for many their lifetime experiences will be influenced by where they started out, or will be contrasted with it, as the respondent in the paper by Savage and his colleagues demonstrates. But mobility can occur whether or not it is recognized in these complex ways, and it is contemporary class position which shapes expectations and life chances. The 'working-class' surgeon may see herself as ill-fitting in her occupational and social group and may relate more closely to her origins, but her income, expected life chances, networks and opportunities will still be those of a surgeon rather than those of a cleaner. The possibilities of achieving different occupational positions clearly vary according to original family circumstances, but that matters because class has consequences.

It is these consequences that are the main subject of this chapter, though they recur throughout the book. First, however, we move from considering how class is felt and expressed to how it is defined independently of subjective orientations. As Bottero (2004) has pointed out, even in the renewal of class analysis (Crompton et al. 2000) it has proved hard to move beyond class categories, and for much research they prove necessary for demonstrating class inequalities. It is therefore to those categories and the concepts underpinning them that the next section turns.

Issues of definition and measurement have been central to debates on class and on class mobility, and these are covered first, before the chapter attends to describing actual class distributions and inequalities between social groups in class distribution. Section 2.3 moves on to a discussion of social mobility, both how it is used and how it varies across groups. Class analysis and the investigation of social mobility are effectively identified with each other when exploring equality of opportunity. Nevertheless, as chapter 1 indicated, equality of opportunity is not a straightforward 'good', but is underpinned by acceptance of a stratified society.

In this chapter, therefore, attention is paid to debates around social mobility and its meaning, including a discussion of Michael Young's meritocratic dystopia, before outlining some of the key findings of social mobility studies on the extent and nature of opportunity in the UK today. Social mobility has typically been measured in relation to men, with transitions from fathers to sons being the basis of analysis. However, this male-centred perspective has been widely challenged (Crompton 2008), and there has been increasing attention paid to women and how, in the context of a rather different class structure, they experience mobility (Payne and Abbott 1990), as well as on the influence of mothers' occupation and education on their children's future class attainment (Korupp et al. 2002). Much less attention has been paid to the mobility of minority ethnic groups. Yet, as this chapter indicates, looking at subpopulations can force new questions to be asked about the relationship between class background and subsequent outcome, as well as about the processes by which class origins come to matter.

2.1 Concepts, definitions, measurement

In his comprehensive study of racial theories, Michael Banton wrote

> There is a growing recognition . . . that part of the present problem is the existence, side by side, of two modes of discourse. One is the practical language of everyday life, employing what are sometimes called folk concepts. The other is a theoretical language in which scientists employ analytical concepts to designate things that the public know under other names. Analytical concepts have to serve purposes different from those served by the words which form part of the practical language of everyday life and therefore may have to be defined differently. . . . Social scientists will meet one frustration after another if they do not learn these lessons or if they try to develop schemes tied too closely to the popular conceptions current in one country or one language. (Banton 1998, p. 3)

While Banton was speaking of 'race', this insight is also true of class and gender. The distinction between everyday use and analytical concept therefore forms the first concern of this and the following two chapters. What is meant for the purposes of the study of inequalities across groups by class? And how do we measure it?

Class has formed one of the core concepts of sociological analysis since sociology took shape as a discipline. Yet despite, or perhaps even because of, this, it is a concept often struggled over by sociologists themselves. It can mean different things depending on context, and different again is the common usage by which people define their own and each other's class. Definitions of class rely on some sense of people's positioning in society and results concomitant with those ensuing from their economic position. How that economic position is conceived will itself vary. Marx defined class as economic, in relation to the ownership of the means of production. By contrast, Weber focused more on people's market situation. Their possession of goods and opportunities for income as well as conditions of the labour market were relevant to class groupings. Given the multiplicity of market situations, Weber argued that social class arises for those collections of market situations within which individual and generational mobility is 'easy and typical'. It is notable that 'immobility' is here part of the definition of class. To find extensive mobility under such circumstances would be to undermine the definition of classes. Frequency of associations, friendships and partnerships has similarly been regarded as fundamental to understanding what constitutes a class position, as Prandy (1990) has argued. By these means proximity of class positions can be established without necessarily requiring a clear set of class boundaries or categories. A fundamental distinction was long held to be that between manual and non-manual workers, though this distinction included status and power elements as well as economic position (Runciman [1966] 1972). With changing occupational structure, the manual versus non-manual distinction may have ceased to be the primary one, though issues of how people are employed and paid and the control they have over their work remain central to contemporary definitions of class position. Goldthorpe argued that the type of labour contract was fundamental. He distinguished in particular between salaried forms of employment (the 'salariat') and waged work. Both Prandy and Goldthorpe used their understandings of class to develop widely used measures of class structure.

In the majority of these formulations, except, partially, the Marxian one, the recognition of one's class is not necessary to act in accordance with it or to experience the life chances associated with it. While the continuing importance of class consciousness has been asserted (Devine 1992), class consciousness is not necessary for their class position still to have a relevance to people's lives. And most sociological research on class and class inequalities assumes, indeed, that individuals' accounts of their own class are not the most appropriate measure (see also Savage et al. 2001). Forms of class consciousness have been shown to permeate people's lives, and class is part of a common vocabulary. These factors may be relevant to interactions between social groups and to cultural practices and behaviours (Le Roux et al. 2008). The ways in which language is classed and the language of class is deployed by different actors in different settings are subjects of sociological investigation in their own right. They are, however, not necessarily pertinent to specific questions relating to structural inequalities, such as whether class inequalities are growing or whether social mobility is decreasing.

Part of what is considered as class in demotic terms is closely connected to issues of status: activities, tastes, behaviours, accent, and so on. These do create distinctions, and people are often alert to subtle variations in order to enact classifications. Le Roux and her colleagues would argue that 'social class divisions can be attributed to the interplay between economic, cultural and social capital, and class divisions should not therefore be conflated with the division of labour itself' (2008, p. 1066). However, many would still maintain the Weberian distinction between status and class: though subtle distinctions of status may be associated with class positions, they do not necessarily define them, or they distinguish somewhat different divisions. John Scott, in his detailed scrutiny of Weber's distinction between class and status, has emphasized this point, echoing the complaint of Banton in the quotation at the beginning of this section:

> The conflation of class and status in the popular discourse of 'class', then, is the reason why contemporary discussions of class have been so confused. Instead of using Weber's concept to dissect the language of everyday life, many sociologists and commentators have simply taken over that language and have incorporated the same confusions into their own work. Mainstream American sociology, for example, equated class with status and simply lost sight of any real concern for structured social inequalities rooted in economic divisions. Equally, it lost sight of the linkages that exist between these divisions and the powers of command. 'Stratification' came

to be seen as an exclusively normative matter of invidious status distinctions. The claim that America is an 'open' or 'classless' society rests as much on this conceptual blindspot as it does on any empirical evidence. (Scott 1996, p. 15)

Perhaps where popular and sociological conceptions of class do overlap, however, is in relation to the recognition that they can shape futures and life chances (Cannadine 1998). When class is denied as a structural force in today's society, it is in order to deny both the inequalities that are supposed to accompany it and the claims of inequality within society. When it is acknowledged as significant – for example, in the recent Equalities Act – it is recognized how powerful different starting points in life are in shaping subsequent opportunities. Recognition of class implies a recognition that people's lives and life chances are heavily structured and that, even if there is substantial scope for individual attainment, opportunities to realize possibilities or to be successful are not equally distributed. It can, but does not have to, lead to a deterministic viewpoint that there is little possibility of escaping the constraints of class. Similarly, recognition implies a version of the world which is inherently unfair and therefore at odds with ideological emphases on individualism, self-realization and the prioritization of agency. This opposition of worldviews underlies why the claim that Britain is a 'classless society' is so contentious. It is not 'simply' a question of self-labelling that is issue, or even the content of those labels.

Measurement of class

So how are these class positions measured, if not by individual perception? Class tends to be constructed from information about people's occupation and, sometimes, the sort of work they do, or from patterns of association between people from different occupational positions. The aim of class schemas is that they should use a set of clear conceptual criteria to allow distinctions to be drawn between different positions or sets of positions (Rose and Pevalin 2001). There are four such schemes currently widely in use to measure people's class:

- Registrar General's social class scheme
- Goldthorpe class schema (also called the Erikson Goldthorpe scheme or CASMIN)
- NS-SEC
- Cambridge scale.

The Registrar General's class classification (see box 2.1) is the oldest of these schemes. It thus represents a division of classes that was prevalent towards the earlier

Box 2.1   Registrar General's social class scheme

I: Professional occupations
II: Managerial and technical
IIIN: Skilled occupations non-manual
IIIM: Skilled occupations manual
IV: Partly skilled occupations
V: Unskilled
Other

> **Box 2.2   Goldthorpe class schema**
>
> I: Professionals, managers and administrators in large enterprises
> II: Semi-professionals, managers and administrators in small enterprises
> III: Routine white-collar workers
> IV: Petty bourgeoisie (farmers, small employers and self-employed workers)
> V: Foremen and technicians
> VI: Skilled manual workers
> VII: Lower working class (semi-skilled and unskilled manual workers)
> The scheme is non-hierarchical but can be conflated into a three-class hierarchical version.

rather than the later part of the twentieth century, and its construction was driven by expectations about uncovering particular class relationships (Szreter 1996). This means that empirically there are often few people in any source of data found in the bottom social class. This, as well as questions about its conceptual basis (Prandy 1999), means that it is rarely used for sociological analysis, where one of the alternatives tends to be preferred. However, it continues to be commonly used in health inequalities research, which is an area in which it was originally developed to discriminate.

The Goldthorpe class schema was based on the assumption of the relevance of the conditions of employment. Thus it separates out 'own account workers' or self-employed and distinguishes between salaried occupations and those which command a weekly wage (see box 2.2). Employment relations are central to this scheme, as they are argued to represent aspects of employment that are relevant to life choices but which are not necessarily visible in nominal position or pay. Thus, the construction of the class takes account of salaried versus wage-based labour, autonomy and managerial responsibility within employment. The Goldthorpe scheme has been very extensively used in cross-national stratification research. It has become the convention in many analyses to accept the central argument for the importance of employment relations, though the conceptual and empirical significance of the emphasis on employment relations has been challenged (Lambert and Bihagen 2007). It has, though, been criticized for the neglect of the agricultural sector, which is significant in many European countries outside the UK, and new versions have been developed to take account of heterogeneity within classes with the expansion of the service class or salariat (Güveli 2006).

For practical purposes, the NS-SEC has now superseded the Registrar General's social class scheme and forms, in both its National (NS-SEC) and European (ESeC) versions, a more up-to-date classification on the basic principles of the Goldthorpe scheme concerning employment relations. For much research, therefore, it has begun also to replace the latter. The NS-SEC also claims to deal with some of the criticisms levelled at the Goldthorpe scheme, in particular the way it does not allow for those out of the labour market and does not well represent the class distributions of women and their associated economic position. It exists in a full fourteen-class version (see box 2.3), which can be collapsed down to a three-class version (through intermediate steps). The fourteen classes also have subcategories for fine grained distinctions.

Unlike the other classifications, which divide people into categories, the Cambridge scale is a continuous scale rather than a set of fixed categories. It is not,

Box 2.3   The NS-SEC

Employers in large organizations
Higher managerial occupations
Higher professional occupations
Lower professional and higher technical occupations
Lower managerial occupations
Higher supervisory occupations
Intermediate occupations
Employers in small organizations
Own account workers
Lower supervisory occupations
Lower technical occupations
Semi-routine occupations
Routine occupations
Never worked and long-term unemployed
[Full-time students]
[Occupations not stated or inadequately described]
[Not classifiable for other reasons]

therefore, possible to summarize it, like the others, in a box. Rather than assuming a qualitative divide between one category and the next, the class structure is conceived as a rank of positions, from 0 to 100, of relative advantage and disadvantage. The ranks are formed by exploring similarity of lifestyle within occupational groupings (Prandy 1990). The Cambridge scale/CAMSIS has separate scales for men and women, thus allowing relationships between men's and women's individual positions to be assessed. Using separate scales, however, does not necessarily resolve the question of the relative position of men and women or make it evident how mobility across generations should be traced.

The issue of the representation of women's occupations and how their class should be treated has been a vexed one for class analysis and estimates of social mobility in particular. Goldthorpe's principal assumption was that women's class position was represented by their husbands. This had the advantage of getting round the conundrum that a substantial proportion of married women – and indeed a much higher proportion at the time of the earlier studies – was not in the labour market at all for a considerable period of their lives. They would thus have no class position. Such assumptions have been extensively challenged on both conceptual and empirical grounds (Crompton 1998). But Goldthorpe has defended his position by arguing that, pragmatically, men's occupations were the best indicator of household class, by suggesting that they were in fact the sole determinants of household class. Obviously while the first argument may be true, the second is not really a defensible position. However, the question of how to take account of household class remains an important consideration for class analysis. A simple approach has simply been to calculate individuals' class positions and to look at the correlations across these. While this is common to much social mobility analysis, as well as to the examination of class inequalities such as health and employment, it neglects the fact that, conceptually, class is best understood as a characteristic of households or families. A care worker living with a doctor is likely to be in a different situation in terms of class position and its impact on life chances than if he was living on his own or with a call centre worker. Class and corresponding life chances are not simply about individual position but are also affected by immediate household and family context.

It is worth noting at this point that most analysis of social position carried out by economists is concerned not with class but with income group or, yet more commonly, individual earnings. This becomes particularly relevant when comparing accounts of social mobility across the two approaches. Economists measuring intergenerational 'social' mobility tend to focus on the relationship between the income or the earnings of parents and children rather than their occupational class. The conclusions drawn from the use of such different measures can vary considerably (as indeed they can between different class measures, though not to quite the same extent). In the US, for example, the story told about opportunity within society is very different if an income/earnings measure is used instead of a class measure (Neckerman and Torche 2007). The discussion of social mobility in this chapter focuses on class measures. But it is worth noting that several influential studies about 'social mobility' have been based on income/earnings measures (Atkinson et al. 1983; Blanden and Machin 2007), and a lot of claims about the extent of mobility or the lack of change come from such studies. Those concerned with class analysis would argue that earnings (or income) measured at a point in time are a poor indicator of overall life chances. These, it is argued, are much better captured by class, which is more closely associated with overall lifetime position. However, it could be countered that direct economic resources are at least a transparent measure of social position.

We now turn to look at the distributions of class and to touch on certain class inequalities. Inequalities across class backgrounds associated with education, early years and health are treated in separate chapters. Here, therefore, we briefly discuss inequalities within classes and some of the features of the occupational distribution of women and minority ethnic groups, before moving on to examine social mobility, one of the central concepts and preoccupations in sociological class analysis, and which, as mentioned in the introduction, has been strongly associated with both social justice and inequality.

2.2 Class distributions and inequalities

Class inequalities have to be seen in the context of dramatic shifts in class structure across the twentieth century – the number of higher-class (professional and managerial) jobs more than doubling over that period. As well as changes in terms of the number of 'good' jobs, there have been changes in the types of job at any given class level, with particular implications for the sorts of work in which women are engaged and their corresponding opportunities. Heath and Payne (2000) illustrated the class distribution across Goldthorpe's seven classes (see box 2.2) for a series of birth cohorts (people born in given sets of years) from the beginning of the last century and for men and women. These distributions are given in figures 2.1 and 2.2. Looking first at the class distribution of men, we see a substantial decline in the proportions in classes V/VI and VII and a corresponding increase in classes I and II. This is the phenomenon of 'more room at the top' that has enabled absolute social mobility

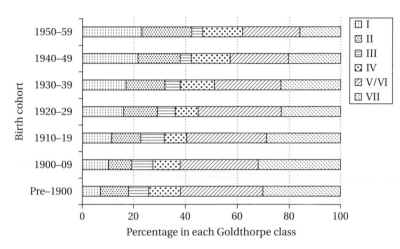

Source: Adapted from Heath and Payne (2000), table 1.

Figure 2.1   Men's social class by birth cohort.

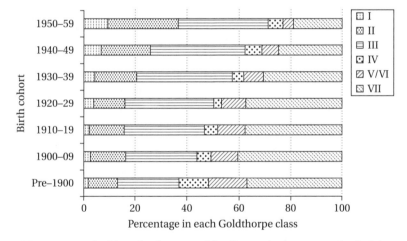

Note: Those women looking after home and family, or who have never had a job, are excluded.

Source: Adapted from Heath and Payne (2000), table 2.

Figure 2.2   Women's social class by birth cohort.

from the working class. Although the seven-class scheme is not strictly hierarchical, classes I and II and V/VI and VII correspond, in the hierarchical three-class version, to contrasting 'service' and working-class positions.

Women, when their class position is looked at on an individual basis, also show the pattern of increases at the top and declines at the bottom. But the gain at the top is much less marked. Instead we see a major growth in the proportion in class III occupations – that is, clerical and service industry forms of work. These expanded dramatically over the latter half of the twentieth century, and are occupations to which

Table 2.1 Change in occupational structure, 1971/81–2001

	Service/ professional	Intermediate	Working/ manual & routine	Unemployed	Other
1971/81	26.3	18.2	49.7	N/A (included in other)	5.8
2001	47.9	18.9	23.3	2.8	7.1

Source: Platt (2005b), table 4.2.

women have responded through participation or, conversely, in which the increased labour market participation of women played a key role in enabling expansion. The organization and structure of the labour market cannot, after all, be separated from the consumption and changing domestic practices of those participating in these new occupational sectors (Glucksmann 1995, 2009).

Even though figures 2.1 and 2.2 clearly demonstrate changes in occupational structure and opportunities over the last century, it could be argued they do not explicitly show how class at a household level has shifted – that is, how occupational structures of households are changing given the combination of workers living in the same family who may have similar or different jobs (Brynin et al. 2009). So, as well as looking at the trends across birth cohorts in this way, it is possible to look at occupational change by considering how one generation's social class distribution (taking account of both partners, where they are in a couple) varies from that of their parents' generation (taking their parents together). By these means we could also address the extent to which the class experience of men and women is shifting over time and whether it is in the same direction. There are different ways of adducing a household class position (Korupp et al. 2002), one of the simplest being to attribute the highest class position of either member of a couple to the pair – the 'dominance approach'.

Looking at a recent cohort of children born in the late 1950s to mid-1970s, and using a simple, three-class breakdown, we can see from table 2.1 how the distribution of their parents' class was significantly different from that of their own. Table 2.1 reflects the increase in proportions in the professional or managerial classes that was a feature of the second half of the twentieth century. Thus, we see that those in the professional or managerial classes made up nearly half of their cohort in 2001, despite the fact that half of the cohort overall came from working-class backgrounds. At a household level, and focusing on a single generational transition occurring at the end of the last century, we can see the changing chances of being in a higher social class *household* which affects both men and women. These chances, compared with those of their parents, of belonging to the professional or managerial classes are dramatic for this generation of children, even if they are not equal across origins. We also see, however, that the chances of being in an unemployed household are substantially higher for the younger generation, reflecting both age-related individual risks – unemployment rates are higher for young people, and younger people are more likely to be living alone, therefore with less opportunity to be protected by a partner's work status – and the polarization of work, with a noted increase in both 'work-rich' and 'work-poor' households (Gregg and Wadsworth 1996; Nickell 2004).

As figures 2.1 and 2.2 indicated, the occupational structures of men and women are quite distinctive when taken individually. Looking at individual occupations within broader categories shows further distinctiveness and differences in occupational concentrations – and in overall occupational segregation. And equally distinctive are patterns across ethnic groups. Occupational segregation has been implicated in both gender and minority group pay gaps. However, different patterns do not necessarily mean unequal ones (Blackburn and Jarman 2006). Occupational segregation is subject to changes in the occupational structure, which has been considered the main factor behind the declines in occupational sex segregation that occurred during the 1990s (Blackwell and Guinea-Martin 2005). Thus, as the service and care sectors have expanded, both men and women and those from different ethnic groups have moved into them, decreasing segregation. Nevertheless, the occupational distributions and trajectories of men and women remain distinctive.

Drawing on work by Louisa Blackwell and Daniel Guinea-Martin (2005), tables 2.2 and 2.3 outline occupational patterns and their variation across men and women and by ethnic group, illustrating the ways in which particular occupations dominated their experience in 1991 and 2001. The types of occupation and the change in their dominance over time are informative about the worlds of men's and women's work at either end of the 1990s. Tables 2.2 and 2.3 reveal the tendency for convergence across the most common occupations, as well as for a decline (in most cases) in the proportion of individuals from each gender-ethnic group concentrated in the most common occupations for their group.

Table 2.2 reveals both the different sorts of occupations into which men are clustered and the different levels of clustering across groups. It also reveals the extent to which the most common occupations have shifted across the ten-year period. Strikingly, in 2001, 53 per cent of Bangladeshi men could be found in the top five jobs they occupied, whereas this was true of only 12 per cent of white men and 13 per cent of black Caribbean men. And there was a very heavy concentration of Bangladeshi men in catering-related occupations. This contrasts with black Caribbean men being in storage occupations and postal and van work and employed as security guards, while the top five among white men included production managers and metal workers. Across all groups of men, however, sales assistants newly featured in the most common occupations in 2001. This reflects the expansion of this sector and also that it was becoming less sex segregated. The appearance of software professionals in the top five occupations for several groups, by contrast, shows the growth of this sector, but primarily among men, as a highly sex-segregated area of work.

Among women, both the level of concentration in a few jobs and the types of job are much more similar across ethnic groups (table 2.3). There is some occupational specificity in relation to nursing among black Caribbean and black African women and catering-related jobs among Chinese women, but a lot of the occupations are similar across all groups, even if there are some changes over time.

Consistent with this picture, Blackwell and Guinea-Martin's overall analysis reveals that ethnic segregation among men and women tends to be lower than sex segregation between men and women and between men and women of the same ethnic group The exception was Bangladeshi men, where ethnic segregation was higher than sex segregation –that is, the difference in their occupational patterns compared with those of other men was greater than the differences between their

Table 2.2 The five most common occupations, 1991 and 2001, by ethnic group: men

Ethnic group	Year	Five most common occupations	Total % in five most common occupations
White	1991	Lorry drivers, managers–services, production managers, metal workers, carpenters/joiners	15.0
	2001	Same, except *storage occupations*, *retail managers* and *sales assistants* replace lorry drivers, managers–services and carpenters/joiners	12.0
Indian	1991	Managers–services, medical practitioners, sales assistants, financial clerks, machine tool operatives	23.9
	2001	Same, except *shopkeepers*, *software professionals* and *retail managers* replace managers–services, financial clerks and machine tool operatives	21.8
Pakistani	1991	Managers–proprietors in services, taxi drivers, sales assistants, machine tool operatives, labourers	25.8
	2001	Same, except *shopkeepers*, *retail managers* and *packers* replace managers–proprietors in services, machine tool operatives and labourers	26.1
Bangladeshi	1991	Cooks, waiters, restaurant managers, sewing machinists, kitchen workers	65.2
	2001	Same, except *sales assistants and kitchen assistants* replace sewing machinists and kitchen workers	52.8
Black Caribbean	1991	Carpenters/joiners, motor mechanics, machine tool operatives, metals workers, lorry drivers	12.0
	2001	Replaced by *sales assistants*, *storage occupations*, *security guards*, *postal workers* and *van drivers*	13.2
Black African	1991	Cleaners, security guards, financial clerks, medical practitioners, nurses	16.8
	2001	Same, except *sales assistants and software professionals* replace financial clerks and nurses	18.8
Chinese	1991	Cooks, restaurant managers, waiters, managers–services, accountants	52.9
Chinese	2001	Same, except *software professionals and sales assistants* replace managers–services and accountants	41.6

Source: Adapted from Blackwell and Guinea-Martin (2005), table 9.

Table 2.3 The five most common occupations, 1991 and 2001, by ethnic group: women

Ethnic group	Year	Five most common occupations	Total % in five most common occupations
White	1991	Sales assistants, cleaners, other secretaries, clerks, financial clerks	28.2
	2001	Same, except *care assistants* replace financial clerks	24.2
Indian	1991	Sewing machinists, managers–services, packers, sales assistants, financial clerks	30.9
	2001	Same, except *clerks* replace managers–services	23.4
Pakistani	1991	Sewing machinists, managers–services, sales assistants, packers, clerks	30.5
	2001	Same, except *educational assistants, care assistants* and *financial clerks* replace sewing machinists, managers–services and packers	26.1
Bangladeshi	1991	Sewing machinists, sales assistants, welfare, community and youth workers, financial clerks, clerks	31.2
	2001	Same, except *educational assistants* and *retail cashiers* replace sewing machinists and welfare, community and youth workers	32.2
Black Caribbean	1991	Nurses, cleaners, other secretaries, assistant nurses, clerks	32.5
	2001	Same, except *care assistants* and *sales assistants* replace cleaners and assistant nurses	29.4
Black African	1991	Nurses, cleaners, catering assistants, sales assistants, other secretaries	32.9
	2001	Same, except *care assistants* and *clerks* replace catering assistants and other secretaries	36.5
Chinese	1991	Nurses, cooks, restaurant managers, sales assistants, waitresses	40.2
Chinese	2001	Same	32.1

Source: Adapted from Blackwell and Guinea-Martin (2005), table 8.

occupational patterns compared with those of Bangladeshi women. Thus, despite some distinctive patterns by ethnicity, occupational opportunities are more heavily gendered than ethnically specific. Moreover, women's occupations tend to be more similar to each other across ethnic groups than do men's. This suggests that gender remains a key structural fault line for occupation and class, but that ethnicity is also highly relevant to men's occupational outcomes and opportunities – and their corresponding experience of the labour market in relation to pay, unemployment risks, pensions, and so on. To the extent that men and women from the same ethnic groups form households together, rather than with men and women of other ethnic groups – and this is the case for most groups, though less so for Caribbean men and Chinese women (Platt 2009b) – these differences between men by ethnic group will also have implications for household class differences and trends. Conversely, the relative similarity between the occupational distributions of women implies that they will have little bearing on moderating or enhancing ethnic stratification within households. So the implications of ethnic differences among men may be highly relevant for stratification at the household level, even if they are less striking than the distinct occupational patterns of men and women when considered separately.

Class has been associated with a range of different outcomes, with higher classes experiencing, on average, better health, greater life expectancy, more qualifications, better child outcomes, and so on. Some of these will be covered in subsequent chapters. However, classes are not self-evident: they are constructs, created by researchers and policy makers for the purposes of understanding cleavages within society and questions of opportunity and inequality. Despite the attention paid to issues of measurement and validation, it is hard to claim that their boundaries are clearly delineated and that the separation between one class and the next is necessarily clear cut, in terms of experiences, identity, cultural practice or income and welfare. They are heterogeneous groupings. Nevertheless, or perhaps because of this, it can be informative to look inside them and to examine the extent of that heterogeneity and to what extent inequalities within classes compare with inequalities between classes. However, when Hills et al. (2010) directly examined income and earnings inequality within as well as between groups, they found in fact that, though there was substantial variation within groups, there was much less inequality within groups than for the population as a whole, and that growing differences between groups were an important factor in accounting for the growth of earnings inequality in recent decades.

This suggests, then, that, despite the variation across groups and the slipperiness of class distinctions and boundaries, classes do nevertheless summarize clear social divisions within society and it is meaningful to talk about differences between them. The differences are particularly pointed when comparing those towards the top of any scheme with those towards the bottom. The potential for classes to represent relatively coherent groupings is critical for the consideration of social mobility and movement between classes, which this chapter addresses next.

2.3 Social mobility

Much class analysis has been dominated by how class background impacts over time on other outcomes. In particular there has been an interest in the extent to which relationships between class position across generations can tell us something about the openness of a society and the extent to which opportunities are systematically structured.

Equality of opportunity as a concept is not only promoted by sociologists, it is also broadly endorsed by politicians and the public. Indeed, the ambition to create a 'meritocracy' of talent, where outcomes are based on an individual's potential and not on accident of birth, is widely espoused and commands considerable consensus. The ideal of a meritocracy has come to seem uncontentious as a vision of a just society. An image where people get their deserts, where no one is held back by irrelevant characteristics or by their background, is seen as being relatively uncontroversial. The attachment to the concept of a meritocracy is, however, somewhat ironic if we turn to look at the antecedents of the term.

The rise of 'meritocracy'

In declaring the aims for his second term in office, the then prime minister Tony Blair argued that

> opening up economy and society to merit and talent is the true radical second term agenda. In the past the idea of meritocracy has been attacked.
>
> But creating a society that is meritocratic is not wrong; it is just insufficient. It needs to recognise talent in all its forms, not just intelligence. And it needs to be coupled with a platform that recognises the equal worth of all our citizens.
>
> But breaking down the barriers to success and allowing people's innate ability to shine through is an indispensable part of building a decent and prosperous country. It cannot be achieved by the Government standing back and allowing a Darwinian survival of the fittest, and pretending that it is meritocracy. It requires an active government ensuring a fair playing field and investing in our people and in our public services to release the potential of all. (Blair 2001)

There are number of things to note about these ambitions. First, the direct use of the term 'meritocracy'; second, the emphasis on equal worth and all forms of talent; and, third, the stress on a level playing field. The latter two elements are ones which Michael Young, who coined the term meritocracy, demonstrated as being easy to say, but, when the implications were explored, the emphasis on opportunity effectively undermined everything it was reaching for. Young's meritocracy was a neologism which parodied both the sociological emphasis on social mobility and problems with the aspirations to achieve a socially mobile society that fed that emphasis. His futuristic book *The Rise of the Meritocracy* (1958) is a humorous dystopia, along the lines of Huxley's *Brave New World*, rather than an optimistic vision of an equal society. Young's meritocracy is defined in the following terms:

> Today [i.e. speaking as if from 2033] we have an elite selected according to brains and educated according to deserts, with a grounding in philosophy and administration as well as in the two S's of science and sociology. . . . Today we frankly recognize that democracy can be no more than aspiration, and have rule not so much by the people as by the cleverest people; not an aristocracy of birth, not a plutocracy of wealth but a true meritocracy* of talent.
>
> *The origin of this unpleasant term, like that of 'equality of opportunity', is still obscure.
>
> (Young 1958, pp. 18–19)

In this work Young goes on to explore in ironic fashion the anti-progressive role of the family in attempting to secure the best for their children and the dissidence of women who (incomprehensibly) resist their role as mothers, selected on the basis of their hereditary intelligence. As soon becomes clear, the principles of meritocracy, if played out to their natural conclusions, can result in some very inegalitarian consequences. Moreover, Young highlights the difficulties with a position that challenges the rights of parents to want the best for their children – a point made more recently and in a more sober fashion by Adam Swift (2003) – and he illustrates the ways in which an emphasis on 'talent', here envisioned as genetic inheritance, can have oppressive consequences. The book also reveals the elitism in the whole notion of 'talent'. Why, as Swift has asked, is it logical that a substantially worse life should be accorded to someone who is less capable than to someone who is more capable? This clearly raises questions about treatment of disabling conditions, for example. Young's meritocracy also highlights the tensions already being felt as to how women should and could balance work and family life in a highly gendered society, and one in which fertility and motherhood were prioritized.

By working through the implications of a 'strong' version of equality of opportunity as if in a record of future society, Young showed how it could present problems for democracy, the enactment of parental aspirations, and the achievement of equality between elite and non-elite groups and between men and women. In line with the nature of the work, the position may have been overstated; but the analysis is nevertheless compelling and clearly demonstrates that, while lack of social mobility may be revealing about systematic class inequalities, the solution to them is not easily found simply in the establishment of a 'level playing field', where such a field is itself shaped by prior experience. Nor is reward for talent a necessary route to a fair society. Instead, social mobility has to be put in the context of other social aims: equality between men and women, equalization of the reward structure more generally, and recognition that parents, even without being overly competitive, are likely to act in what they consider the best interests of their children, and that they do so to the extent that they are able and that their resources – social and cultural as well as economic – allow (Bourdieu and Passeron 1977).

An overview of social mobility at the turn of the twenty-first century revealed the ongoing nature of the concerns that Young had highlighted and the problem this presented for the clear commitment to implementing social mobility (Aldridge 2004). Aldridge reverted to the issue that supporting parents to help their children, including helping them to avoid downward mobility, might be a clear policy aim but one that was unlikely to increase social mobility. He also raised the problem of the extent to which, once achieved, social mobility – in either direction – should be expected to persist over the life course. If you start to make an effort later in life, surely you should be able to move up in the class structure. Or, if you are a barrister, but become lazy, should you be forced down to become a sales assistant? Of course, neither of these scenarios is likely to happen, life chances are cumulative, and it is hard to shift positions which have been acquired as the result of longer-term processes. But if such transitions are impossible, then is a society really a meritocracy? If they are possible, however, they may create so much instability that insecurity outweighs any concerns regarding equality of opportunity.

Moreover, what rarely gets mentioned, at least among its political proponents, is that there is a downside to social mobility. It is impossible to have equality of opportunity without also having downward mobility. Downward mobility can also be destabilizing and create unhappiness (after all, the presumption is that, if merit is rewarded, then one has only oneself to blame for 'failure'), and it potentially breaches an implied contract that people should be able to remain at least at the level of their parents. Hout (2003) has suggested we should think in terms of 'taking turns', and swift transitions between generations might well mitigate much of the distress caused by downward mobility: 'I may have done badly but my kids are doing alright'. But it is hard to see how such a scenario could be guaranteed.

Two further issues give pause to general endorsement of social mobility. First, the assumption of returns to talent plus effort may not sufficiently acknowledge that women's lifetime occupational trajectories are also heavily influenced by having children. They may lose class position because of taking time out of the labour market. Is that an appropriate penalty for lack of 'effort'? And, if not, how should the particular occupational path still typical of mothers be considered within the meritocratic ideal?

Second, that which is rewarded by the market – and therefore regarded as 'talent' or 'ability' – changes over time as well as being shaped by historical factors. Is it clear that those who become barristers have more ability than those who become teachers? The differential rewards would suggest that this is the case, but different sorts of 'talent' and access to different sorts of training make a direct comparison on objective grounds almost impossible. Other than evaluation through actual rewards such as pay, it is a hard case to argue. There is surely an element of being in the right place at the right time for certain forms of success, while certain forms of talent – one might think of Mozart – are not necessarily guarantors at least of commensurate economic rewards, even when one has the opportunity to realize one's talent at a practical level. Of course, the emphasis on talent and potential obscures the fact that merit, more tightly defined, is supposed to represent intelligence (or ability, capability, etc.) *plus* effort. But though there have been some attempts to evaluate the effort part of the equation and its contribution, the overall emphasis has been on the reward of ability, and there is neither clarity concerning, nor consensus on, how 'easy' success through natural facility should or could be compared to hard-won achievement. In practice, as the discussion of gender and education in chapter 6 notes, achievement requiring effort is frequently rated as being of lower value than 'natural ability'.

Social mobility debates and findings

Given all the difficulties with the concept of meritocracy in particular, but also social mobility more widely, we might question the amount of energy and ink that has gone into the study of social mobility. And, indeed, Ken Roberts has explicitly questioned this preoccupation from within the sociological study of class. He asks

> why so many sociologists continue to lend support to measures that are supposed to equalise opportunities. Sociologists should know that the best way to change mobility flows is to change the structure of opportunities itself. We are more likely to reduce unemployment rates among the least-qualified by reducing general unemployment than by providing the least qualified with yet more education and training. (Roberts 2001, p. 223)

Instead, though, there has been detailed consideration and debate around how best to tackle the conceptual and methodological issues raised in relation to social mobility, while the implicit importance of the enterprise remains unchallenged. Rather than seeing unemployment as a challenge to an emphasis on equality of opportunity, the ability to incorporate unemployment within an analysis of mobility is seen as a practical problem of incorporation or recognition – or, alternatively, a distraction from the central focus, even if in a liberal economy it should instead be regarded as a fundamental component of the class structure. There are different positions on practically how best to treat the unemployed within studies of social mobility. They are generally excluded as lacking a class position, yet the exclusion of unemployment as an outcome in the measurement of social mobility can alter the results, since unemployment – and among the unemployed, long-term unemployment – is a much higher risk for those from lower social class backgrounds (Aldridge 2004; Miller 1998) or particular ethnic groups (Platt 2005b). Mobility studies thus risk portraying only a partial picture of the potentially most serious way in which class origins shape occupational or class outcomes. And with the polarization of work within households, and the tendency of employment rates to be resistant to recovery, this remains a concern in periods of relative prosperity, not only in periods of recession.

In addition, the implications of the extent of the dispersion – the range of difference between the various class positions, between the top and the bottom – clearly have a bearing on the interpretation of what observed social mobility means. Mobility is presumably rather different if class positions are fairly close than if there is a huge gap between the life chances at the top and the bottom (Westergaard 1995). Similarly, social mobility may disguise or not be very revealing about situations of entrenched disadvantage of particular groups and their opportunities. For example, it might transpire that people from working-class groups and ethnic minority origins fare no worse than other working-class people. But if there is a far higher proportion of a particular group from the working class, then the fact that they have mobility chances compared to others in the working class may not be that encouraging in a long-term perspective.

And, just as allocating class to women has been a point of considerable dispute more widely, it is heightened in the study of social mobility in relation to whether it is the association between the outcomes of fathers and sons, or fathers and children (both sons and daughters), or mothers and daughters, that is of interest. Traditional studies of class mobility have tended to examine only fathers and children, often fathers and sons (Goldthorpe et al. 1987). But, with the increase in the number of women in the workplace and in the proportions of people living singly and for longer, such a focus can no longer – if it ever could – be claimed to be informative about society as a whole (Ganzeboom et al. 1991). Indeed, research has shown that the treatment of mothers can substantially alter social mobility stories (Beller 2009).

If the avoidance of downward mobility is the main aim for parents and their children, Breen and Goldthorpe (1997) have theorized why the risks associated with different educational strategies may indeed be non-symmetric between higher and lower social classes. This therefore goes some way towards explaining continuing differentials in educational outcomes and consequently in relative social mobility across groups.

A final vexed issue in the study of social mobility is the practical one that occupations and their position in the hierarchy change. Some jobs disappear, and new ones are created. How is it possible to measure transitions comparably in such circumstances? Old systems of measurement may no longer be appropriate in new circumstances. Even when jobs look as if they are the same, they may have altered in terms of conditions of service status, and so on. So apparent immobility may in fact reflect mobility, and vice versa. This has been illuminated by historical studies of social mobility and the creation of temporally specific and harmonized class schemes (Lambert et al. 2007).

In both acknowledging and attempting to address these issues, the study of social mobility has continued to be central to understanding the role of class within society and the extent to which societies are open (and promote opportunity) or closed (and inhibit it). Social mobility tells us something about the way society is organized and reveals sometimes counter-intuitive processes at work that affect possibilities and the realization of aspirations. Moreover, analysis of social mobility can be informative in revealing differences not only over time, where a lot of emphasis has been placed, but also between groups. Are some social groups more mobile than others? And, if so, what does that tell us about opportunities and constraints? This is a point to which I return below when discussing ethnicity and social mobility.

A fundamental distinction to make about the analysis of social class is that between absolute and relative mobility. Someone's absolute chances of social mobility are determined in large part by the occupational structure: if there is an increase in professional or managerial jobs and a decline in working-class jobs over time, then, necessarily, some people with working-class backgrounds will have to experience upward mobility – there is simply more room at the top. By contrast, relative social mobility refers to the chances of someone moving into a professional class from working-class origins compared to the chances of someone from a professional class background remaining there. Even if those from a lower social class background experience substantial absolute upward mobility, their relative chances of ending up in a higher social class position may still be smaller than those who started off more advantaged. Studies have tended to focus on relative chances; but what may matter to individuals may be their absolute experience of class – whether or not they have done as well as or better than their parents – rather than their relative position.

It is also important to bear in mind that, while most of the focus is on intergenerational mobility (i.e. that between parents and children), intra-generational mobility (mobility within the life course) may also be an important indicator of opportunity or constraint within society.

Mobility and education

Equality of opportunity is supposed to be delivered predominantly through an egalitarian educational system that allows everyone the possibility of achieving the qualifications that will lead them to a 'good job' and a good – or higher – class position. Thus there is an emphasis on education. If achievement is gained through education, then, it is argued, no one can complain about what happens to them and all can realistically aim for the top. Overall, education has been effective in providing a route to occupational outcomes that can be shared across those from different backgrounds (Ganzeboom et al. 1991). Part of the effect of social class background can, nevertheless, be fed through educational achievement, not only through private schooling but through particular choices of secondary schooling and support for learning. Thus education does not form a transparently egalitarian route to outcomes but is itself subject to the stratification processes that mean it can be better exploited by those already more advantaged, and that particular educational structures, such as those that promote parental choice, can exacerbate such processes (Ball et al. 1995).

The belief in the equalizing potential of education was certainly behind initial investigations of social mobility which explored both whether education was equally accessible and produced equivalent opportunities and its importance as a mediating factor in class mobility. The close association assumed – and demonstrated – between educational opportunity and upward social mobility means that its role in class outcomes is part of the discussion of social mobility. It is perhaps not surprising, then, that the seminal early study of mobility carried out by Glass (1954) was attempting to assess the extent to which the new education system, instigated by the Education Act of 1944, had created a new way to the top for working-class children. Was it enabling clever children from less advantaged backgrounds to succeed educationally? And did this then give them a better start in adult life? At an absolute level, the expansion of the education system between 1930 and 1960 meant that there were more children in education and more working-class achievement overall. But how were working-class children doing relative to middle-class children? Were they being equipped to take advantage of the changing class structure, with its move towards more skilled jobs and fewer unskilled jobs, which was beginning to occur in the postwar decades?

These were the questions that Glass set himself in his 1954 study of social mobility. He showed that the 1944 Act was not levelling social differences in favour of ability as much as had been hoped for from the system. He looked at entrants to grammar schools in the existing tripartite system and found that numbers tended to reflect class hierarchies: a predominance of middle-class children and a small proportion of working-class children. He made a case that this was nothing to do with intelligence, though he was concerned that the 11 plus examination to assess eligibility for grammar-school education selected out working-class children through forms of question that were aligned with middle-class culture and knowledge (compare the discussion of Bourdieu in chapter 6). This was a concern that continued throughout the life of the 11 plus examination. Glass also found that working-class children seemed to 'fit in' less well than their middle-class counterparts and that teachers seemed to regard them as 'ill-fitting'. Such themes and observations have persisted into analysis of contemporary educational institutions (Ball 2006; Reay 2005). In Glass's study, the working-class children had the highest relative aspirations – but these did not necessarily seem to come to fruition.

Glass also looked at the jobs of fathers and sons to consider occupational mobility, and the result of this study was to suggest (with some cautions and reservations) that there was a distinct lack of mobility, or occupational freedom as he saw it. He was writing in the period before comprehensive education and in the time of tripartite education, with grammar schools at the top of the hierarchy. He summed up the situation overall that making it into the grammar system did assist with occupational mobility – though not conclusively so – but that the grammar system was itself dominated by those from higher social classes, for whom it was experienced as normal and aligned with their background and expectations. The system enabled them to achieve levels of upward mobility that meant that, even with an expansion of higher social class jobs, they still went on to dominate the professional and managerial classes.

More recent research (Smith 2000) indicated that increasing qualifications at all levels meant that the relative chances of people from different social backgrounds of acquiring such qualifications remained relatively constant. There has been a great expansion in educational achievement as a whole, but relative chances have remained very similar. Later changes in educational policy, especially those emphasizing market processes and parental choice, have done little to shift these systematic differentials (Ball 2008).

Class mobility

The contrast between high levels of absolute achievement or mobility and lower or negligible levels of relative achievement or mobility is reflected in recent studies of occupational social mobility across the generations. Heath and Payne (2000) traced the patterns of mobility of a series of cohorts of men and women to identify both their absolute chances of upward mobility and their relative odds of achieving a higher social class position. Table 2.4 summarizes the amount of class stability and absolute upward mobility for men and women according to the decade they were born. It indicates that mobility rose for both men and women across this period and is related to the description of the changing class structure. Recent work by Goldthorpe and Mills (2008), however, looking at a range of sources and for outcomes in the 1970s to early 2000s, suggests that, while women have continued to make absolute gains, the upward mobility of men has levelled off.

When looking at relative mobility – that is, the chances of ending up in a particular class, given your class background, compared with the chances of someone from a

Table 2.4 Upward mobility and stability among men and women, by cohort (%)

Birth cohort	Men		Women	
	Stable	Upwardly mobile	Stable	Upwardly mobile
Pre–1900	43	27	31	24
1900–09	39	29	29	22
1910–19	38	30	26	27
1920–29	35	39	28	23
1930–39	34	38	22	29
1940–49	28	42	20	33
1950–59	35	42	17	36

Note: Only information on those stable and upwardly mobile is supplied. The remainder were either downwardly mobile or experienced horizontal mobility – i.e. they changed class to one that could not unequivocally be rated as higher or lower.
Source: Adapted from Heath and Payne (2000), tables 6 and 9.

Table 2.5 Odds ratios of service-class outcomes, comparing those with service-class and working-class origins

	Men	Women
1900–09	10	17
1910–19	19	15
1920–29	14	15
1930–39	10	7
1940–49	6	11
1950–59	8	6

Source: Adapted from Heath and Payne (2000), tables 12 and 13.

different class background – the results showed that outcomes were far from being independent of class origins. For example, 20 per cent of those who ended up in the highest social class had their origins in that class and 15 per cent had their origins in the working class. But because the highest class had been small and had expanded and the lowest class had been large and had contracted over time, this meant that 46 per cent of those with their origins in the highest social class remained there, while only 9 per cent of those originating in the lowest social class experienced mobility into this class. The standard way of describing the relative chances of different positions is to look at the ratio of the odds for a particular outcome across two groups. Larger odds mean that the chances of a particular outcome are greater for one group than for the other. Table 2.5 shows Heath and Payne's calculations of the odds ratios over time, which illustrate the relative chances of being in the highest social class dependent on class background. Grouping outcomes into three possible ranked class positions, they show that, for men from the youngest cohort, the odds of being in the higher class when coming from that class were around eight times greater than for some-one from a working-class background. For women the odds were around six times greater. Heath and Payne's results appeared to imply, nevertheless, that there had been some decrease in the association between class origins and class destinations over time or, put another way, that there had been an increase in relative mobility.

However, looking specifically at relative chances, Heath and Clifford (1996) judged that there had in fact been 'constant relative chances'; and Marshall et al. (1997) argued that there had been a 'generally unchanging relationship between class origins and educational achievement' over different cohorts. Some have therefore attributed Heath and Payne's (2000) results in part to sampling error given the relatively small sample sizes on which they were based. Goldthorpe has consistently argued, and claims to have demonstrated, that there is comparatively little change in relative chances of movement from the lower classes into the service class compared with retention in the service class of service-class children. He first put forward this claim in a 1972 survey (Goldthorpe et al. 1980), and again when updated with 1983 data (Goldthorpe and Payne 1986; see also Goldthorpe et al. 1987). In both cases, they argued that relative mobility had remained remarkably constant over a period – that mobility was not increasing. Erikson and Goldthorpe (1992) also made this claim in a comparative context when they argued for the existence of 'a constant flux' across a number of European countries. Countries might have different patterns of occupational mobility but the trend was considered to be remarkably similar. The corollary, though, that Goldthorpe and his collaborators have emphasized in recent work is that, equally, there is no evidence for a decline in social mobility. In a paper comparing results from a range of different sources, Goldthorpe and Mills (2008) challenged the idea that there had been a decline in social mobility and instead argued the case for remarkable stability over time. In the context of substantial political anxiety about social immobility, they submitted that there was nothing particularly distinctive about the current period and that studies suggesting a decline were potentially misleading. Nicoletti and Ermisch (2007) have also made the point that the pattern of mobility is not clear cut and that comparing just two points and inferring a trend from them is unreliable in the face of variation in both directions. The longer-term evidence also suggests that society has not become significantly more open (Prandy and Bottero 1998), but it may not have become more closed either.

Ethnicity and intergenerational social mobility

We saw earlier how the class positions of different ethnic groups vary substantially. But it is not clear from those distributions from a single point in time what the experience of social mobility is for minority ethnic groups. There has been far less investigation into the mobility of ethnic minority groups. However, analysing mobility processes across subpopulations can reveal the extent to which assumed class relationships can be generalized and can be informative about the extent to which society is 'open' on more than one dimension.

Here, the findings from some key studies are briefly summarized. Overall they suggest that there are different patterns of mobility for some minority groups and that in some cases this translates into inequality in access to higher social class positions.

Heath and McMahon (2005) used pooled data from the General Household Survey for 1985 to 1992 and covering Great Britain to examine social class outcomes (access to the 'salariat' or the professional/managerial social class), taking account of social class background. They found that, among first-generation men, there were no differences in chances of access to the higher social class (or 'salariat') among the Irish compared with the white British, once class background was taken into account, whereas the chances for Indians, Caribbeans and Pakistanis were lower. First-generation Irish and black Caribbean women had greater chances of access to higher social class outcomes, controlling for background, and Indian and Pakistani women had lower chances than white British women. Thus there appeared to be a minority or migrant disadvantage for men but for only some groups of women.

Among the second generation, Heath and McMahon found that Irish and Indian men had superior chances of ending up in higher social classes compared with white British men of the same cohort and controlling for class background, but Caribbean men had worse chances. For second-generation women, however, ethnicity no longer played a significant role in outcomes once class background was controlled. This can be compared with a similar result found in analysis of different data (Platt 2005a).

These findings suggest that class background may have less salience, and constrain chances less, for some ethnic groups than others. This may be partly to do with differential rates of downward mobility on migration across groups (Heath and Ridge 1983). That is, if minority groups tend to end up in some of the less desirable jobs on migration, but some come from lower social class positions and some from higher, the mismatch will be greater for some groups than for others. However, those who came from more privileged backgrounds, even if these are not reflected in their post-migration outcomes, may retain and transmit some of their cultural and social – and economic – capital. Recovery of the underlying class position is then more likely among the children of those who experienced such class suppression on arrival. The fact that class processes appear (more) comparable across women is likely to reflect the more restricted class distribution of women overall. Nevertheless, the fact that class processes appear to operate differently for men and women indicates that the intersection of migration background and class position has different consequences for men and women: we cannot conceive straightforwardly of an ethnic penalty or advantage in class mobility, but need to focus on the ways in which class effects are moderated by both ethnicity and gender simultaneously.

Of course, looking simply at social class background does not take account either of how that class background is – or is not – mediated through education or the extent to which these results are explicable on the basis of different levels of qualifications according to ethnicity and sex. Further analysis followed up the question of the extent to which class background was protective for minority as well as majority groups (Platt 2005b) and explored the relationship of education to mobility (Platt 2007b). However, since it used a household definition of class, the analysis could say little about gendered differences in class mobility across groups. The starting and ending positions of the minority groups are illustrated in figure 2.3, which shows the proportions from each group ending up in each social class; conversely, for each 'destination' we see the proportion coming from each origin class. The increase in room at the top means that a substantial proportion of those with working-class origins from all groups ends up in the top social class. But the sizes of the bars for the top social class differ quite substantially across the group. Moreover, the extent to which the top social class is dominated by those of working-class origins also varies.

Detailed analysis demonstrated that upward mobility (i.e. conditioning on class origins) was greater among the Indian, Caribbean and white migrant group than among the white non-migrant majority, but was lower among the Pakistani group. When the role of education in mediating these differences was considered, it was found that the greater levels of relative mobility among Indians, Caribbeans and white migrants could be understood in terms of educational attainment. In fact, levels of educational attainment among Indians suggested that they should perhaps have experienced even more upward mobility. Among the Pakistanis, however, lower relative rates of upward mobility were despite, not because of, their educational qualifications, and they should have experienced much more upward mobility than was in fact the case. Thus they appeared to experience closure in terms of upward mobility that was not experienced by the other minority groups. Moreover, investigation of the role of class background found that, while it was important in retaining advantage for the white majority and in helping the more privileged Indians, Caribbeans were not 'protected' by higher class origins. The story was therefore one of diversity, which partly vindicated the role of education as a route to mobility among migrants and partly found it insufficient to account for the outcomes across groups. Moreover,

Figure 2.3

White migrants	Routine/manual	
	Intermediate	
	Prof/managerial	
Pakistanis	Routine/manual	
	Intermediate	
	Prof/managerial	
Indians	Routine/manual	
	Intermediate	
	Prof/managerial	
Caribbeans	Routine/manual	
	Intermediate	
	Prof/managerial	
White non-migrants	Routine/manual	
	Intermediate	
	Prof/managerial	

Legend: ☐ Higher social class origins ⊠ Intermediate class origins ▨ Working-class origins

Horizontal axis: 0 10 20 30 40 50 60 70

Source: ONS longitudinal study, author's analysis.

Figure 2.3 Distributions of class destinations by origins, England and Wales, 1971/81–2001.

there was no clear evidence of a minority group effect that could be generalized across groups.

The study illuminated the important role of educational qualifications in achieving class mobility for those in relatively marginalized positions. It also demonstrates that education is less important for those in privileged positions – class background for the white majority mattered in terms of their chances of higher class outcomes over and above the role of education. However, the fact that education did not 'work' for all minority groups challenges us to think more carefully about how its role as a route to mobility for minorities actually operates. It has been claimed that certain groups have a particular commitment to education (Francis and Archer 2005; Modood 2004), but the theory of migrants' educational investment and empirical evidence across groups in terms of educational practices and aspirations indicate that group-differentiated arguments on the valuation of education are hard to sustain (Platt 2007c).

The fact that higher social class origins 'matter' only for some also requires that we reflect more carefully on the mechanisms through which class origins result in more advantageous outcomes. It highlights the assumed processes that take place within advantaged families to ensure that children have better chances and challenges us to explain how they can be differentiated by group. Thus, as well as demonstrating the importance of investigating the intersections between stratified positions to obtain a fuller understanding of the social world, it also underlines how exploring such intersections can challenge conventional wisdom about overarching processes such as class mobility.

The exploration of class mobility across groups can, therefore, help to reformulate our understanding of class. If social class mobility works differently for different groups, then its central role as an indicator of the openness or closed nature of society perhaps needs rethinking. Or, at least, our judgements on the latter may need to take into account not only the experience of women, but also the differentiated experience of subpopulations, such as minority ethnic groups. A more open society on ethnic lines may be one in which class structures across groups reflect those in the society overall, while a high degree of social mobility may nevertheless come at the expense of minorities. When conceiving what is more equal in class terms, it is important to consider who is affected by patterns of mobility and immobility and how. Moreover, the varying relationship between education and social mobility across groups suggests that relationship between class and education is not singular. Formulations of the interconnectedness of class and education need, on the one hand, to take account of the ways in which education can be used by minorities to bypass constraining class structures and the status quo and, on the other, to recognize that neither educational attainment nor class privilege may be sufficient to ensure successful outcomes for those in marginalized positions. Some of these issues are picked up in other ways in chapter 6. Meanwhile, they suggest that the analysis of social mobility still has many more questions to answer.

Questions for reflection

1 What is class?
2 Should openness in society be a key aim or should the reduction of inequalities between groups be prioritized?
3 If gaps between social classes are reduced, should we worry about social mobility?
4 Should unemployment, as a predominantly temporary experience, fit into a study of social class mobility and, if so, where?
5 What does the study of ethnic group social mobility tell us about the class structure?

Further reading

Crompton (2008) provides a detailed overview of the development of class analysis, measures, debates and renewal, as well as the development of ethnographies of class. A rich account of recent thinking on class that pays attention to class identities and culture can be found in the edited volume by Devine et al. (2005). Bottero's (2005) book on social inequality provides a good introduction to the theoretical debates on class, stratification and class measurement. For a thoughtful and illuminating account of how to approach social mobility from a qualitative perspective, it is well worth reading Bertaux and Thompson's (1997) volume.

3 Gender

> They're walking around with manicured nails, perfect nail varnish, perfect make-up, hair perfect and by the time they're 30 they look about 60 cos they've worn so much shit on their faces they've ruined their skin altogether. They speak through their noses, they look down at you as if you're common as bloody muck and a few years before they were no bloody better. They've landed themselves a cushy little job and married a bloke with some money.

> He will try to say we're working class; we go to work everyday, and I say oh yes, we've got the care, the nice home. . . . Working-class women, I'd think council estates, living off benefits, middle class have choice.

These two quotations come from a study of the classed identities and aspirations of working-class and middle-class women (Hebson 2009). They highlight the discomfort and resentment associated with class positions that has been a focus of recent work of a number of sociologists, such as Sayer, Reay, Savage and others (Devine et al. 2005; Reay 2005; Savage et al. 2001; Sayer 2005). They also draw attention to the processes of attempted boundary setting that have been emphasized elsewhere (Sayer 2005). Hebson's article explores how aspirations are located in relation to class identities, which are used both to root achievement and to denigrate (as well as to valorize) others not facing the same network of opportunities and constraints, intimating the ways in which structural constraints are adapted to or rationalized or interpreted in terms of individual positions, linking to the broader discussions of women and work to be found in this chapter. Moreover, these quotations point towards how internally differentiated women can feel, foregrounding the heterogeneity among women that is theme of this chapter, and which is explicitly treated in its final section. There is the recognition that, while some women may have choice, others do not. Income differences and housing position are seen to affect women specifically in particular ways. These are aspects of gendered inequalities that are followed up in later chapters.

Hebson's article also reveals some of the ambivalences in women's relationship to work, including the insecurity they face, where men's work is still the dominant reference point: women do well, the first speaker claims, by finding a man with money. We can see in these quotations how a partner's work status is referred to and used as a point for defining women even among women who are themselves in employment. Women's relationships to each other, including antagonistic ones, are shaped by perceptions of men's labour market position and women's historically and normatively more tangential relationship to paid work.

In these short examples of the way women talk, about themselves, their work and other women, we can see some of the complexity of their experience of inequality and their struggles to make sense of it, a process which can itself contribute to the durable nature of some of the fundamental inequalities they face, such as in the labour market.

In what follows we move away from women's actual voices, but, when discussing differences between women, women's 'preferences' or the enduring nature of the unequal domestic division of labour and women's dual burden, we can hear their engagement with possibilities and constraints and 'what makes sense'.

3.1 Definitions, concepts and coverage

I start by considering the definition of gender. Gender is probably one of the most abused terms in common usage. It is often used as a simple substitute for 'sex' and it is also commonly employed to refer simply to women. Its use highlights the problems that arise when terms that are developed to convey specific conceptual claims are incorporated into everyday language as a substitute for others, without in fact transforming what they replace. Thus gender often becomes a 'polite' word for sex, without necessarily incorporating a recognition of the constructed nature of gendered distinctions. In this it is similar to those uses of 'ethnicity' which employ the term as a substitute for 'race' without recognizing the reasons for the rejection of race terminology, and thus perpetuate them (Carter and Fenton 2009). The analysis in this book will principally be drawing out inequalities between women and men, and primarily those in which women are disadvantaged, but it is important to note that that is not a necessary implication of a gendered analysis. Even though it is not a specific focus here, one advantage of the concept of gender is that it encourages a study of masculinity as well as of femininity, and the ways in which inequalities constrain patterns of both male and female experience and behaviour (Haywood and Mac an Ghaill 2003): it promotes an exploration of the relations between the sexes as well as of the social position of women (Connell 2005). Nevertheless, like class and ethnicity, gender is a contested term in its conception as much as in its use.

Ann Oakley is widely credited as having introduced the concept of 'gender' into the social sciences. She distinguished between the biological 'fact' of sex (itself not a clear, binary distinction) and culturally specific expressions and expectations of 'masculinity' and 'femininity', which are justified by association with biological sex and therefore appear immutable. She exposed the process by which the 'lines are tied between the act of giving birth and the act of cleaning the house' as determined by a form of social ascription unrelated to individual capacities and open to challenge (Oakley 1972). That is, what is seen as masculine or feminine, or as men's work or women's work, is not dependent on biological differences but is a construction that has come about through the way society has developed, and which will not necessarily be replicated across other societies. Oakley and others argue that the matching of male and female to gender roles occurs through socialization. Gender is thus an analytic term, whereas sex is the descriptive term that applies to the differentiation between men and women.

However, this distinction between sex and gender has been broken down by the recognition that sex differences are not absolute, and that a restriction to two sexes is itself a construction that denies the plurality of sexes (Fausto-Sterling 2000). Thus what we see as sex differences are related to the social forces which construct them: sex and gender are implicated in each other. Feminist and postmodernist analysis has thus criticized the attribution to sex of fixed biological difference and the perpetuation of a dichotomy rooted in a hegemonic male view of the world. If gendered differences are not fixed or necessary, neither are sex differences. Such critiques can be seen as part of feminism's engagement with – or contribution to – postmodernism and to be linked to a wider critique of categories that sees such divisions as part of power structures that determine meanings and constrain knowledge (including sociological knowledge), and that therefore require deconstructing and destabilizing as a form of liberation and of the better representation of a shifting and complex social world.

This body of work has been important in stressing the diversity of women's experience; it has also challenged the essentializing tendencies born of assumptions of the homogeneity of women that can be found not only in traditional 'male' sociology but also in overarching theories of male power and domination, or more specifically patriarchy (Pateman 1988; Walby 1990). While Walby articulates a system of domination of women that operates across a series of domains, including paid work, unpaid work and the cultural sphere, this system implies a relatively singular conception of gender relations. Instead, those challenging the validity of such singular categories as men and women pay attention to the specificities of meaning for those located in particular situated contexts. They thus tell the particularized stories of those who are positioned in relation to a variety of mutually constitutive social groups and experiences, and of the complexities of their social engagement.

The relevance of specific contexts to the realization of gender is also fundamental to Butler's influential work on performativity (Butler 1990). For Butler, gender is created and re-created within specific sets of social relations where gender is performed. 'Doing' gender involves the rehearsal of a 'script', which is itself largely predetermined through dominant discourses. Gender is attached not to particular bodies but to acts of speaking and communication. Her development of ideas of performativity has been influential in challenging essentialized ideas of masculinity and femininity, which she associates with proponents of theories of patriarchy. Moreover, she argues that a recognition of gender as a performance allows for subversion of the 'scripts' by altering the performance. This reinterpretation has not been without critics: some reject the reduction of gender to language (which, they argue, ignores the importance of bodies and embodiment); and some question the possibility of challenging inequalities through an emphasis on the performance of gender. How the subversive possibilities of gender performance can be achieved given the assumed prior of the dominant scripts has also been questioned.

Oakley subsequently defended her original discussion of gender and of the gender/sex distinction against postmodern critiques as representing a valuable sociological concept. She argues that it retains a crucial role in identifying and exploring persisting material inequalities and their ideational causes (Oakley 2005). In this view, then, gender analysis is associated with uncovering inequalities between men and women that are structurally embedded. It is in these terms and with this understanding of gendered analysis that this chapter proceeds. Employing such a concept of gender, as being located and revealing of inequalities, does not need to assume homogeneity among women – or, for that matter, among men – but it does imply that we can name groups and discuss experience across categories, even if that risks marginalizing the experience of some of those not named or ignoring the distinctiveness of specific individual intersectional experiences.

It is important to be sensitive to the extent to which a study of inequalities between men and women requires a recognition of historical and cultural variety and change rather than a universalizing analysis, but this does not necessarily imply a rejection of the categories of men and women so much as an acknowledgement of the necessary heterogeneity of those categories. Indeed, Crenshawe (1991), in developing the concept of intersectionality, suggests that the use of categories is critical in order to address inequalities of marginalized groups. There is, she says, 'the power exercised simply through the process of categorization; the other, the power to cause that categorization to have social and material consequences' (1991, p. 1297). While both may be important, Crenshawe suggests that the major problem is not 'social categorization as such, but the myriad ways in which those of us so defined have been systematically subordinated' (ibid., p. 1298). A comparable point has been made by Fraser (2000) in her discussion of the decline of attention to redistribution, as identity politics took centre stage. Despite the importance of recognition of identities, it has been asserted that we still need to pay attention to people's and groups' material circumstances, circumstances that can also determine whether recognition is achievable (Byrne 2005).

I now turn to a consideration of certain inequalities between men and women and how they can be seen as gendered. The discussion that follows focuses on the interrelated issues of the labour market and domestic work and emphasizes heterogeneity among women. Nevertheless, even in looking across the experience of different women, there are limits on the extent to which it is possible to reveal the whole variety of configurations of experience and their complexity. Thus there is a tendency to focus on averages, despite what they exclude, and to concentrate on experiences that are common across many women, even if they do not reflect the full diversity of women's experience.

Women and inequality: an overview

Employment inequalities between men and women cover the areas of participation, unemployment, hours and timetable, occupation and pay. That is, women are less likely to be in employment than men and when employed are more likely to be working part-time. Men are more likely to work irregular patterns and to undertake shift work. In the UK, men's unemployment rates are also higher than those of women, though in many other countries the opposite is the case. Women are more heavily concentrated at lower occupational levels (see also chapter 2), and men and women are to a certain extent occupationally segregated. Chapter 2 showed that occupational segregation between men and women has been declining over time, though it is higher than segregation among men or among women of different ethnic groups. Women can expect to earn less than men on average, and this pay gap is more, not less, evident when we compare those with the same levels of qualifications and broad occupational grouping (Longhi and Platt 2008).

The differences in pay between men and women can be understood partly in terms of occupational segregation and differences in part-time work rates, which themselves reflect the gendering of employment and of the division of domestic labour. Family circumstances, work history, and the demands of the domestic sphere are also directly implicated, as is occupational or class position. Despite the increases in women's labour market participation, the rise in the number of women who delay starting a family or do not have children, and some equalization in the sharing of household labour (Fisher et al. 2007; Gershuny 2000), it is still true that women remain over-whelmingly responsible for dependent children and for providing and organizing their care, with the consequences for other aspects of their life that such responsi-bilities bring. Changes in the form of the family, such as the growth in same-sex civil partnerships with and without children, have impacted on these general patterns only at the margins. Other changes, meanwhile, such as the increase in numbers of lone parents – or, more precisely, of women who will experience lone parenthood at some point – have tended to add to women's domestic responsibilities as well as their attempts to manage the 'double burden' of work and family life. Alongside changing patterns of educational qualifications and the structure of employment, family, class and life stage are factors relevant to women's chances of being in paid work and what that work is. The cumulative impact of differing responsibilities in relation to family and home and the gendered nature of employment trajectories results in diverg-ing pay and income across the life course. Thus the gendering of both work and the domestic sphere can lead to lifetime differences in the economic well-being of men and women, an issue addressed in more detail in chapter 5.

However, there are substantial differences between women, and it has been argued that greater equality between the sexes in some areas may come at the cost of greater polarization between men and between women living in or moving into different sets of circumstances. Women have particular, classed experiences of the labour market and the demands of home life, as well as, before that, of educational systems. And these critically influence their subsequent opportunities. As patterns of paid work become arguably less gendered, are they becoming more classed?

The remainder of the discussion pursues these points, with brief illustrations of inequalities between men and women. It is followed by a more detailed discussion of domestic work, which is a persistent source of inequality between men and women and which interpenetrates occupational and labour market experiences, but which has traditionally not formed a core element of sociological analysis of inequality. This includes some consideration of how we measure both what happens in the domes-tic sphere and what its value is. The final part of the chapter returns explicitly to the issue of heterogeneity among women and reflects on diversity in occupation and employment among women, and its implications.

3.2 Gender inequalities in work

Employment and part-time work

The gender employment gap – the difference in employment rates between men and women – stood at around 12 per cent across the European Union in 2009. That is, despite their increasing levels of participation, women of working age continue to have a lower chance of being in paid work than men of working age. There is some variation across countries (as we can see in figure 3.1 from a selection of contrasting EU countries, plus Norway, Turkey and the US), but in the vast majority of countries the employment gap is substantial. Of the countries illustrated, only in Lithuania is there a marginally higher share of women than men in work.

Nor do these differences necessarily reflect differences in unemployment – that is, those looking for a job but unable to get one. In fact, as we can see from figure 3.2,

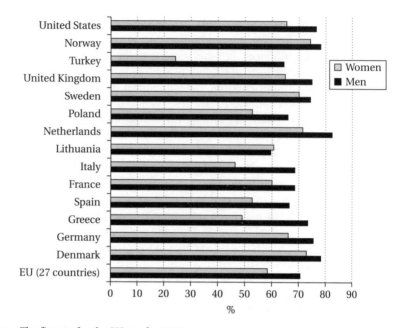

Note: The figures for the US are for 2008.
Source: Eurostat data.

Figure 3.1   Employment rates of men and women in selected countries, 2009.

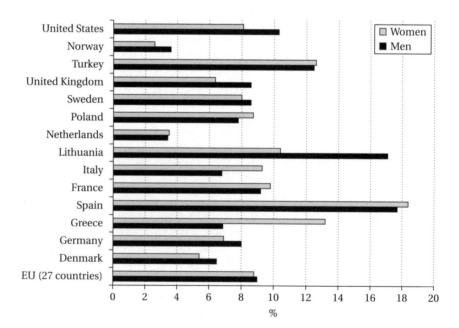

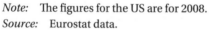

Source: Eurostat data.

Figure 3.2   Unemployment rates of men and women across selected countries, 2009.

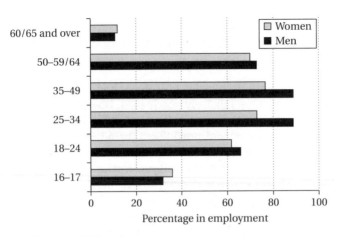

Source: Adapted from ONS (2008).

Figure 3.3   Employment rates by age band, men and women, UK, 2008.

the unemployment rates of women are frequently lower than those of men, including in the UK. While the employment gap between men and women in the UK is substantial, it is not as large as that in the Southern European countries of Spain, Greece or Italy, though it is greater than that in the Scandinavian countries. According to UK figures, around 79 per cent of working-age men and 70 per cent of working-age women were in employment overall in 2008 (ONS 2008). Figure 3.3 shows how this breaks down by age, with the biggest gaps in participation being in the middle years of life, at ages twenty-five to forty-nine. Even though women are more likely to be in employment at this period than at other periods of life, when they may be studying or retired, in this mid-life period men's employment rates are close to 90 per cent, whereas those of women peak at 77 per cent. This does illustrate rates at a single point in time, however; and it may be that women's employment among the younger cohorts currently in education may rise to rates above those of their mothers' generation, given the fact that women's employment has been steadily increasing over time and across cohorts.

For those women in work, half of the jobs in 2008 were part-time rather than full-time. Rates of part-time work are particularly high among women with dependent children. Part-time work occurs predominantly in particular, relatively poorly remunerated occupations. It is not an option across the occupational structure, and can thus account in part for women's occupational segregation. As well as typically attracting low pay, the fact of having been in part-time work can have long-term consequences on wages and therefore on lifetime incomes (Manning and Petrongolo 2008; Olsen and Walby 2004). It is worth noting, however, that while women are strongly over-represented in part-time work, men are more likely to be working atypical hours, shifts or overtime. This is reflected not only in longer hours but also in when those hours occur (Drew and Emerek 1998). Drew and Emerek conclude that

> A pattern emerges in which men's work, whether in full-time typical employment or atypical shift/weekend working, allows them to best meet the 'male breadwinner' role while women's working patterns, much of which occur outside

'typical' employment, facilitate their reconciliation of work/household commitments and thereby reduce their earnings and impede their career advancement.
(Ibid., p. 94)

Irregular working is not a prerogative of women, and many shift-work jobs typically carried out by men are relatively poorly paid. However, additional hours and
overtime may raise the remuneration, bringing earnings in line with those of other
male-dominated occupations and providing a 'bread-winner' wage (Lewis 1992).
There is therefore an imbalance in working hours that can be seen as particularly
pertinent to the lower-skilled, lower-prestige elements of the labour market, with
women doing fewer hours in jobs with little prospect of advancement and men doing
longer hours in jobs with demanding and anti-social schedules.

However, despite the poorer pay and long-term penalties for women associated
with periods in part-time work, there has been an observed 'paradox' across a range
of studies. Women in poorly remunerated part-time work nevertheless seem to prefer
that work and to have higher job satisfaction (Booth and van Ours 2008; Hakim 1991).
Hakim, in her 1991 study, observed that there appeared to be a minority of work-
committed women and a majority of women whose primary motivation was family
oriented. She used this to explain their satisfaction with 'low-quality' jobs, arguing
that it was time to recognize women's agency in making choices that were, from a
more male-focused view of the labour market, not optimal. From this she developed
her theory of women's labour market 'preferences'. Expanding from a consideration
of two groups of women to three, she argued that women are either family oriented,
career oriented or adaptive (Hakim 1998, 2000), and that the type of woman will
determine both the sort of job she is in and her satisfaction with it as meeting her
preferences for combining – or prioritizing – work and family.

In stating the tenets of her theory, Hakim argues that women's heterogeneity both
accounts for their different occupational outcomes and degrees of occupational
segregation and has helped to maintain male priority and power, since men's aims
are more homogeneous. Women's interests are not common, but will depend on
the 'type' of woman or how her preferences balance family interests, which may be
tied up with the activity of a partner, and individual interests. In this way her position
echoes some of the longstanding feminist debates dating back to the nineteenth century, which struggled to align the interests of single women, who looked for a 'level
playing field', with those of married women, whose well-being was bound up in their
family circumstances. However, she also links her theory to the contemporary stress
on choice and individualism and personal direction associated by Beck, Giddens and
others with postmodernity and contemporary affluent societies.

Preference theory has been subject to substantial critique and challenge. For
example, McRae (2003) has argued that differences in employment trajectories
cannot be put down to preferences, and has reasserted the significance of constraints
in determining outcomes. Crompton and Harris challenge the underpinnings of
the theory more directly, on the basis that it would seem ultimately 'to rest upon a
psycho-biological classification of female "types" whose origins remain obscure'
(1998b, p. 144). They argue that the occupational outcomes of both men and women
have to be seen in terms of the interplay of choices with the structures which make
them viable or not – and which shape them (Crompton and Harris 1998a). Thus,

while acknowledging women's heterogeneity, they question the amount of latitude allowed to women's ability to make entirely self-directed choices. Moreover, preferences are not directly measured, but are effectively inferred from the realized choices, risking a certain circularity in the account. Nevertheless, it is certainly clear that differentiated occupational choices, with some being more 'sex typed' than others, are made early on and before girls have direct experience of the labour market (Polavieja and Platt 2010). This suggests that heterogeneity in occupational choices does precede the constraints of family life or the realization of occupational possibilities.

The debate is fruitful in bringing to the fore the tension between questions of agency and structure and how they impact on women, as well as registering the extent of heterogeneity among women and the importance of the ways in which work and family life articulate with each other rather than being regarded as distinct domains, as they have been in traditional models of careers and employment trajectories. Particular work arrangements may be experienced as suiting women and men and their family life, even if that means obliging (or enabling) women to take on low-paid, dead-end or part-time work. These women may not *want* to be low paid but may acknowledge that the arrangement across family members and the overall household budget provides a solution to the management of work and family life.

The temporal perspective is important here. Part-time work, including the occupational downgrading that often accompanies it, labour market withdrawal and interruptions to employment have long-term effects on women's earnings and on their incomes more generally. But at a single point in time it may make economic sense at a family level, over and above or alongside any preferences or family interests it meets, for a woman to reduce her hours once there are young children in the home.

It is also worth noting that 'poor' jobs are not randomly distributed across women of different social classes, as we might expect if selection into them was driven purely by family orientations and working preferences. There are, for example, big differences by household occupational class as to whether a woman is in full-time or part-time work, ranging from a fifth of those in professional or managerial class households to over half of those in routine or semi-routine class households (Hills et al. 2010). On the other hand, ethnic minority women are less likely to work part-time (Dale and Holdsworth 1998). In some households, buying in care to enable continuous work may simply not be an economically viable option. Thus 'preferences' must be considered as acting alongside the realities of overall household income and a partner's occupation and remuneration. Conversely, for some women, working at all will be less about pursuing a career than about supplementing family income, which may necessitate full-time hours in the absence of other earners or if household income is low.

Occupational segregation

Women are more likely to end up not only in part-time jobs but also in particular occupations. This is partly a consequence of the pattern of working hours, since part-time work is easily obtainable only in certain occupations, but it applies more generally. There is a strong gendering of occupations, which has been related to both

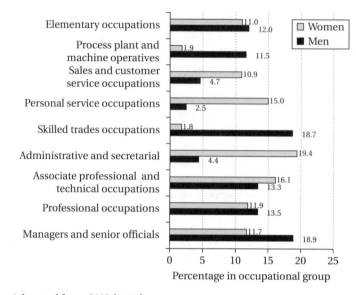

Source: Adapted from ONS (2008).

Figure 3.4   Occupational distribution of men and women, UK, 2008.

lower pay and more limited careers for women. Figure 3.4 shows the differences in occupational distribution across men and women, and we can see that there is substantial variation. Men are substantially more likely to be managers, to be in skilled trades and to be process plant and machine operatives. Conversely, women are much more likely to be in personal service occupations, administrative occupations and sales. This is consistent with the finer grain of the most prevalent occupations illustrated in chapter 2. It also shows the extent to which occupations are gendered, with women more likely to be in caring and clerical occupations and men in managerial or skilled manual occupations.

It has been argued that occupational segregation is fundamental to structural gender discrimination in enabling differential pay and limits on advancement and promotion (Rubery 1998). There is some basis for these claims in the fact that 'women's' occupations are often lower paid than 'men's', and those in which women are concentrated can offer fewer benefits. Moreover, historical analysis has shown the ways in which occupations such as clerical work have been subject to status – and therefore pay – regrading as the proportions of women in them have increased (Lewis 1984).

Nevertheless, the relationship between occupational segregation and women's employment outcomes is not clear-cut. As Blackburn and Jarman (2006) have pointed out, distinguishing between horizontal and vertical forms of segregation is important. Additionally, it is not obvious how one should work out what pay in an occupation 'should' be in the absence of segregation. Polavieja (2005), for example, has suggested that the specialized skills required in occupations with a high concentration of women may, on average, be lower, with consequent impact on pay. Lower levels of specialization have been attributed to the likelihood of women to experience a career break and thus having less to gain from building up skills within a particular workplace. These arguments bring us back to the interconnectedness of work histories and family lives. However, though there is increasing recognition of the extent of the discontinuities in women's employment and their significance for earnings, careers and employment trajectories (Jacobs 1995; Jenkins 2009b; Olsen and Walby 2004), arguments that stem from lower specialization imply that women have predicted the discontinuities in their careers and made employment choices accordingly, which may not be a realistic assumption (Hakim 1995).

In addition, there is the paradox that the extension of personal service work, which involves a range of 'caring' jobs, has come about partly through the extended participation of women in employment. The development of this sector, characterized by flexibility and low pay, has been necessitated as women in work need to buy in care (in the absence of men providing it). But it is then women who predominate in this area of work: women tend to take responsibility for caring, whether it is in the private domain of the household or in the area of paid work, a process that Gonzalez et al. (2000) refer to as 'gender coding'. Gendered patterns of work facilitate the entry of women in the labour market and thereby a partial transformation of the workforce. But the costs may be occupational segregation and potentially a large sector of women working in poorly paid and relatively poorly valued jobs.

Pay

Much of the discussion so far has turned on the quality of the job in terms of rewards. We now look directly at pay, and specifically at the 'gender pay gap' – that is, the proportion by which women's average full-time earnings fall short of men's. The gender pay gap in the UK has now been relatively stable, at around 16 to 17 per cent, for a number of years. In 2009 it was 16.4 per cent. If we look at median earnings, the gap is somewhat lower: in 2009 it was 12.2 per cent. But if part-time and full-time work are combined, the median pay gap rises to 22 per cent and the mean pay gap to 20 per cent. (See box 3.1 for a discussion of pay gaps and the different ways they are measured.) This is not simply because women in part-time work are paid less on average than men; in fact, the gap between part-time workers is less than the gap between full-time workers. The issue is that part-time work generally, whoever is doing it, tends to be low paid, and women are much more likely to be in part-time work than men.

The overall mean pay gap of 20 per cent compares with an EU average of 18 per cent, though in some countries, such as Belgium and Portugal, the gap is half that, while in Italy it is only 5 per cent. As figure 3.1 shows, women's employment rate in Italy is among the lowest in Europe, yet those women who are in work achieve, on average, earnings that are very close to those of men.

Pay gaps are sometimes taken to be evidence of discrimination in employment. However, that is a misunderstanding. Pay gaps include all the reasons that lead to women on average being paid less well than men. In fact, if the pay of men and women with the same characteristics (age, education, health status) and family circumstances are compared, the gap of married or cohabiting women relative to married or cohabiting men increases to around 25 per cent. This is illustrated in

Box 3.1   Pay gaps

The average (or mean) pay gap refers to the percentage by which the pay of women is lower than that of men. To take a purely notional example, if men's average pay is £10 per hour and women's is £8.50, this would give a pay gap of 15 per cent.

Median pay gaps are calculated in the same way, but instead of taking the average they take the mid-point of pay. The median is the value at which half the group's pay is higher and half is lower. Median pay is usually lower than mean pay, because a small number of high earners pull up the average. Median pay also tends to be closer than mean pay for men and women because the mean is affected by very high earners and there are more high earners among men. Again, simply for illustration, if men's median pay is £8.00 and women's is £7.20, this would give a pay gap of 10 per cent (i.e. £8–£7.2 – 80p – /£8.00).

It has been common practice in the past to calculate pay gaps on the basis of full-time earnings only. The assumption has been that, because of the differences between full-time and part-time work and associated pay, a comparison of full-time pay gives a better impression of what is going on in the labour market. However, it has also been argued that, because rates of part-time work form an element of labour market inequality, when considering pay gaps we should consider the pay of all earners, whether full-time or part-time. When part-time and full-time work are combined, pay gaps at both the mean and the median become larger, because the greater numbers of women in lower-paid part-time work reduce the mean and the median more for women.

For comparisons it is necessary to be aware which midpoint (mean or median) is being used and whether full-time or all earnings are being included.

All these calculations are based on hourly rates of pay. However, it is possible to calculate weekly pay gaps as well. These are greater than hourly pay gaps even when only full-time earnings are considered, because women in full-time work still do fewer hours on average than men in full-time work.

figure 3.5, which shows the predicted pay in pounds sterling per hour of men and women who are white British, aged forty to forty-four, Christian, born in the UK, non-disabled, without dependent children, with middle-level (level 2) qualifications, and in mid-ranking occupations. Men in different partnership situations can all expect to have higher pay on average than women. While women in same-sex couples fare better than single women or those in heterosexual partnerships, they still face substantial pay penalties of around 20 per cent of the pay of men in couples. Societal and structural constraints and discrimination, as well as different choices, narrow the options and opportunities for all women, it would seem.

It appears that the gendering of work and family life, including the ways in which it leads to interruptions in employment and the greater tendency to work part-time, is more important in limiting pay than the individual actions of employers in penalizing women or barring their progression and promotion. If the composition of women workers is broken down further, the minority of those who are well qualified and without children and caring responsibilities have employment and pay trajectories

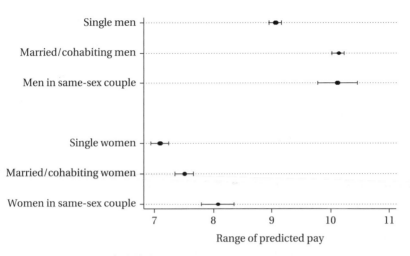

Source: Longhi and Platt (2008), figure 4.3.

Figure 3.5   Predicted pay of men and women in different partnership circumstances and holding characteristics constant, Great Britain.

that are similar to men in a comparable situation. At the same time, for men, having a family is associated with higher pay.

This is not to say that discrimination against women in employment does not occur. There is clear evidence that it does, and that the 'glass ceiling' continues to operate. But it is important to look at the wider context of employment inequalities and social structures – in which discriminatory behaviour takes place – as well as at the specifics of discriminatory employers and workplace cultures.

It is clear from the preceding discussion that the major factor implied in gendered patterns of work and pay is the unequal division of family responsibilities and, in particular, the birth and presence in the household of children, particularly young children. The gendering of both employment and the domestic sphere shapes the inequalities women suffer in these domains. This has consequences that can reach into later life and old age, since incomes in mid-life have long-term consequences: 'the impact of motherhood on women's relative pay is not a matter of a one-off shock from which there is gradual recovery (which is what happens with employment), but is a picture of continuing decline through most of the first childhood' (Hills et al. 2010, p. 367). We see some of these consequences for women in chapter 6.

The next section therefore looks in more detail at the domestic sphere: how it has been conceptualized and how inequalities in domestic work have been measured, and the implications of these inequalities. As some of the preceding discussion has implied, the extent of gendered inequalities in employment is also intimately connected to heterogeneity among women and the development of inequalities between them. The examination of domestic work is therefore followed by a consideration of the diversity among women that the simultaneous and intersecting demands of paid work and family responsibilities can help to engender and maintain.

3.3 Gender and domestic work: women's double burden? ▓▓▓▓▓

In 2000, a survey of 21,500 individuals across Europe found that

> the 'double burden' of work and domestic responsibilities is still shouldered largely
> by women – 41% of female respondents said that they took care of the children (24% of
> men), 64% of women did the cooking (13% of men) and 63% did the housework (12%
> of men). (Paoli and Merllié 2001, p. 40)

A subsequent survey in 2005 showed that women were still doing the bulk of domestic work, with around three times the number of hours spent on weekly unpaid work as men (Parent-Thirion et al. 2007). In this section we scrutinize what is meant by domestic work and how it is measured. Domestic work more generally and housework are often conflated. One of the issues is what should and should not be included in a measure of domestic work. We start, therefore, with Ivan Illich's definition of housework: 'any *labor* by which the consumer transforms a purchased commodity into a usable good. . . . The time, toil and effort which must be expended in order to add to any purchased commodity value without which it is unfit for use' (Illich 1982, p. 47). This could include, for example, turning a potato into chips or making up a bed.

Domestic work is seen as a fundamental and distinctive part of industrial economies. Ann Oakley, however, was one of the first sociologists to draw attention to it as a specific domain of sociological inquiry (Oakley 1974a, 1974b). She developed an analysis of housework as a form of *work*, but one that is physically demanding, isolating and emotionally draining. She also attempted to quantify the hours spent on housework. Illich drew on Oakley's innovative analysis in his development of the concept of 'shadow work', where he highlights the link between domestic work and the industrial, or post-industrial, era.

Though some would regard domestic work as a descendant of the gendered division of labour that took place within the productive unit of the family in pre-industrial societies, analysis by historians of housework and the recognition of the transformation of the sphere of *paid* work would lead most to argue that there is a significant break between these forms and modern unpaid work. To quote from Illich again:

> the difference between housework past and present cannot adequately be put into
> traditional language, nor satisfactorily expressed in the categories of class analy-
> sis or social-science jargon. . . . What housework is now, women of old did not do.
> However, the modern woman finds it hard to believe that her ancestor did not have
> to work in a nether economy. Irrefutably, the new historians of housework describe
> the typical activity of the housewife as something unlike anything women have done
> outside industrial society. (Illich 1982, pp. 47–8)

The meaning of housework sets it apart from other forms of work even as it comes into being through the transformation of the economy and the specific features of employment in an industrial and post-industrial society. So what is the work that occurs within the home or that constitutes unpaid work? Various arguments have been developed about what should and should not be included. Measures and typologies can include cooking, caring for children, caring for older people, washing and ironing, do-it-yourself activities to maintain the home, gardening, or production of fruit and vegetables. National and local contexts can also make a substantial difference to what it makes sense to measure as unpaid work. There are debates about the relevance of each of these potential components and how they can be meaningfully conceived as 'housework'. Childcare is sometimes deemed a chosen form of activity rather than a 'chore', though some try to distinguish between activities that involve playing with children and those which involve the personal care of children and elders. Nevertheless, the presence of children will clearly increase the amount of general housework (cooking, cleaning, washing, etc.) that has to be done. Cooking is sometimes differentiated from other forms of housework such as ironing or vacuuming because it has distinctive patterns in the male–female division of domestic work and because, while day-to-day cooking, including the feeding of children, tends to be done more by women and could be considered a chore, cooking for guests or special dinners may increasingly be carried out by men. These forms of cooking can have very different meanings. Different national conventions around hospitality and eating habits may also affect what is required from cooking and how the activity is interpreted. Some measures therefore try to get at the function of the activity over and above the activity itself by, for example, asking for whom it is done.

As well as the types of activity considered, there follows the issue of how to measure the amount of time spent on any activity to allow a measure of inequality, especially as more and more households have dual earner couples among whom a more even division of labour might be expected. One approach is simply to ask people how much time they spend on particular activities or what the share is between themselves and their partner. The other is to attempt to measure directly what people do and how long they spend doing it by the use of time diaries. In many surveys the respondent is asked how much domestic work they do and how much their partner does. Sometimes just one person is asked; in other cases both partners are asked. Unsurprisingly, in the latter case the two answers do not tend to show a very good match. Nevertheless it has been argued that by averaging the two responses it is possible to get a reasonably reliable measure for each partner (Laurie and Gershuny 2000). And even when responses differ, on average they show that women do more of the domestic work than men. Other measures try to break down a whole twenty-four-hour day into the sorts of activities that occupy it. The use of a full-day approach enables total work, paid and unpaid, to be estimated by summing the two parts.

What is clear is that, however it is measured, there are distinct inequalities in housework tasks and that, moreover, the free time available to women when paid and unpaid work are both deducted is less than that for men (Lader et al. 2006; Parent-Thirion et al. 2007). This, then, constitutes the double burden, where participation in the labour market among women does not mean that men show a commensurate participation in unpaid work. Figure 3.6 illustrates time spent on household chores as they were divided among men and women on average in the UK in 2000.

These inequalities in the amount of time spent on domestic work have shown some change over recent decades. This is partly on account of a reduction in the amount of unpaid work that takes place overall, which itself has in part been influenced by changes in technology (Gershuny 2004). The additional income gained from participation in employment can be spent on 'labour-saving devices'. Glucksmann (1990) drew attention to the interconnectedness of the spheres of (paid) production and unpaid domestic work, whereby employment on production lines in an era of mass production provided the resources for purchasing such products. And she went on to

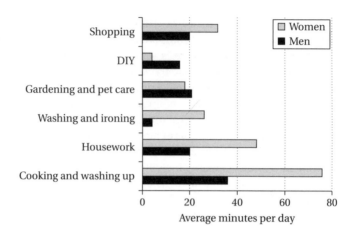

Source: UK Time Use Survey 2000, adapted from ONS Time Use Survey 2000 web dataset (available at www.statistics.gov.uk), table 14.

Figure 3.6   Division of household chores by sex, UK, 2000.

develop the concept of the total social organization of labour, which allows a consideration of the relational aspects of all elements of labour (Glucksmann 2000, 1995).

Technology can, though, be a double-edged sword, as increasing ease of cleaning and so on has been accompanied by a commensurate increase in standards or requirements for particular levels of cleanliness. Nevertheless, domestic appliances have in many ways transformed the domestic economy. Buying in care also reduces the demands on women to provide that care, and thus reduces inequalities between men and women since, when the total amount of unpaid work decreases, women's share tends to decrease as well. But such buying in of care may establish new inequalities among women and may increase the extent to which the socialization of children and primary caring responsibilities is associated with women. As Jensen points out,

> almost without exception, [the child(ren)] will be taken care of by women, either their own mothers or women who get paid for the work. Due to the feminisation of public sector healthcare, children will come across female dentists, doctors and social workers. Importantly, the teaching during a child's first years at school has increasingly become a *female* profession. (Jensen 1999)

Overall, there is remarkable persistence in the gendered division of labour; and though there have been some slight changes in the balance, most of the reduction in inequalities in the domestic sphere that have taken place have come not through men doing more, but through women doing less (Gershuny 2000; Laurie and Gershuny 2000). However, when couples are looked at over time, there does seem to be a gradual process of adjustment (what Gershuny refers to as 'lagged adaptation'), which means that the division becomes more equal between couples. And, when looking at cohorts rather than cross-sections of the population, there is some evidence that younger generations are moving towards a more equal division of domestic work.

Another major cohort difference, however, is that there are simply fewer female family members available to provide care, particularly that care directed upwards to the older generation. This is in the context of changes in fertility, increasing longevity and hence a growing elderly population. In Britain at the beginning of the twentieth century there were on average seventeen female relatives to every person over sixty-five; at the turn of the twenty-first century there were three. The decline simply in numbers of women *potentially* available to care may affect the extent to which elder care within the family is gendered, though not necessarily the extent to which care that is bought in is gendered. The issue of the need to find care from outside the home, both as a result of the relative increase of the older population and as women progressively combine paid work with family, brings us to the question of who carries out that work, and the implications for inequality.

3.4 Gender, class and caring: inequalities between women

The links between paid and unpaid work clearly begin to emerge from the preceding discussion. Lyon and Glucksmann (2008), in their comparative analysis of 'configurations of care', have argued that work can only be understood by exploring the different domains in which similar activities take place – across unpaid and paid work and across the informal and formal sectors, which also involves identifying those who are carrying out the work. Caring work may have moved from being unpaid to being paid and from domestic to public settings, as well as in some cases from the public to the private sectors, but the activities remain gendered – and frequently marginalized, especially in relation to elder care. Women may be argued to be the beneficiaries of the increase in paid-for care as it enables increasing labour market participation, and this has been particularly important for those engaged in full-time work and aiming to maintain continuous careers. But they are also the main providers: according to recent estimates, around 90 per cent of care workers were women (ibid.). Even in the absence of children and childcare responsibilities, women can be affected by gendered expectations of responsibility for elder care, and, as a result of 'gender coding', even in the presence of work they may be expected to find the means of providing it (Gonzalez et al. 2000).

In countries where welfare states are less developed and which have strong traditions of familialism (Leitner 2003; Lewis 2000; Pfenning and Bahle 2001), this need has been met in particular by migrant carers, supplementing paid carers found among women from lower social classes. Women (and men) from other countries are contracted to work at the interface between the family and the public domain of the labour market (Bettio et al. 2006), often occupying a marginal status in terms both of the work they do and of their status within the country. This is a phenomenon which has received substantial attention in the literature, as regards both the composition of new migrants and the particular economy of the care sector (Passerini et al. 2007). Migrant carers are not such a dominant feature of the accommodation of the 'dual burden' in the UK, partly because the transition into employment began sooner, partly because of the large, female-dominated part-time sector, and partly because of the more comprehensive reach of some aspects of the welfare state. The healthcare sector in the UK, including care homes, depends on a large flow of migrant workers. Nevertheless, even with a more formal and formally regulated care sector, the beneficiaries of paid-for care and those who deliver it are typically from different ends of the class spectrum, and income and earnings inequality between women is increasing. Moreover, the UK, as the discussion in chapter 2 indicated, is also seeing a move of working-class men into the service sector. There is a growing divide between full-time, well-paid professional women and a poorly paid insecure group of women workers who are partly employed delivering care to those who can afford it. In this context, does it make sense to talk of women's relationship to work and care as a whole, or are we in fact seeing very different types of women's experience of paid work, unpaid work and their intersection? Does greater equalization between men and women in the higher social classes, and the potential for women to move into previously masculine domains, come at the cost of greater inequality between well-off and less well-off women? Those activities carried out by less well-off women are marked by the attributes of feminized work, such as low status and low pay, even as more (working-class) men also move into these occupational domains. We could see this as a move towards greater class distinction as the price for greater equality between men and women. Alternatively, can it be construed as part of a move towards greater inequality between men and women that nevertheless has the potential to transform the experience of women more widely?

An intersectional perspective provides the potential for highlighting heterogeneity among women. Exploring the intersection of different women in different positions or with different characteristics can help to describe inequalities and the ways in which they are shifting over time (McCall 2005). Such an approach has the potential to demonstrate the very different configurations of paid and unpaid work – their demands and rewards – faced by women from different social classes (Fagnani 1998), as well as different family circumstances, migrant statuses and minority positions. But to evaluate these distinctions requires a further step of attempting to theorize – and predict – their implications.

Focusing on the experience of women entering the upper echelons of the employment hierarchy (British and French women in banking and medicine), Le Feuvre (1999) addressed the question of whether their access to traditionally masculine jobs could be considered an attack on gendered employment structures and the gendered organization of society more generally, despite the fact that it still leaves an over-representation of women at the bottom of the hierarchy. She considers four ways that this feminization (in terms of increasing numbers of women moving into senior professional and managerial positions) has been conceptualized: feminization as gender reproduction – that is, the downgrading of jobs as – or so that – women can enter them; feminization as feminitude, whereby 'feminine values' are incorporated into the occupational structure without altering gendered relationships; feminization as virilitude, where women are represented as taking on male-gendered characteristics in order to fulfil the requirements of the position; and feminization as gender transformation, whereby the occupational structure and aspects of a gendered society is changed by women's entry into hitherto unreached areas. She argues that this last form of feminization is transformative not because the women become 'like men' but because the gendered spaces that are open to people are shifted by these processes, and consequently so are the social meanings attached to being a man (or a woman).

Le Feuvre argues that it is possible to see these transitions of women into the most high-status domains as transformative; and she contends that they have an impact over and above the individual successes that they represent and the polarization between women by which they may be accompanied. This potential, nevertheless, is built within the operation of a classed society, and the process of transformation requires an exploitation of resources that a gendered division of labour offers to women juggling the double burden at a level of privilege and affluence. Reductions in inequality at one level may come at the expense of the increase in inequality at another, but Le Feuvre's analysis suggests that this is not necessarily a zero-sum game.

What is required is recognition both of the intersection of gender and power and of the inequalities engendered, so that they can be questioned rather than being subsumed into an overall story of average progress. It is important to reveal the shifting configuration of inequalities at the intersections of different provisionally employed analytic categories, but, as Crenshawe (1991) pointed out, it is also necessary to consider the wider implications of these shifting inequalities and to explore the possibilities that, once recognized, they may form the bases for coalition as well as division and challenge.

Questions for reflection

1 To what extent does segregation contribute to women's employment inequalities?
2 If the price of greater equality between women and men in the domestic sphere overall is greater inequality between women from social groups, is that a price worth paying?
3 How easy is it to classify differences between domestic work and other work?
4 Is there any means to move away from 'shadow' work, or is it the necessary corollary of a capitalist society?
5 What are the implications for an analysis of inequalities of working-class women and men servicing the employment/lives of middle-class men and women?
6 Does recognizing domestic work (and childcare in particular) as being carried out predominantly by women essentialize differences between men and women?
7 How might women's preferences contribute to their inequality?

Further reading

Ivan Illich's discussion in *Gender* (1982) is thought-provoking and brings his particular understanding of domination and inequalities to bear on the subject. McCall (2005) provides a valuable intervention in considerations of intersectionality; by making the links between method and complexity, she sets out an analytic strategy which aims to reveal rather than assume inequality. Abbott et al. (2005) provide both a general overview of gender inequalities that go beyond those treated in this chapter and an account of feminist approaches to uncovering and explaining them.

4 Ethnicity

Society views me as Black which means that I have to be equipped to deal with that reality and accept it.

I personally forget most of the time that I have an ethnicity, but I am lucky to have been successful academically and study in a world where I don't feel that such things are important.

In ethnicity, it brings me back to the values. Ethnicity propels you proper on how you must live, and work is included it's not separated.

I don't think much about my ethnic group. . . . It's the obvious thing for me, I'm white, I cannot change it and probably it influenced who I am at the moment, shaped me somehow, but I just don't know.

The first two quotations come from a study of 'mixed-race' young people where differences in sibling identifications and their relationship to issues of choice in identity are explored (Song 2010). The last two quotations come from a study of the 'dimensions of ethnicity', carried out to develop survey questions on ethnic identity (Nandi and Platt 2009). They are deployed here to illustrate a number of points that this chapters pursues. The first quotation identifies in direct terms the ways in which structural constraints shape the lives of minority group members – that is, how people and their ethnicity are constructed within societies and how these constructions are replicated in the words, actions and assumptions of individuals with whom they engage. Such structural influences result in substantial inequalities across groups, as the chapter demonstrates. The second quotation highlights the intersection of class and ethnicity in people's lives and the differentiated experiences that stem from those intersections. In the third quotation, the respondent registers the fact that ethnicity is or can be experienced as permeating all aspects of life, from professional identities to patterns of association and value structures. And the final quotation emphasizes the significance of normalized white 'ethnicity' that does not need to express itself relationally despite its profound significance for outcomes and opportunities.

What is also apparent from the contexts in which these quotations are embedded are the different meanings attributed to ethnicity, whether it is seen as ascriptive or chosen, something that is not only central to a subjective sense of self but which also informs – or even determines – all other aspects of life. Respondents are drawing on the range of understandings of ethnicity that are available to them, and that enable them to make sense of their sense of themselves and how others relate to them. 'Commonsense' notions are not themselves uniform and were highly contested in the course of the discussions from which the latter two quotations derive. Moreover, the extent to which they map on to sociological understandings also varies substantially. It is therefore to the thorny issue of what ethnicity and ethnic groups are that we turn first.

4.1 Ethnicity: definitions and measures

An ethnic group is, theoretically, one in which the association with both a particular origin and specific customs is adopted by people themselves to establish a shared identity. Ethnic groups are therefore self-conscious and claimed identities, and include the various 'white' populations of Britain. The UK's ethnic groups encompass the whole of the British population, while minority ethnic groups or ethnic minority groups refers to those which are numerically in the minority and which can be seen to be in a minority position in terms of power relations. For this is an alternative meaning of the term 'minority' and one which is incorporated along with the strict numerical one in the formulation 'minority ethnic groups'. In this way, women also, even if they constitute a numerical majority, can be conceived of as minoritized.

Weber's writings form a valuable starting point in attempting to define ethnic groups, and identify the key elements of identification with common descent – whether real or imagined. He introduced the concept of ethnic groups in the following terms:

> We shall call 'ethnic groups' those human groups that entertain a subjective belief in their common descent because of similarities of physical type or of customs or both, or because of memories of colonization and migration; this belief must be important for the propagation of group formation; conversely, it does not matter whether or not an objective blood relationship exists. Ethnic membership (*Gemeinsamkeit*) differs from the kinship group precisely by being a presumed identity, not a group with concrete social action, like the latter. (Weber 1978, Vol. 1, p. 389)

These elements have been developed and extended in further discussions of ethnicity and ethnic group. For example, Schermerhorn (1978) defined ethnic group as:

> a collective within a larger society having real or putative common ancestry, memories of a shared historical past and a cultural focus on one or more symbolic elements defined as the epitome of their peoplehood. Examples of such symbolic elements are: kinship patterns, physical contiguity (as in localism or sectionalism), religious affiliation, language or dialect forms, tribal affiliation, nationality, phenotypical features, or any combination of these. A necessary accompaniment is some consciousness of kind among members of the group.

Again the emphasis is on common descent, shared 'memories' (whether strictly actual or not) and self-consciousness of the identification with the group. Ethnicity and being part of an ethnic group is about being aware of and claiming a particular group affiliation. The importance of perception and imagining of antecedents is also core to Anderson's (1991) notion of 'imagined communities'. As well as defining ethnicity by 'a sense of belonging', others have defined groups relatively – that is, in relation to how they construct difference from others and establish boundaries for the groups (Wimmer 2008). This is a perspective that is associated with Barth's work (Barth 1969), where he focuses on the social processes of incorporation and exclusion that maintain ethnic groups as distinct.

There is often a perceived link between ethnic identity and national identity. National identity, in particular what Smith (1991) refers to as 'ethnic nationalism', is much concerned with the assumption (or construction) of a shared past built around common culture and symbols. The parallel between national and ethnic identity was made by Weber; though he also highlights the slipperiness of both terms and their susceptibility to disappear if pressed too closely: 'The concept of the "ethnic group", which dissolves if we define our terms exactly, corresponds in this regard to one of the most vexing, since emotionally charged concepts: the nation, as soon as we attempt a sociological definition' (Weber 1978, Vol. 1, p. 395).

Ethnicity and nationality are in fact often regarded to a large degree as inter-changeable. Once a person is away from their country of origin, their nationality may be taken (and be taken by themselves) to be their ethnicity, both because of acknowledged commonality within the group and on account of acknowledged dif-ference from others. Thus, discussion of Polish or Italian or Turkish communities (outside Poland, Italy and Turkey) often implies the sense of shared belonging and of common antecedents. Within countries of origin, though, much greater differen-tiation and subtler or simply alternative distinctions may prevail across a range of domains, such as language, religious affiliation, etc.

Conceptually, then, ethnicity relates to a contingent identity, in the sense that it is not fixed but is subject to an individual's consciousness and claiming of their identity and the ways in which this can be shaped by group processes that form and police the boundaries of groups. Membership of an ethnic group is not fixed in time and people's sense of their ethnicity may develop (Phinney 1990). And identities may not be exclusive (Song 2010b). Contextual factors may be highly relevant for what is felt or expressed at a particular moment or location. People will express (and feel) different aspects of identity as being significant/important at different times and at different scales – local, regional, national, transnational. Nevertheless, what is often considered as being essential to ethnicity is the fact of its boundedness. Even if it forms a temporary boundary, ethnicity is often experienced in contrast to what it is not. As Barth pointed out, ethnic groups are formed by their distinction from others, rather than by the 'content' of ethnicity. This is also a perspective common to the psychological literature, where ethnic identity is regarded as possible only as part of a contrast with another group. This implies that ethnic groups can be seen in terms of membership and non-membership, even if within that various processes may restructure the boundaries at different points in time or at different locations at the same point in time.

Identity interacts with ascription or the ways in which people allocate others to groups. This can be seen in the ways in which systems of ethnic categorization have developed, such as those used in censuses or surveys or on monitoring forms. People are expected to match themselves to predefined categories (Burton et al. 2010). That system of categorization can influence the ways in which individuals think about themselves, as it shows the ways in which they have been conceived. For example, a woman from a minority ethnic background within Nigeria might have a strongly developed ethnic identity and might initially be confused by or resist the expectation in the UK census definition to define herself as 'black African'. Over time, however, she may regard this as how she is located within UK society by others, and experience shifting levels of identity and self-expression according to context.

Ethnicity and ethnic group membership, then, may be properties of all people, but they are nevertheless situational and relational (Alam and Husband 2006). Though we may tend to think of ethnicity as a fixed characteristic, its salience and what is taken to be one's own ethnic identity or primary identity will vary with context.

The language of race

It has been widely accepted for many years in this country that to speak of race is inappropriate because races do not exist. Introductions to the topic of ethnicity or 'race', in inverted commas, normally initiate their discussions with this point. As Cornell and Hartmann put it, 'most contemporary scholars dismiss the entire idea of race as a meaningful biological category that can be applied to separate groups of human beings' (1988, p. 23; see also Law 1996, p. 5).

Banton (1998) has comprehensively described the development and transformation of the use and meaning of the term 'race' and has shown how the current, unacceptable, usage derived from a concern with 'types' that came to underpin racial thinking. The typological construction depended on a very loose concept that had no basis in fact. It was the foundation and the consequence of an ideology that argued for the innate superiority of some 'races' over others and the naturalness of ensuing conflict. To that extent its use cannot be justified and should not be maintained. However, as David Mason (1995) has pointed out, in practice the demotic use of the term 'race' and the way it features in the language of policy renders it difficult to avoid altogether. The need for communication tends to mean that some accommodation often has to be found, though this is not uncontested (Carter and Fenton 2009).

The situation is further complicated by the fact that, though races may not exist, racism, in the sense of treating someone in a manner informed by an ideology of race, and racialization, whereby groups can become constructed as forming races, do. Mason has proposed that, in relation to the terminology and usage of race, we should recognize that

> race is a social relationship in which structural positions and social actions are ordered, justified, and explained by reference to systems of symbols and beliefs which emphasise the social and cultural relevance of biologically rooted characteristics. In other words, the social relationship of race presumes the existence of racism. (Mason 1995, p. 9)

For many analysts, 'race' remains an issue to engage with on account of the fact that people recognize phenotypical differences and interpret them as having significance. People continue to act and speak as though races exist. Those subject to particular classifications based on the assumption that races are meaningful may find their lives significantly and crucially affected. Moreover, the language of race is ingrained in policy and law, and therefore can be bound up with possibilities of redress. Some sociologists, therefore, defend the use of the term race for social scientific purposes and on pragmatic grounds, and outside the UK it is in common usage. For example, researchers in Canada and the US claim that the debate has been held and that we know, as sociologists, that races are not biological entities; therefore the term 'race' can be freely used to mean a structuring experience of perceived physical and/or cultural difference without connoting biological essentialism.

Nevertheless, in this book, while there will be some discussion of racism and racialization, I will be operating not with the language of race but that of ethnicity. Ethnicity itself is not unproblematic, of course, and its effective substitution for 'race' can mean that it retains many of the same problems (Carter and Fenton 2009; Fenton 2010). There is a danger in that, acknowledging an element of substitution or translation between the language of race and ethnicity, no revision of the conceptual problematic of 'race' is undertaken, and the interpretation of social relations and divisions on which it is based are not subject to reconfiguration. Rather, the same problems are simply transferred to an alternative terminology, but less explicitly so. Strong preconceptions of the subject under discussion (what minority groups we are talking about) and the naturalization of certain group divisions may well lead to lack of rigour in the application of the language of ethnicity or the interpretation of ethnic inequalities. It is therefore important to be alert in identifying ethnic differences and inequalities, what, if anything, is implied by such differences about ethnicity and ethnic groups, and to what extent notions of ethnicity itself can help us to understand them or instead confound explanations that should more properly be situated in differential class, geographical or social locations (Karlsen and Nazroo 2006).

Ethnicity and religion

There is an increasing trend to analyse within-country minorities and the inequalities they experience in terms of religious affiliation. One approach is to use religious affiliation as cognate to ethnicity – that is, as representing a meaningful and bounded group, at least for the purposes of analysis of ethnicity. This can be observed particularly in relation to the analysis of Muslims. Following the furore over Salman Rushdie's *The Satanic Verses*, the concept 'Muslims' as a meaningful and distinctive but highly contested section of British society became more fully developed (Modood 1992). However, this did not mean that at the level of policy Muslims were recognized as a minority for equality purposes. Such a development only occurred in 2003, with the incorporation of regulations on religion for minority ethnic groups into anti-discrimination legislation on employment that dates back to 1976. In fact, there has been considerable resistance to acknowledging the claims of religious minorities as being on a par with ethnic minorities, as Tariq Modood (1998) has discussed and challenged. This resistance, alongside a conceptual fixing of what it means to be Muslim, has been distinctive of the period following the attacks of 11 September 2001 and the London bombings of July 2005 in the national discourses of many countries, as well as in the formulation of research questions and engagement (see the discussion in Levey 2009). Islam is taken to be an overarching identity, linked to consistent and stable values and practices, and at the same time conceived as a grouping that should not be sanctioned through explicit incorporation or recognition. In policy and practice, however, there have been moves to recognize religion as being on a par with other 'protected' statuses – or sources of inequality – such as sex, ethnicity and health, most recently in the 2010 Equalities Act. Modood (1998) argued that a multicultural state should recognize religious minorities as well as those defined in terms of country of origin, colour or particular cultural practices. From a concern with inequalities and redistribution, recognition may not be an end in itself, but it is critical to addressing inequalities at a policy and legal level (Modood 2009). Moreover, without a prior conception of 'groups' and analytical attention to them, it is not possible to identify whether there are inequalities that require attention. (See also the discussion in chapter 3.) Conceptions of religious affiliation can be argued to influence experiences of inequality, such as differential employment outcomes, through, for example, the social networks provided by religious affiliation or through discrimination based on religion (Clark and Drinkwater 2007; Purdam et al. 2007). Nevertheless, it can still be hard to conceive how it is that religious affiliation in itself shapes life chances and the experience of inequalities. Moreover, it transpires that much analysis of 'Muslims' is in fact heavily ethnicized in the UK. It is the two main Muslim groups, Pakistanis and Bangladeshis, rather than the overall population of Muslims that are typically the focus of analysis (Open Society Institute 2004), or, alternatively, studies implicitly exploring the role of religious affiliation in creating constraints concentrate on these two groups (Dale 2002; Tackey et al. 2006).

Another approach is to use religious affiliation as revealing heterogeneity within groups and to explore the experience of those defined at the intersection of ethnicity and religion – for example, distinguishing Indian Hindus from Indian Muslims or white British Christians from white British Jews or white British with no religious affiliation. There is also an increasingly prevalent recognition that identifying minority groups through both their religious affiliation and their ethnicity acknowledges the way that these can be mutually constitutive and, from an inequalities perspective, overlap conceptually. Thus there is frequently discussion of Pakistani Muslims (Thapar-Bjorkert and Sanghera 2010), which brings with it not only an emphasis on their dual sources of identity (Jacobson 1997, 1998) but also acknowledgement that their particular social location is bound up with the joint experience of national or ethnic origins and religious group and history, as they are experienced within the specific UK context (Alam and Husband 2006). Attention is increasingly being paid to diversity within as well as between groups, and it is becoming clear that employment patterns vary in distinctive ways within groups by religious affiliation (Dobbs et al. 2006). Given the crudeness of the ethnic group categories in common use (as discussed further below), exploring the intersection of ethnic group and religious affiliation can give some purchase on groups more tightly defined who have common and distinctive histories, migration experiences, settlement patterns or occupational concentrations (Longhi et al. 2009). Regardless of any causal impact of religious affiliation, if collections of individuals are more properly defined as meaningful social groups at the intersection of ethnicity and religion, and if exploring intersections can reveal and shed light on processes of inequality, then it may be appropriate to conduct analysis in terms of ethno-religious groups (Brown 2000; Lindley 2002).

Measuring ethnicity

So what happens when the attempt to capture people's ethnic identity for the purposes of identifying inequalities takes place? We then move to a system of categorization that has only a loose connection with the conceptual basis of ethnicity. This can be problematic in terms of having a sense of what inequalities between such categories are actually measuring. If we identify categorical differences in, say, employment, education or income, what do these mean and what do they tell us about ethnic stratification or the mechanisms by which the observed inequalities come into being and are sustained? The categories offered may also well create dissonance with the self-perception of those who are asked to place themselves in one of the groups.

Expressed or chosen identity is often not captured in sources of information about inequalities across ethnic groups. Despite multiple studies demonstrating the complexity and multiplicity of people's identities (Aspinall 2000; Tizard and Phoenix 1995;

Song 2010), measurement of inequality typically requires stable but crude measures which can only approximate to some key distinctions between groups more properly defined. For example, such measures can capture those distinctions that occur at the intersection of a number of common aspects of 'identity', which might include immigration history, forbears' nationality, region of origin, religion and skin colour. The combinations will, however, vary for the different categories in an attempt both to represent distinct histories and to be recognizable to those responding to them (Bulmer 1996). In standard census and survey questions, options are predefined with only limited scope for qualifying them. The extent to which they are adequate to represent self-expressed identities while allowing for 'objective indicators' to measure inequalities across groups is a subject of ongoing debate (Modood et al. 2002). Existing systems of categorization have been continually contested and critiqued – even among those who support the collection of 'ethnicity data' (Butt et al. 1991; Simpson 2005). Others reject any attempt at 'racialized' categorization (Gilroy 2000).

The nature of, and problems with, the first census question on ethnicity which underlies the further development of commonly used categories of classification has been extensively considered (Bulmer 1996; Coleman and Salt 1996; Karn et al. 1997), with Ratcliffe (1996) going so far as to assert that the one thing the question does not measure is ethnicity. The (often unspoken) assumption is that what constitutes the 'non-white' population is self-evident and that its interest is equally self-evident (Mason 2000). In this process, 'ethnic group' becomes racialized and identified with minority ethnicity (Ballard 1996a) and 'white British born' becomes ever more normalized by its exclusion from ethnicity (Bhavnani et al. 2005). The potential that is offered by the increasing range and longstanding existence of ethnic classifications for understanding and monitoring equality also, therefore, presents a potential danger in relation to 'essentializing' groups (Bonnett and Carrington 2000); and, by encouraging explanations of differences in outcomes to be sought in ethnic differences, they may promote 'cultural' or racialized accounts over structural ones and thus even potentially reinforce disadvantage (Nazroo 2003a).

Despite these problems, it is the standard ethnic group categories as developed for the 2001 census and applied in a range of surveys and other forms of information relevant to inequalities that are used in this book. There were sixteen categories in the final version of the question as employed in England and Wales. However, much of the research reported covers only a subsection of these groups. The full list and the distribution of the ensuing 'groups' across the populations is given in table 4.1. It should be borne in mind, though, that use of these categories is largely pragmatic. They are informative to the extent that they can reveal inequalities and help us to understand underlying processes. However, their use is not intended to imply that they represent meaningful ethnic groups according to the conceptual basis on which the sociological understanding of ethnicity has been developed. Allying pragmatism with rigour is, nevertheless, the form in which much analysis that has shaped our understanding of the social world has proceeded.

4.2 Ethnic groups and diversity

Ethnicity and inequality are interlinked across a range of domains. Indeed, part of the understanding of ethnicity is linked to the marginalization of particular groups.

Table 4.1 Distribution of ethnic groups across England and Wales, 2004–8 (%)

Ethnic group	All	Adult men	Adult women	Children < 16
White British	84.6	85.6	86.1	80.9
Other white	5.2	5.9	5.8	3.5
Mixed white and black Caribbean	0.4	0.1	0.2	1.1
Mixed white and black African	0.2	0.1	0.1	0.4
Mixed white and Asian	0.3	0.1	0.1	0.8
Other mixed	0.2	0.1	0.2	0.5
Indian	2.1	2.0	1.7	2.3
Pakistani	1.6	1.2	1.1	2.8
Bangladeshi	0.7	0.4	0.4	1.3
Other Asian	0.7	0.7	0.7	0.8
Black Caribbean	1.0	0.8	0.9	1.2
Black African	1.3	1.0	1.0	2.2
Other black	0.1	0.1	0.1	0.2
Chinese	0.5	0.5	0.5	0.3
Other	1.4	1.4	1.3	1.7
All groups	100	100	100	100
(N)	(397,668)			

Source: Adapted from Platt (2009b), table 1 (from Household Labour Force Survey 2004–8).

Some of these (education, poverty, health) will be touched on in subsequent chapters. The experiences and outcomes of minority groups are subject more and more to both research and policy attention, with a particular focus on certain domains such as employment, education and social relations or 'cohesion'. An ever growing range of data to draw on both increases and is driven by the expanding evidence based on ethnic inequalities, since initial recognition stimulates and is critical in developing sustained interrogation and interpretation of ethnic inequalities. In this chapter we focus on an area where ethnic inequalities have received perhaps the most extensive and detailed treatment – that is, different ethnic groups' relationship to the labour market and experience in employment (Platt 2007c).

However, it is first worth gaining some basic understanding of the distribution and key demographic features of the UK's ethnic groups, since these both shape the possibilities for exploring inequalities (for example, the relatively small number of older people in some groups limits our detailed understanding of their circumstances) and can inform some of the starting assumptions in interpreting inequalities (for example, descriptions of family structure have informed the frameworks for analysis of educational and employment inequalities for some groups).

Who are the UK's ethnic groups?

Table 4.1 illustrates the categories into which the UK's ethnic groups are divided. Slightly different sets of categories pertain in Scotland and Northern Ireland, though

Box 4.1   Sources of variation across the UK's minority groups

Group country of origin
Date/period of main migration
Main areas of settlement
Occupational 'niches'
Impact of de-industrialization
Extent of geographic dispersal
Return or onward migration
Language (and fluency in English)
Family structure
Social contact and intermarriage
Proportion UK born
Age

there is substantial harmonization in relation to the larger categories. These categories are intended to reflect populations that vary across core elements linked to domains that shape ethnicity and ethnic identity, such as country of origin, language, religion, nationality and prior colonial relationships, with a particular emphasis on distinguishing by physical appearance and skin colour (Coleman and Salt 1996). While the categories are internally heterogeneous to a certain degree, they also differ from each other in some key ways, summarized in box 4.1. These differences are pertinent for the ways in which the group histories have developed and for the extent and experience of inequality within and across the groups. Thus it is clear, given the categorization in terms of country or geographical region, that country of origin varies across these groups, and with that the main period of migration for those in the different categories, with black Africans being more recent and black Caribbeans representing the oldest, *postwar* migration stream. Distinct migration histories resulted in distinctive settlement patterns in different parts of the UK, and location in areas of particular industries was also linked to particular 'niche' skills for some groups. For example, Pakistanis moved particularly to the areas of textile industries (Smith 1977). Where de-industrialization has particularly affected such industries – for instance, with the textile industries of the northern English towns – those groups have been particularly severely affected. Period of migration and location has also had long-term impacts on housing experience and inequalities (Phillips 1997).

Despite substantial outmigration from original areas of settlement and a trend to move from inner cities to more suburban areas (Finney and Simpson 2009; Simpson and Finney 2008), the geographical location and concentration of groups still differs quite substantially, partly as fertility and new migration 'refreshes' the ethnic composition of traditional areas of settlement. Thus there is distinctive residential clustering, which varies in extent and area according to ethnic group, alongside clear patterns of dispersal (Phillips 1998).

Many minorities come from countries that have had longstanding relationships with the UK from the colonial period. For many, therefore, English is already a first or an official language. Others, though, may come to the UK with little or no English,

Table 4.2 Percentage of the UK's main minority ethnic groups born in the UK

Ethnic group	All	All	Women	Men	Children
	UK born	UK born or arrived<14	UK born	UK born	UK born
White British	98	99	97	97	99
Other white	46	54	39	41	68
Indian	43	56	21	19	86
Pakistani	56	67	26	22	92
Bangladeshi	52	68	14	9	94
Other Asian	23	38	7	7	63
Black Caribbean	63	73	49	46	95
Black African	35	50	11	12	73
Other black	66	76	42	48	90
Chinese	25	38	11	10	78

Note: The vast majority of the mixed groups are UK born and are not included here, partly on account of small sample sizes.
Source: Pooled Household Labour Force Survey datasets, 2004–8, own analysis.

which influences possibilities for social contact and, in some cases, employment – or limits the particular type of employment. Those who are well qualified from non-English-speaking countries, including the new migrants from Eastern Europe, may also arrive with English-language skills, while others from the same country will not.

Family structure and demography vary substantially across groups. Demographic patterns are linked to migration history and to the proportions born in the UK. Indeed, some of the categories in the more recent census classifications, notably the 'mixed' categories, have largely come into being to reflect UK-born populations who cannot easily locate themselves within uniform categories. For example, we can see from table 4.2 that while, as might be expected, almost all of the white British majority were born in the UK, this was the case with only a quarter of the Chinese and 'other Asian' groups. Around half of Pakistanis and Bangladeshis were born in the UK, but these were predominantly children, whereas nearly two-thirds of black Caribbeans – nearly half the adults – were.

There has been a tendency in a large strand of research to argue that being born outside the UK is a strong determinant of labour market chances, as a result of factors such as having qualifications from other countries which are not easily recognized; having a different first language; having experience in a different labour market, which may not be given so much credit by employers; not having 'home-grown' networks for information and job search assistance; and having different assumptions and expectations about types of labour market participation and about women's involvement in the labour force. Thus migrant status is often a major focus for studying labour market inequalities, since it is anticipated that the reasons, if clearly identified, can be located and reveal the ways in which characteristics lead to common outcomes across groups. Conversely, the assumption would be that such

Table 4.3 Age and family structure of selected ethnic groups

Ethnic group	Mean age, years	Family structure (%)				Mean family size	Families with 4+ people (%)
		Single	Couple, no deps	Couple with dep. children	Lone parent		
White British	40	36	35	20	9	2.2	16
Indian	33	30	30	33	7	2.6	28
Pakistani	26	24	19	45	11	3.2	43
Bangladeshi	24	20	14	52	14	3.6	49
Black Caribbean	35	41	14	16	28	2.1	16
Black African	26	44	9	25	22	2.4	24

Source: Adapted from Platt (2009a), tables 2 and 3, from pooled Household Labour Force Survey datasets, 2002–5.

migrant-centred accounts cease to be relevant for those born in the UK, who will engage with – and be treated by – the labour market in the same way as the majority population of the equivalent age and characteristics. Certain explanatory factors (for instance, qualifications obtained in another country) cease to be relevant. However, a migration focus is limited because there are by now substantial proportions of the UK's minorities who are born in the UK. Moreover, as the following discussion demonstrates, it is not just – or even predominantly – among those born in other countries where inequalities in labour market experience are found. And, indeed, there are frequently closer parallels in the experience between migrant and subsequent generations from the same ethnic group than between those of the same generation, whether migrant or UK born. Thus a migration-centred conceptual focus, while it can contribute to understanding certain patterns in labour market experience, does not provide a comprehensive framework for understanding ethnic employment (or other) inequalities.

An alternative has been a recourse to 'cultural' explanations of ethnic inequalities – accounts which are often embedded in perceptions of family structure, fertility and values. Table 4.3 highlights average differences in age and family structure across ethnic groups. The age structure is revealing about the extent to which minority groups make up a larger proportion of the next generation than they do of the current generation. It brings into sharp relief the patterns of school achievement, since they will heavily influence the extent to which contemporary group experiences are or are not transformed in subsequent generations. Chapter 6 illustrates the outcomes by ethnic group for those currently going through school; and it is informative to know that minority groups make up a much higher proportion of school-age children than they do of adults – and especially of older people.

In terms of family structure, table 4.3 reflects certain conventional understandings of different ethnic groups that have been used to structure debates on inequalities relating to them, often at the expense of consideration of other characteristics. Thus the high rates of lone parenthood among black Caribbean families have been represented both as intrinsic to this group and as highly problematic, in particular, for the boys growing up in them. The wider constructions relating to the 'problem' of lone parents (Lewis 2001) take on particular forms when linked to ethnicity (Reynolds 2005) and tend to locate forms of structural disadvantage within the family. Chapter 6 explores this issue in more depth. On the other hand, the larger average family sizes of Pakistanis and Bangladeshis have been linked to 'traditional' values, themselves regarded as being heavily implicated in women's labour market participation. While these differences in family structure do impact on poverty risks for both groups (Berthoud 2005), they are not the sole factor, nor for Pakistani and Bangladeshi families even the dominant factor in the very high rates of poverty among those two groups. Moreover, patterns of family structure are dynamic; they change over time, and thus cannot be used to define the meaning of a group except highly contingently. The interaction among family life, partnership and work is shaped by, as well as results in, inequalities, through differential opportunities, responses and possibilities, different rewards for work and educational qualifications, and different starting points. This is not to deny that there may be preferences for larger rather than smaller families, or that women exercise agency when bringing children up on their own. However, without a recognition of how both play off each other, there remain difficulties in linking differences between groups in one domain causally to observed inequalities. Moreover, it is important to be alert to the ways in which such causal narratives replicate particular racialized patterns of thinking, which persist, even if at an understated level in much discussion of ethnic difference.

4.3　Ethnic minorities in the labour market

Interpreting ethnic differences in labour market outcomes

Ethnic inequalities can be found not just in rates of participation in paid work (among those of working age), but also in the relative proportions in employment and self-employment, in the distribution of groups across occupations and their concentration within particular occupations, and in pay. In attempting to understand the sources of such inequalities and the extent to which they can be attributed to particular experiences of minority ethnic groups, the dominant approach has been to try to determine the extent to which absolute differences can be explained through differences in characteristics across groups. That is, if we can observe average differences in age, qualifications, length of time in the UK, fluency in English, geographical area and employment rate in local labour market, and so on, across groups, can these allow us to account for differences in employment, pay or type of work? All of these factors, it is argued, particularly qualifications, but also age, local employment rate, and so on, can and do legitimately affect employment. Therefore once these are held constant in comparisons, either there should be no difference or we are left with relative inequalities, an effect that can be attributed to 'ethnicity'. That leads then to the question of how we interpret the ethnic effect. This is complicated by the fact not only that observed differences across groups are very substantial, but that the residual effects of 'ethnicity' also vary substantially and significantly by group. Should we, as is often done, then interpret these relative inequalities as discrimination? Heath and McMahon have argued that, rather, we should consider them as an 'ethnic penalty' which can and almost certainly does include discrimination, but which may also capture other employment relevant factors that have not been measured:

> We use the expression 'ethnic penalty' to refer to all the sources of disadvantage that might lead an ethnic group to fare less well in the labour market than do similarly qualified Whites. In other words, it is a broader concept than that of discrimination, although discrimination is likely to be a major component of the ethnic penalty. (Heath and McMahon 1997)

They say, then, that we should be cautious in how we treat such ethnic effects, since the direct route by which they come about is not evident. Moreover, in order to account for the variation between groups it would be important to develop an idea of differential discrimination linked to specific ethnic groups. Some analysts, nevertheless, conclude that ethnic penalties are clear evidence of labour market discrimination and regard the ethnic effects as the end point of demonstrating a stratifying society. By contrast, others reflect on how the penalties could instead demonstrate reasonable bases for differences in outcomes that are simply not measured, such as preferences around particular types of work undertaken; willingness to travel substantial distances; (lack of) particular skills we do not know about; or (lack of) job relevant experience, which is often poorly measured. For these researchers, relative ethnic inequalities remain a challenge to better frameworks of explanation and better specification of differences between groups, with the expectation that, with sufficiently good measurements, ethnic group differences will be subsumed within them and leave only the different generic routes to unequal outcomes to be addressed. What is clear from extensive research is that ethnic effects are typically found across groups in studies of ethnicity and employment, indicating systematic disadvantage, and that the principal aim of most labour market analyses is to uncover – or demonstrate the absence or potential for explanation of – relative differences between minority and majority groups.

The predominant emphasis on uncovering ethnic effects is perhaps open to question. First, the focus on relative chances in the labour market should not distract us from the very large absolute inequalities faced by minorities. These can be argued to be of concern however 'explicable' they are. Second, if ethnic penalties are not self-evidently demonstrating discrimination, absolute differences and the factors that appear to 'explain' them are not free of the influence of discriminatory actions and structures. For example, differences in work histories may reflect the cumulative impact of discrimination and lack of opportunities or increased risks of unemployment leading to long periods out of work, even if the work history record then appears to 'justify' lower pay or position. A focus on individualized experiences and relative chances may both obscure discrimination and indicate it without sufficient evidence. Third, while a focus on relative differences can reveal the factors that are implicated in fundamental labour market inequalities, such as qualifications or age, if groups compared vary dramatically in terms of these characteristics, then an analysis which looks at net effects is not especially meaningful. For example, it may be that it can be shown that graduates over forty from all groups have equal outcomes, but if there are very few such people within a particular ethnic group, then it does not constitute an appropriate comparison.

For all these reasons, it is important to retain a sense of the size, scale and nature of absolute inequalities as providing a context for understanding ethnic

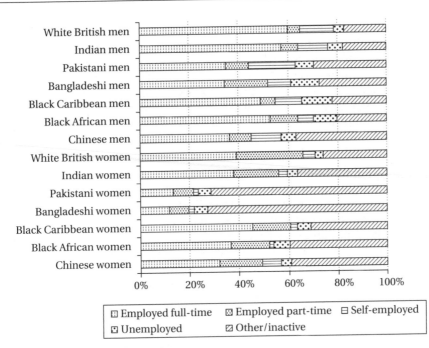

Source: Longhi and Platt (2008), figure 2.1.

Figure 4.1 Employment status by sex and ethnicity, Great Britain, 2004–7.

penalties. It is to illustrations of these absolute differences in labour market outcomes that we turn next. When moving to explanations we can then take account of the key factors that are associated with them, but also how they may reinforce each other.

Inequalities in work and pay

First we look at economic activity and inactivity across groups. Economic activity covers both those in paid work and those who are unemployed but looking for work. Those who are not seeking work, whether for family, health, or other reasons, are counted as economically inactive. However, the boundaries are not necessarily that neat. Some who are not looking for work may be happy to have a job if they thought they could get one; others may have been discouraged by long periods of fruitless search. The greater social acceptability for women of 'looking after home and family' has been shown to lead some to redefine themselves as inactive if they face a long spell without work, with no substantial change in their activity or desire to have a job. Men are less likely to do this, but if suffering health problems may equally use health as an 'explanation' for non-participation, even if their problem was already present while they were in work. Therefore, whether unemployment or simply non-work is the appropriate measure of disadvantage is a moot point (Berthoud and Blekesaune 2006). Figure 4.1 illustrates patterns of employment and economic activity across ethnic groups and for men and women separately.

We can see from figure 4.1 that there are strong differences in full-time employment rates across both men and women from the different groups. We can also see clear differences in unemployment, self-employment and part-time work. Though part-time work is more common in general among women – it is white British women who show the highest rates – the high rates of Bangladeshis stand out among men. As chapter 3 discusses at more length, engagement in part-time work has been argued to represent preferences among those women who prioritize family over work. While this is not uncontested, it may account in part for the high rates of self-employment among white British women. Other groups of women may face a more discrete choice between full-time work or not working, both through preference and because, in the absence of a reasonably well-paid partner, taking up typically low-paid part-time work does not make economic sense at the household level (Platt 2006). For men, it is difficult to see part-time work as reflecting a choice, and is more likely to represent a constraint on obtaining a job with more hours. For those with health conditions or disabilities, which tend to be higher than average among Bangladeshi men, part-time work *may* offer an adaptive solution. There is little evidence as to whether or not this is the case.

Self-employment is much more common among men than women, and is highest among Pakistani men. This relates partly to occupational patterns, and it has been pointed out that the advantages that are traditionally associated with self-employment are not found in many of the self-employed occupations, such as chauffeuring and taxi driving, that are particularly prevalent among Pakistanis. Rather than self-employment representing a positive choice of autonomous work, the evidence suggests that it should be understood as a constraint – a form of paid work that is adopted in the light of lack of other possibilities (Clark and Drinkwater 2000). From this perspective, differential rates of self-employment can also be read as employment inequalities.

Unemployment rates differ substantially across ethnic groups. Those for Bangladeshi and black Caribbean men stand out, but they are also high for black African and Pakistani men. They are lower among women, but it is clear that minority group women face higher unemployment rates than majority group women. The relatively high rates of unemployment among Pakistani and Bangladeshi women are striking given their low levels of employment and high rates of inactivity. It is not simply that inactivity is an alternative for them to unemployment, or they would have low unemployment rates alongside their high inactivity rates.

Figures 4.2 and 4.3 simplify the picture from figure 4.1 by detailing just those in some form of paid work and ranking them according to the proportion employed. This allows us to see clearly the very differences across groups, even after the introduction of specific policies to raise the employment rate of minority ethnic groups, following a review of their labour market experience and the establishment in 2003 of an Ethnic Minority Employment Task Force. Figures 4.2 and 4.3 also show that to talk of a minority group employment rate is misleading, since the diversity *between* groups is so great (Platt 2007a).

Over time there has been some closing of the employment gaps between minorities and the majority, but the gaps for those groups with the lowest employment rates remain large. Particular attention has been drawn to the differences between women, with very low employment rates among Pakistanis and Bangladeshis. These low rates have been subject to substantial investigation and a number of initiatives

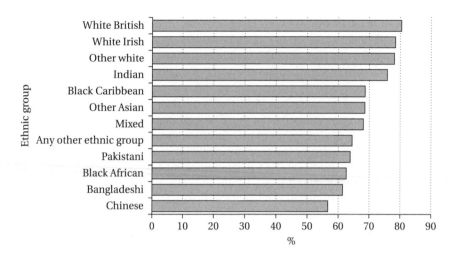

Source: Adapted from Platt (2007c).

Figure 4.2   Men's employment rates by ethnic group, 2004.

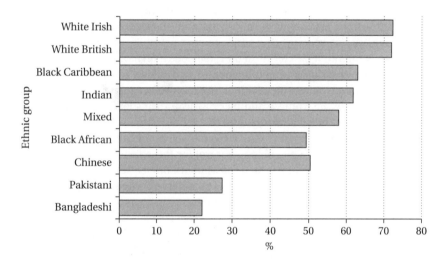

Source: Adapted from Platt (2007c).

Figure 4.3   Women's employment rates by ethnic group, 2004.

to reduce the barriers to employment. Low participation is frequently interpreted as stemming from the predominantly Muslim faith of these groups, which is interpreted as being associated with a rejection of engagement in the public sphere for women, a reluctance to combine work and family responsibilities, and restrictions on the sorts of jobs that they are willing to take up, exacerbated by relatively low levels of qualifications. However, there is substantial evidence that low participation is a specific feature of contemporary working-age women, many of whom have migrated as adults. For younger generations, and particularly for those born in the UK, there appears to be substantial convergence in expectations of participation and actual engagement in the labour market (Dale et al. 2006, 2002b; Georgiadis and Manning forthcoming), and acquisition of qualifications has been fastest among these young women (Bagguley and Hussain 2007; Lindley et al. 2006). As Georgiadis and Manning point out, this convergence has not come at the cost of substantial declines in religious affiliation or religiosity among younger Pakistani and Bangladeshi women. The majority still regard themselves as Muslims even if their behaviour and expectations – and skills – are very different from those of their mothers' generation. This highlights the difficulty of attempting to use particular characteristics or dimensions of minority position, and in particular religious affiliation, as a means of accounting for specific inequalities. Profession of a religion does not necessarily imply a static and consistent set of values. Nor is it specifically the common fact of religious affiliation to Islam that renders Pakistani and Bangladeshi women's employment participation so low. Religious affiliation has to be explored in relation to other factors, such as ethnicity, country of birth and upbringing, qualifications and contemporary family status. Moreover, assumptions about religious affiliation can help to compound the inequalities that they supposedly explain, through discrimination, low expectations, and neglecting the structural constraints and household level economics that inhibit labour market participation.

We can see, moreover, that, while the low employment rates of Pakistani and Bangladeshi women stand out, those of Pakistani, Bangladeshi, black African and Chinese men are also very low. The employment rates of Pakistani and Bangladeshi men are rarely interpreted in terms of their religious affiliation, even if religious discrimination may contribute to employment disadvantage. In addition, by looking across the four groups, it becomes evident how important age structure is to employment rates. Much of the Chinese and black African men's lack of employment can be attributed to their being students. And the demographic profile of Pakistani and Bangladeshi working-age men is also skewed towards the younger age range. This leads to the attraction of being able to control for these factors and to make comparisons across otherwise similar men (or women), but it also raises the question of what are the most appropriate comparisons to undertake when looking at the labour market – for example, whether to exclude students or to focus on those of a particular age range – in order better to understand the specific causes of inequality. We can also see the differences and similarities between labour market experiences of men and women. Since families are made up largely from within a single ethnic group (Platt 2009b). The experience of other members of the household is relevant to individuals' possibilities and strategies for employment. And, since families are largely made up from a single ethnic group (ibid.), it makes sense to consider the labour market experience of men and women from the same group side by side.

We see, then, that employment inequalities are substantial between the majority and minorities and vary substantially across ethnic groups. They also raise questions about how we interpret economic activity, unemployment and different forms of employment and whether they have the same interpretation across different groups. We also see that extrapolating to causes or potential causes of labour market inequality is not straightforward and needs to take into account the specific intersections of dimensions of ethnicity and the dynamics of identification and social location.

Concentrating now just on those in employment, we go on to look at inequalities in pay. Table 4.4 gives hourly rates of pay among men and women by ethnic group. It

Table 4.4 Pay of men and women in full-time work, by ethnic group

	Women	*Men*
White British	10.84	12.94
Indian	11.09	13.49
Pakistani	9.61	9.98
Bangladeshi	10.63	10.24
Black Caribbean	11.14	12.27
Black African	10.23	10.63
Chinese	11.72	13.00

Note: Hourly pay is in £s at 2007 prices.
Source: Adapted from Longhi and Platt (2008), table 3.1.

shows that, while men tend to earn more than women from the same ethnic group, this is not the case for Bangladeshi men, and men from several groups appear to earn less on average than women from other groups. Because they are based on small samples we cannot rely fully on the precision of these estimates for all comparisons within and between groups and sexes, but there are nevertheless some clear differences which it is possible to draw out.

First, the rates of pay show us something of the scale of the differences between groups, even among those in full-time work. There are clear pay differences relative to majority group men both for white British women and for men and women from most minority groups, with only Indian and Chinese not experiencing pay disadvantage. The disadvantage for some groups relative to majority group men are clearly sizeable, Bangladeshi and Pakistani men and Pakistani and black African women standing out for their lower rates of full-time pay. What is also evident is that, for most minority groups, women's pay is not significantly worse than that of men and may even be better. This contrasts with the substantial pay gap faced by white British women. It is relevant to think again of how employment and pay relate to one another. Those in groups with very low employment rates may be willing or able to enter the labour market only when they can command a reasonable level of pay. It is also worth bearing in mind the differences in demographics that we saw earlier on. There will be a higher proportion of older women among white British women than there are in other groups, often with interrupted work histories, who may have relatively poorly paid opportunities. Young people, however, have the lowest rates of pay. It is during the years in between that both men and women reach their optimum earnings levels. They also have higher qualifications on average and will thus have higher earnings potential than previous, less well-qualified generations. Thus, differences in pay cannot be interpreted simply as evidence for the presence or absence of employment discrimination but have to take account of who is in work and whether they are being rewarded commensurately with their skills and qualifications. In fact, analysis suggests that there are major ethnic penalties in pay for some groups, such as Bangladeshi men, and even those well paid, such as Indian men, are receiving lower rewards than they might expect given their occupations and skills (Longhi and Platt 2008).

Explaining labour market inequalities

We have seen that there are striking inequalities, or at least differences, across ethnic groups among those of working age in employment, self-employment, unemployment and pay. We go on to consider why and how these differences arise. Box 4.2 lists some of the key factors that have been identified as contributing to employment inequalities across ethnic groups. All these have been shown to have a bearing on labour market inequalities to a greater or lesser extent. However, a number of them are specific to those who migrated as adults, such as UK labour market experience and English-language fluency. It is important to remember that differences in employment and pay disadvantage are not just a first-generation problem, affecting those who have migrated from another country, and for whom entering a new employment context might be expected to be more challenging. Indeed, a substantial amount of research on the UK's minority groups has focused on issues of migration and the expected disadvantage that is assumed to derive from the fact of international relocation. At the same time, continuing relative as well as absolute disadvantage into the second and subsequent generations is evident from the research literature. I touch here on some of the research that has distinguished immigrant and second-generation employment outcomes, exploring a number of the factors contained in box 4.2. Since there is not the scope here to do justice to all of the posited routes to unequal outcomes, I therefore concentrate on research that relates to (a) behaviour or networks in terms of job search activity, with a particular focus on the migrant generation, and (b) skills, in terms of English-language fluency and educational qualifications, with a particular focus on those born in Britain. The final section then returns to the thorny issue of employer discrimination and the associated evidence and how we can evaluate it.

It is widely accepted that migrant networks differ from those of the majority and that there is a tendency in all groups for them to be bounded – that is, generally group-specific – though with considerable variation within that overall picture (Platt 2009c; Zhou 2005). The implications of such differences in networks may be relevant to their general well-being if they affect possibilities for social participation, and so constitute inequalities in their own right (Cheong et al. 2007; Platt 2009c), or they may be of interest to the extent that they contribute to inequalities in other domains, such as in the labour market or education (Platt and Thompson 2007; Thapar-Bjorkert and Sanghera 2010) or in the extent to which there are implications for society more generally (Letki 2008; Zetter et al. 2006). However, the significance of networks for understanding inequalities and the mechanisms by which they operate are perhaps not as evident as the extensive research and policy interest in social capital would imply. It is argued that immigrants will have less knowledge or fewer options in relation to searching for jobs, with consequent impact on their unemployment rates. They may have limited knowledge of local labour market institutions or smaller social networks, or be looking in particular sectors of the labour market. Battu, Seaman and Zenou (2004) argued that personal networks are a popular source of job search for men and women, but that Pakistani and Bangladeshi groups and those born outside the UK were disadvantaged in the labour market as a result of relying on them. By contrast, Frijters, Shields and Wheatley Price (2005), using the same data, found some differences in job search behaviour across their four broad

Box 4.2   Potential reasons for differences in work and pay

- Qualifications
- Experience in the UK labour market
- Employer discrimination
- Occupational segregation/specialization
- Geographical location and industrial decline
- Self-employment and niche employment
- English-language fluency
- Job-specific skills
- Living in disadvantaged (low-employment, low-pay) areas
- Access to jobs or vacancies, networks
- Different job preferences
- Poor health (potential consequence as well as cause of labour market inequalities)

groups of immigrants (South Asians, blacks, whites and others) compared with white non-migrants. However, they found that, for all groups, personal contacts were the most effective way of gaining employment and that choice of methods when search-ing for jobs could not explain the immigrant groups' 'penalty' in the longer time it took to leave unemployment. Heath and Yu (2005) considered whether networks for job access had potential for accounting for why the outcomes for some minority groups were better than for others. Their evidence does not point to job search activ-ity or approach as playing an important role in differential employment outcomes. There seems, therefore, little evidence to support the contention that the way jobs are approached or the way people exploit their networks is pertinent to understanding labour market inequalities.

It is often argued that immigrants' pay gaps might be related partly to lack of skills, little knowledge of the language of the host country (Chiswick 2008; Dustmann and Fabbri 2003; Shields and Wheatley Price 2001), or different education received in their country of birth and not recognized in the host country. Conversely, it is argued that the second and subsequent generations, having been born in the UK, should not suffer from these labour market disadvantages. Hence, we would expect second-generation immigrants to fare much better in the labour market than those of the first generation. In fact the empirical evidence shows ongoing disadvantage or ethnic penalties (Dustmann and Theodoropoulos 2006; Heath and Cheung 2006, 2007), though typically less than in the first generation. On other measures, however, and for some groups, the outcomes are actually worse for those who have been born or brought up in the UK than for their migrant parents or grandparents. Berthoud (2000) showed how young Caribbean men fared particularly poorly in the labour market, and this has been reinforced by more recent studies. Moreover, at times of high unemployment or recession, young people are very badly affected and minor-ity group members are also much more vulnerable to job loss (Berthoud 2010). For those both young and from a minority group, the prospects can be particularly poor – and may have long-term consequences for future job opportunities and hence lifetime incomes. Though there is some catch-up in better economic circumstances, the evidence suggests that it is not as great as the loss that occurs when the economy slumps (Lindley 2005). Thus young people who have lived through a period of unemployment may find that the impact stays with them in more prosperous times. The poorer outcomes of those minorities born in Britain challenge conventional skill and education-system based accounts of labour market differentials.

There could nevertheless be explicit differences in qualifications, which may in part be a legacy of the disadvantage faced by the migrant generation, to the extent that parental resources and qualifications play a role in their children's educational success. Heath and McMahon (1997) used the 1991 census (for England, Wales and Scotland) to examine the role of educational attainment in social class outcomes for the second generation. They found it played an important role in contributing to the patterns of occupational class outcomes, but that an 'ethnic penalty' still remained for black Caribbean, black African, Indian and Pakistani men relative to British-born white men. They found a similar story for the ethnic penalties experienced by second-generation women from the different ethnic groups, though minority group women were even more disadvantaged in relation to avoiding unemployment. They concluded that 'being born in Britain is not associated with any improvement in competitive chances' (1997, p. 108).

Clark and Drinkwater (2007), using data from the subsequent census, also found that education played a strong role in explaining employment chances, but that a big gap remained between the chances of certain minorities and the white majority. Thus there did not appear to be a trend towards reducing the gap and equalizing outcomes. Comparison of women's outcomes a decade apart using pooled Labour Force Survey data also showed both the increasing relevance of educational qualifications and the persistence of an ethnic penalty over time (Lindley et al. 2006). Indeed, the study showed that the extent of differences in employment rates that could be attributed to observed differences between white majority and minority groups actually decreased over time, leaving a larger role for an 'ethnic penalty'. So, while Pakistani and Bangladeshi women have made the greatest gains in educational qualifications (Bagguley and Hussain 2007; Dale et al. 2002b; Lindley et al. 2006), and while the differences in employment rates between the highly qualified and the unqualified are starkest for these groups, outcomes do not mirror very closely patterns of educational success and failure. Greater investment in education would appear to bring diminishing returns for some groups.

Given that unemployment rates tend to be higher in youth, Berthoud (1999) analysed employment penalties among five groups of young men: white, Caribbean, black African, Indian, and Pakistani or Bangladeshi. This enabled him to compare those born or raised in Britain with those who migrated after the age of sixteen without the confounding factor that immigrants tend to be older than British-born minorities. There were substantial variations in qualification levels among the young men according to their ethnic group. Both white and Caribbean young men were consistently less likely to be unemployed the more highly they were qualified. To a certain extent, then, high unemployment rates among Caribbeans could be attributed to qualification levels. On the other hand, their chances of unemployment were still greater than those for the white group at all qualification levels.

The finding of a strong role for education in employment outcomes but a persistent ethnic penalty was also found in a number of other studies, and it was clear that it affected the UK-born as well as non-UK minorities, specifically those from black, Indian and Pakistani groups (Blackaby et al. 1997, 1999, 2002, 2005). Moreover, periods of unemployment were found to last longer and the chances of gaining employment were lower for British-born ethnic minorities (all grouped together) compared with the majority group, despite the fact that their higher qualifications and younger age profile should have improved their chances (Frijters et al. 2005).

The consistent message from analysis is that, while many factors in the list in box 4.2 have been shown to be relevant – sometimes highly relevant in the case of qualifications – to differential employment outcomes across groups, they cannot fully explain them. Behavioural accounts, such as those dealing with job search activity, tend to be able to account for fewer differences, as do accounts which imply distinct ethnic 'preferences'. These are anyway hard to evaluate separately from the constraints that may engender them. For example, individuals may 'prefer' to work in a non-discriminatory workplace and thus receive lower pay as a consequence, but that is not a very meaningful construction of preference. Education and qualifications are clearly critical to reducing employment inequalities among minority groups. However, it is equally clear that, while they may be necessary to close the gap, they are not sufficient to equalize chances across groups. The complex relationship between qualifications, histories, and cumulative effects of disadvantage make it difficult to illuminate the precise ways in which outcomes fall short, but a role is clearly indicated for discrimination, both direct discrimination and the wider prejudicial environment. Such discrimination has tended to be assumed to be racial, thus based on the perceived minority ethnicity and 'otherness' of minority ethnic groups. But increasingly ways are coming to the fore in which it might make sense to think of discrimination as being cultural, motivated by perceptions of particular groups and their assumed practices, including their religious affiliation. This involves understanding how difference is recognized, constructed and reformulated and how it leads to prejudicial attitudes (Abrams 2010). But it also involves an attempt to grasp the scale and extent of it to evaluate potential impact and, if inequalities are to be reduced, to target it more effectively.

The final section of this chapter therefore explores the ways which have been used to demonstrate and enumerate the extent of minority discrimination within the UK labour market.

Discrimination and ethnic labour market inequalities

Employer discrimination can rarely be covered directly in the sorts of studies just discussed, which depend mostly on large-scale surveys and report the perspectives of individual respondents. Instead, this body of research provides a clear indication of the ways in which minorities are structurally disadvantaged in terms of labour market outcomes. We now, therefore, turn directly to the role of discrimination in perpetuating employment inequalities. The consensus is that it exists, but it is harder to measure than characteristics that are located 'within' individuals, such as their health status, qualifications or occupational class. Box 4.3 summarizes the approaches that have been used to ascertain labour market discrimination, each of which is discussed in turn.

Box 4.3   Ascertaining discrimination

Calculating from survey data the remaining ethnic effect after taking account of employment-relevant characteristics
Measuring public attitudes
Asking people whether they have been discriminated against
Using the evidence from tribunals
Discrimination tests on employers

Discrimination in employment has been illegal for decades, and legislation exists to penalize racially motivated crimes. Nevertheless, there is little doubt that discrimination continues to operate to limit the life chances of those in a range of marginalized positions. Definitions of discrimination and institutional racism and the legal framework have been extensively rehearsed elsewhere (Bhavnani et al. 2005; Connolly 2002; Goulbourne 1998; Parekh 2000). These discussions have highlighted how an individualized approach is rarely sufficient to capture the ways in which racism and discrimination permeate organizations, institutions and social interactions. This is one of the reasons why attempting to ascertain the discriminatory actions of employers at a particular moment can give only a very partial picture of how discrimination operates and how it impacts on life chances across the life course and in cumulative fashion, and thus how disadvantage is perpetuated. Nevertheless, gaining some clarity about individual acts of discrimination can help us understand the employment context better and give a greater purchase on occupational patterns, choices and constraints.

An indication of levels of employer discrimination can be identified using people's perceptions of personal experience. For example, Modood (1997) used responses on perceived job refusal, with Caribbeans, at 28 per cent, the most likely to identify discrimination, followed by African Asians, Indians, Chinese, and Pakistanis and Bangladeshis. More recently, the Home Office Citizenship Survey canvassed perceptions of discriminatory job refusal. Here it was black African men (26 per cent) and women (16 per cent) who were most likely to identify job refusal on racial grounds (Heath and Cheung 2006). Over 10 per cent of Caribbean and black mixed-race men also perceived they had been denied a job on racial grounds, with smaller, though still substantial, proportions of Indian and Pakistani men and Caribbean women (around 9 per cent), followed by around 7 per cent of Bangladeshi men and Indian and Pakistani women, and 6 per cent of Bangladeshi women. Analysis of the 2005 survey, not disaggregated by sex, found that, of those who had been refused a job in the last five years, around 17 per cent of Indians and Pakistanis, over 20 per cent of Caribbeans and nearly 30 per cent of black Africans felt that the refusal had been on racial grounds (Kitchen et al. 2006).

The difficulty is that people's perceptions may not be accurate; and identifying whether you have been discriminated against at the point of selection (either invitation to interview or following an interview) is very hard to ascertain, given that it is almost impossible to know what the competition is. Such perceptions give some indication of the obstacles perceived by those seeking jobs, but they are further complicated by the fact that there may be less experience or perception of discriminatory job refusal in highly segregated job markets. Such occupations might be the most disadvantaging, as through lack of alternatives people end up in jobs that have low rewards where, because they are not 'desirable', issues of competition don't arise. Thus increasing perceptions of discrimination in employment could, paradoxically, be a result of a more open labour market with greater opportunities for minorities to compete with the majority (Modood 1997).

Perceptions of discrimination within employment – for example, in relation to promotion – are likely to give a much clearer indication of actual discrimination. Some complaints will reach tribunal, and tribunal cases and investigations of employers by the Equalities and Human Rights Commission may give some indication of the nature of such experience. But few cases reach tribunal, and, again, there is the issue that people may be more likely to proceed with cases where they have greater faith in the effectiveness of the system. Tribunals and actions against employers are likely therefore only to be indicative rather than clear evidence of differences in discrimination experience between groups or over time.

Surveys of prejudiced views may act as a general barometer of discriminatory attitudes in the population. According to the British Social Attitudes Survey, at the beginning of the 1990s, 36 per cent of the population considered themselves to be racially prejudiced. This declined to 25 per cent by the end of the decade before rising again to 32 per cent in the early years of the twenty-first century (Rothon and Heath 2003). This rise is consistent with a perceived increase in racial prejudice found in the Home Office Citizenship Survey (Kitchen et al. 2006). Around 30 per cent of those of working age in 2003 viewed themselves as racially prejudiced (Heath and Cheung 2006). However, the relationship of such generalized prejudice to employer discrimination can only be oblique – only those in a position to appoint or refuse a job can do so, and even prejudiced individuals may not appoint on that basis. However, these figures may also act as indicators of potential discriminatory attitudes in the working environment and at least link to apparent preferences for, or concentrations of, minority groups in less prejudiced environments, specifically in public-sector rather than private-sector occupations (ibid.). Even if employers do not directly discriminate, awareness of their potential to do so, avoidance of prejudiced environments, or past bad experiences may lead to evasive strategies where the risks are felt to be considerable.

Finally, recruitment tests are considered to represent objective measures of discrimination. These take the form of submitting otherwise identical (in terms of work experience, nature of qualifications, relevance for the post, etc.) pairs of applications to employers, simply including a signal (usually via means of inventing the applicant's name) that one of the pair is from a minority group. Any difference in rates of calls to interview can then be attributed straightforwardly to discrimination. Such tests have been used on a number of occasions in the past and in a range of countries, and have always tended to identify some degree of employer discrimination. After a long gap, such a recruitment test was recently carried out in the UK, commissioned by the Department for Work and Pensions. Wood et al. (2009) found from this exercise a net discrimination rate of 29 per cent. Put another way, they concluded that an ethnic minority applicant would have to submit sixteen applications to obtain an interview where a white applicant would need to submit nine. The case for the existence of employer discrimination is then fairly clear. It may be less clear what can be done about it, or how to move towards a more equal society if the exclusion of minority group members is made to seem a rational option or can simply take place unconsciously.

We have seen that minority groups face substantial disadvantage in the labour market in both absolute and relative terms, but that there is substantial diversity in the experience of different minority groups (Modood et al. 1997). There is also heterogeneity within groups as defined by existing categories, and outcomes can be differentiated by sex and by generation; but the intergroup differences are clearly evident and are consistent across a range of studies. The ways in which labour market context and minority origins intersect vary according to the clusters of characteristics associated with particular groups. This in turn lends some support to the distinctions between the groups that are identified through the use of the existing categories. If inequalities were not identified between categories, then the rationale of construct-ing the social groups in this way would be less apparent – at least for an analysis of inequality. As it stands, we can observe substantial disadvantage, and recognition is a prerequisite for intervention or action (McCall 2005).

Nevertheless, it is also important to bear in mind that the construction of groups is not necessarily a reflection of identity as people would wish to claim it, and the associations we observe do not necessarily stem from anything inherent to the groups themselves or to ethnicity. Instead, it is worth considering that how groups are classi-fied is also likely to be influenced by their socio-economic location and that the power of choice over identification and group location may well be associated with greater advantage (Manning and Roy 2007). It is also important to recognize that particular ethnicities often have different patterns of experience if women and men are explored separately, challenging the possibilities for group-based accounts of inequality. The significance of the intersection between gender and ethnic group is one that recurs in subsequent chapters, and is part of the complex story of ethnic inequality in the UK.

Questions for reflection

1 Is ethnicity a useful concept?
2 What is missed by existing measures of ethnic group?
3 How far are ethnic labour market inequalities related to ethnicity?
4 Why is labour market disadvantage so different across different ethnic groups?
5 Why might discrimination vary across minority ethnic groups?
6 What are the benefits of a structural versus an individualized approach to ethnic inequalities?

Further reading

Fenton (2010) provides a comprehensive and critical discussion of the concept, defi-nition and use of 'ethnicity'. Platt (2007c) offers a detailed review of labour market inequalities as well as differences in poverty across ethnic groups, while Heath and Cheung (2006) explore labour market inequalities in relation to the evidence on dis-crimination. Parekh's (2000) report still stands as a thoughtful and comprehensive account of inequalities faced by minorities in the UK and ways in which to address them. Dobbs et al. (2006) provide a straightforward account of variation and inequal-ities across the UK's ethnic and religious groups.

5 Youth and Age

So I was doing nannying for 3 days a week and working as a supervisor at [shop] most of the weekend and the rest of the time, to save for India. And then I went to India for 3 or 4 months. And came back and didn't really do anything. Signed on for a bit. And decided that I was going to do a Masters in something I think and opted for fashion . . . Didn't get in, got completely disillusioned by it and completely broke down and stuff like that. So just little bits of childcare stuff, and what else? I became a florist. Then I went to India for 6 months. Came back, signed on for a bit, went back to the floristry for 3 years . . . then I did a Masters degree.

I try not to let it dwell on my mind but like most people when you're laying in bed at night and everything is going through your mind and you can't get to sleep 'cos it's all – and that's when you think about it. You think 'oh God am I going to get through this week'.

The first quotation comes from a study of fractured transitions (Bradley and Devadason 2008). It documents the lengthened transitions from states of childhood/ youth to those associated with adulthood, especially in terms of moves into full-time, life-time jobs. Kara's account reflects the multiple transitions to which Bradley and Devadason draw attention, with moves occurring both into and out of employment within early adulthood, and the high probability of some experience of unemployment during these economically marginal years. It also reflects the ways in which the expansion of education extends periods of transition and mobility among young people, potentially enabling quite dramatic shifts but also being a focus for aspirations which can be bitterly disappointed. The authors contrast these multiple moves with the more focused trajectories of other respondents, highlighting diversity in youth transitions as well as their fractured nature.

The second quotation comes from a study of early retirement (Archer 2003). It expresses the financial uncertainty and anxiety of a woman who has no independent pension income, is currently on a low income and, 'if anything happens', is highly vulnerable to the risks of poverty in later life. While she has made a 'choice' to leave the labour market and lives with a partner still earning, her life-course earnings have left her without financial resources of her own on which to draw, and her time in employment has not provided her with security for old age. Her recognition of her own dependence, a dependence that may be insecure, causes her sleepless nights.

Between them, these two quotations therefore highlight forms of instability and anxiety at different points in the life course. Age-related inequalities in employment and earnings are particularly striking among younger people, and women face substantial poverty risks in old age. Both of these areas are addressed in this chapter. But life-course trajectories are diverse and fragmented, not only at the beginning and end of working life but throughout the middle years. Inequalities can accumulate across those with different patterns of lifetime income and earnings, but they can also stem from unanticipated interruptions which fracture apparently steady trajectories, such as divorce or sudden loss of employment. This chapter therefore explores and illustrates ways of looking across life courses and the inequalities engendered over time.

5.1 Inequalities across the life course

In his study of poverty of 1899, in which he first introduced the systematic measurement of poverty as a lack of income, Seebohm Rowntree drew attention to the cycles of income experienced across the life course. He noted that poverty affected people at certain life stages, alternating with more affluent periods: thus childhood, the period of bringing up children, and old age were all times of want, while young working life (before children) and later working life (after children were themselves earning) were times of relative prosperity (Rowntree 1902). He also noted that, while he was measuring those in primary poverty at a particular moment in time:

> Many of these will, in course of time, pass on into a period of comparative prosperity; this will take place as soon as the children, now dependent, begin to earn. But their places below the poverty line will be taken by others who are at present living in that prosperous period previous to, or shortly after, marriage. Again, many now classed as above the poverty line were below it until the children began to earn. The proportion of the community who at one period or other of their lives suffer from poverty to the point of physical privation is therefore much greater, and the injurious effects of such a condition are much more widespread than would appear from a consideration of the number who can be shown to be below the poverty line at any given moment. (Ibid., pp. 137–8)

Rowntree illustrated this point with a graph showing the transitions above and below his 'poverty line' (see figure 5.1).

Because of the cumulative impact of family structure, Rowntree showed how less prosperous times could build up over the lifetime of individuals. He concluded that 'every labourer who has as many as three children must pass through a time, probably lasting for about ten years, when he will be in a state of "primary" poverty' (1902, p. 135). His insight concerning the importance of understanding experience in a life-course perspective and recognizing that people's experience was not fixed but changed with circumstances, even if those circumstances (marriage, children, old age) were seen as generally predictable, was probably largely intuitive rather than empirical. That is, it is not clear that the graph illustrated in figure 5.1 could be shown to derive directly from his poverty estimates (Hatton and Bailey 2000). But it was a significant insight, nevertheless, for understanding patterns of experience across the life course: that people are not simply born into a state and remain there, but their experiences and opportunities change and develop – or decline – over time. This was to become a feature of subsequent sociological analysis.

The fact that Rowntree could draw his illustration of working-class life courses based on an expected pattern of transitions draws attention to the assumption that particular stages of life succeed each other in predictable and coherent ways and at relatively fixed times. Thus, in a traditional, stylized perspective, it was expected that the school years were followed by employment, leaving home, marriage, children,

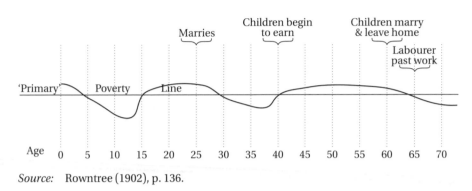

Source: Rowntree (1902), p. 136.

Figure 5.1   Rowntree's perspective on the life-cycle alternation of poverty and prosperity.

children leaving home, retirement and, eventually, death. It is acknowledged that this traditional pattern no longer exists – and there is substantial debate as to whether it ever really did for a large minority of people. Sociological attention was subsequently directed to the shifts in both timing and order of transitions and how these came about. For example, an extension of 'adolescence' was effectively achieved through the increase in the school leaving age, first to fifteen in 1944 and then to sixteen in 1971. Debate and analysis has taken place over what these shifts have implied for the meaning of expected life stages (Irwin 2005). The interest in life-course transitions has also been associated with the development of research on 'youth' specifically, including the influential work associated with the Birmingham Centre for Contemporary Cultural Studies. Youth has come to be a significant life stage, and for many there are delays to those events that are supposed to end it. Work is delayed by education – or unemployment; and marriage takes place later than it did in the post-war era. Attention has also been paid to the ways in which other transitions overlap one another. For example, parenthood might precede marriage, and leaving home does not necessarily follow getting a job. As Iacovou puts it,

> In terms of living arrangements, the most important components of the transition to adulthood are the transition out of the parental home, the transition from single status to living with a partner, and the transition from childlessness to parenthood. These transitions do not constitute a perfect definition of the transition to adulthood: some people never make one or more of the transitions, some people make a transition only to reverse it later (e.g., by moving back to the parents' home or by splitting up with a partner), and some people make and reverse transitions repeatedly. (Iacovou 2002, pp. 44–5)

Indeed, although the average age at leaving home is substantially lower in the UK than in some Southern European countries, many men, in particular, nevertheless remain in the parental home well into their twenties; and different patterns of transitions can be linked to wider inequalities in family income or ethnic background (Aassve et al. 2006; Iacovou 2002).

Thinking about inequalities in individuals' experiences as they grow up or grow older also involves finding different ways of summarizing people's experience over time, as well as the cumulative inequalities or disadvantages they experience when considered from a temporal perspective. In 1941 Rowntree attempted to refine these observations on periods of need in a life-course perspective by counting just how many people might encounter poverty at some stage, and concluded that 52.5 per cent of the working class (according to his definition of that class) would pass through poverty at some point. He also tried to refine his estimates of the length of time that children, specifically, might spend in poverty and predicted that 89 per cent of children whose fathers were employed but on low wages would be impoverished for more than five years and 66 per cent for ten years or more (Rowntree 1941, p.159). He was thus able, according to his measure and definition, not only to put a figure on all those affected but also to estimate durations. These issues are relevant to poverty analysis today and, more generally, to methods and approaches that have been developed that allow us to look at periods of life or life stages as a whole (Mayer 2009).

In this chapter, taking both a shorter- and longer-term perspective, we look at the inequalities in early life and the role of social background and touch on the associations between earlier disadvantage and later life outcomes. But we also turn to the other end and look at older people. What are the differences in life-course experience that have led to differences in outcomes for older people? What is their experience and how does it vary? These questions drive the second part of the chapter.

Coverage of inequalities in youth and age is preceded by a reflection on inequalities across the age range and their interpretation. For, of course, youth and age are not directly connected, in that the young people who are growing up today are likely to be different when they are older from those who are currently pensioners. This draws our attention to the importance of distinguishing age from cohort effects. When we summarize the experience of people at different ages, it is easy to assume that what we are seeing are *age* differences – that is, that as the twenty-year-olds become forty or the thirty-year-olds become sixty they will have the same outcomes, experiences or opportunities as those currently forty (or sixty). In fact, though, what we may be seeing is *cohort* differences – that is, those who are currently twenty are reflecting the experience of those born twenty years after those who are currently forty, and growing up twenty years apart has made their life chances qualitatively different. For example, the employment rates or pension entitlements of younger women may well be very different from those of their mothers when they reach their mothers' age. Box 5.1 summarizes the common distinction between age, period and cohort effects. In fact, both age and cohort are likely to influence an individual's situation at a particular point in time. To illustrate the differences, it is necessary to follow individuals as they age and explore their individual trajectories, and how they differ by background and by cohort. The third section of this chapter deals with inequalities in the middle of life.

It is also relevant, when we think about life-course trajectories and how they are unequal or become unequal over time, to consider the role of particular events and how they act as 'triggers' for changes in experience, so that people find themselves moving from one 'track' to a very different one. Such triggers might be the onset of chronic ill health or disability, a change in employment, or the impact of divorce on family income. A more positive trigger might be receipt of an inheritance, which provides some financial security and the positive consequences that go with that. Research on triggers is referred to briefly in the final section of the chapter. But we start with some general illustrations of age differences in particular outcomes.

Inequality at different ages

If we compare groups of people at different ages, we can see how their outcomes in different areas vary. For example, the average pay of young adults is low; the chances of disability increase with age; among those above retirement age, those who are substantially older are more likely to be poor; proportions in employment are higher in mid-life, though the patterns are different for men and women; and so on. Examples of age-related variations are illustrated below. For example, figure 5.2 shows how the pay of both young men and women up to the age of twenty-four is substantially below that of older age groups.

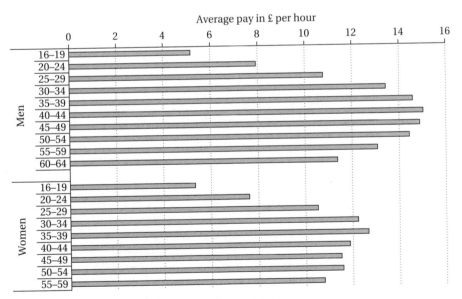

Source: Adapted from Longhi and Platt (2008), table 3.5.

Figure 5.2   Pay across age groups.

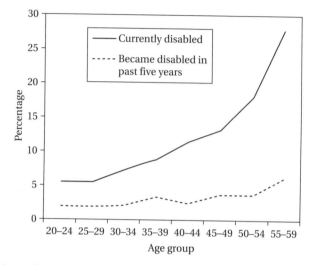

Source: Berthoud (2006), figure 3.1.

Figure 5.3   Prevalence and 'incidence' of disability, by age group.

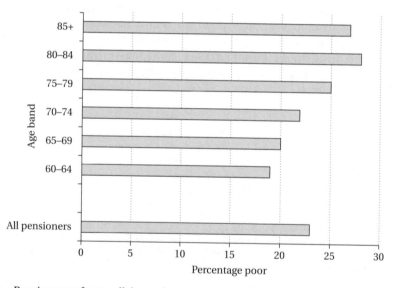

Note: Pensioners refers to all those above pension age (currently sixty for women and sixty-five for men).
Source: Adapted from DWP (2009), table 6.5.

Figure 5.4   Poverty risks of pensioners, by age band, 2007/8.

Figure 5.3 shows the sharp increase of disability that occurs after the age of fifty (Berthoud 2006). The lower line suggests that this increase stems not from a particularly strong increase in the risk of becoming disabled at any age, but because disability tends to be a permanent or long-term state so that more people become disabled over time.

Figure 5.4 shows how the poverty risks of today's youngest pensioners are fairly low – about the same as the risks for the population as a whole – but that they rise dramatically among older pensioners, particularly among those over eighty. However, those who were between sixty and sixty-five in 2008 were born into very different circumstances – the late 1940s – than those who are over eighty and were thus born in the late 1920s.

These age-related patterns are informative about individuals of different ages concurrently. It does not mean that their employment, income and health trajectories will follow those of their predecessors (Jenkins 2009b). The next section therefore examines the experience of those who are currently young, but where we can observe how their experiences are developing over time and the influence of social class background. This is then contrasted with the picture of inequalities among older people.

5.2 Inequalities in youth and age

Children are born into a wide range of family circumstances in terms of social class, ethnicity, income, family structure (whether lone or couple parent), and so on. The overarching perspective taken in intergenerational social mobility studies takes this starting point as given and then seeks associations with outcomes, when the children are themselves grown up, to ascertain the extent of immobility or lack of opportunity. But how soon do these differences in life chances emerge? And what are the processes by which they do or do not develop into lifetime inequalities? The literature from a range of countries, following the early trajectories of birth cohorts of children, suggests that social background matters for very early educational outcomes and that these initial differences tend to widen throughout childhood (Goodman et al. 2009). Differences start early but seem, in most cases, to be exacerbated through the first school years rather than being mediated by state school systems. Of course we do not know what would happen in the absence of state provision of education; and the important role of opportunities for academic development in the middle years of childhood have been emphasized (Feinstein 2003b).

Looking in detail at the contribution of family background to early years outcomes, it has been shown that a mother's education is strongly associated with the school readiness of her children and that income affects speed of development (Hills et al. 2010). Goodman et al. (2009) demonstrated that, though differences between social groups (specifically, groups defined by parental social class, income bracket and education, or living in a deprived area) tended to widen over childhood, there was some convergence in the final two years of compulsory schooling – a catch-up effect. The divergence throughout childhood was driven more by increasing attainment at the top (the most privileged end) of the distribution rather than by reductions at the bottom. While the focus of analysis of inequalities is often on the bottom of the distribution, it is worth noting how they can be influenced by processes at the top.

Interestingly, one case where early disparities reduced over time was among ethnic minority groups, where large initial gaps at age three in cognitive skills were found to reduce over the school years. Compared to these social class and income differences, the gender gap was much smaller and moved around more, with girls' initial academic advantage declining in the early school years and then recovering, but only taking off in the post-primary period.

Feinstein, looking at a cohort of babies born in 1970, found that social class differences in test scores reflecting cognitive ability were already clear at twenty-two months, and he noted that attainment at that age was associated with subsequent academic performance and participation in higher education (Feinstein 2003a). Moreover, his study showed how there was nevertheless movement in test scores up to the age of ten, with those who had low initial scores but came from advantaged backgrounds tending to move up and those with high initial scores but from disadvantaged backgrounds tending to move down. The result was that, while within classes initial higher achievers performed better than initial low achievers at age ten, those who came from advantaged backgrounds but performed poorly at twenty-two months had, by age ten, overtaken in terms of academic performance those who came from disadvantaged backgrounds but had performed highly at twenty-two months.

Background matters, then, for early years and childhood outcomes directly, which will have implications for the future. There is also a body of evidence which shows how disadvantage in childhood has long-term consequences in its own right in terms of poorer later life outcomes on a range of measures (Duncan et al. 1998; Ermisch et al. 2004, 2001).

It is clear that the circumstances into which children are born are highly unequal, and in ways that have consequences across the childhood years. Social background is not a one-off influence on life chances but can have an impact over time. Moreover, what happens in the school years is important and can make a difference for the future. Interestingly the partial 'catch-up' observed at the end of compulsory schooling by Goodman et al. (2009) reveals the extent to which the effects of social background are not all one way, and that there are possibilities of reversing them. A similar catch-up pattern in the GCSE outcomes of some minority ethnic groups has also been observed (Wilson et al. 2005). However, it is hard to identify the processes or mechanisms which lead to this reversal.

Turning to the other end of the life cycle, there are distinctive gender inequalities in age, some of which have been linked to life-course patterns and labour market and domestic inequalities. Older age, then, represents the net outcome of various life-course processes. These inequalities can be observed in health, income and wealth. And women have more years to live through than men, which can also influence their circumstances in later old age. In 2006–8, life expectancy at birth in the UK was 77.4 for men and 81.6 for women (ONS 2009) – that is, a baby girl born at that time could expect to live to nearly eighty-two and a baby boy to seventy-seven. Among those already sixty-five, men had a life expectancy of a further seventeen years and women another twenty years. There is a clear gap between men and women, though it has declined over the last few decades. On average, women have higher life expectancy than men across the world, though the gap tends to be higher in developed countries (where it averages around seven years) and narrower in less developed countries, averaging around two years in the least developed countries (United Nations Department of Economic and Social Affairs, Population Division 2007).

This brings us to the paradox that, although they have longer life expectancy, women have greater sickness or morbidity and are more likely to suffer from disabling conditions. Arber and Ginn (1995) explain this as resulting in part from the fact that conditions that disable women are less likely to lead to death, so that the more serious disabling conditions that men experience reduce their life expectancy relatively, but also mean that they are not living with a disabling condition. If years of *active* life are measured against total years of life, then women's advantage over men is substantially reduced. Older women are more likely to be disabled than older men. Although the 'active life expectancy' of women is still longer than that of men, the expected period of terminal disability and dependency is about twice that for men.

Active life is, moreover, not only a health and social care issue, it can also affect available income. Living becomes more expensive if quality of life is to be maintained as capacity diminishes – for example, getting in help, making adaptations to the home, being more reliant on cars and taxis, and so on, are all extra costs of disability (Burchardt and Zaidi 2005).

Men and women's experience in old age crucially depends on their lifetime experience – the amount they have contributed or that has been required that they contribute to pensions, and the amount of assets and savings that they have managed to build up. Both employment and the way in which pensions relate to employment are therefore critical in terms of maintaining living standards in old age. How well and how long those resources last also depends on how long there will be a call on them, with older pensioners tending to be poorer than younger ones, as we saw in figure 5.4. The result, given the gendered nature of employment, pensions and participation, is greater poverty for women in old age. Rates of pensioner poverty are 19 per cent for couples, 21 per cent for single men and 30 per cent for single women (DWP 2009). Box 5.2 summarizes some of the key factors relating to gendered inequalities in later life.

Ginn and Arber (1996) have shown how pension income varies according to women's lifetime experience and how pensions policy contributes to the inequality in entitlement between men and women after working age. They relate women's lower entitlement to wider gender disadvantage in the labour market and the gendering of pensions. The factors associated with a low pension income for women include reduced years of employment, discontinuous employment, lower contributions, low earnings, and any cuts in earnings that result from a career break. Though career breaks and part-time work were most heavily implicated in differences in income, even women who had worked full-time were living on lower pensions than men. But the tendency of the more valuable occupational pension schemes to require particular years of service and, in the past, to exclude part-time workers has militated particularly heavily against women's accrual of substantial pension entitlement.

Bardasi and Jenkins (2002) have looked at the role of work histories in determining income in retirement in the UK, following individual women and men over time and using their lifetime histories to understand their outcomes. They found that women's substantially lower income could be related to various disadvantages in the marketplace. Both family and employment had an impact on how well women fared in later life.

The lower average earnings of women also impact their potential to accrue assets or savings and thus buffer themselves against the decline in income they face in older age. Warren et al. (2001) showed that the assets of pension-age women averaged only around 90 per cent of the assets held by men. Despite relatively low individual pension entitlement, women may be financially protected if they are and continue to be married during retirement; but women who have been married and become divorced are likely to be worst off of all, with few individual resources to fall back on and greater likelihood of interrupted work histories.

Box 5.2   Factors influencing the economic vulnerability of older people and the gendered differences in old-age poverty

Work histories – interrupted or continuous (particularly linked to time taken to care for young children)

Earnings

Part-time work

Marriage

Assets and savings

Inheritance

Emphasis on the importance of lifetime experience also draws attention to the significance of class: women are worse off to the extent that they have lower earning power and/or employment which is more likely to lead to disability in old age. This is a class issue, and in fact gender differences, though they remain if we compare men and women of a similar class, are dwarfed by differences between classes, with very disparate abilities to earn, save, build up a comfortable home, and so on (Evandrou 2000). Issues of health and morbidity are, like life expectancy itself, affected by the lifetime experience of men and women and their class and economic background: poorer women and men tend to have higher mortality, but they also have higher morbidity and greater loss of capacity, particularly if they have previously been engaged in manual work. They are thus more likely to be exposed to the extra costs associated with disability and loss of capacity mentioned above. At the same time, disabled people are themselves less likely to be signed up to a pension scheme and to be accumulating assets for later life, so that chronic illness can also contribute to as well as stem from poorer socio-economic position.

The experience of older people earlier in their lives in terms of earning power, marital status and child-bearing is thus crucial in the extent to which they are in poverty in old age. The influence of these factors is shaped by the way societies construct and enable particular forms of working – and family – lives and also how, and the extent to which, specific systems such as national insurance and pension systems contribute to the redistribution of income across the life cycle. Old age is the focal point where all the aspects of a woman's life and experience come together.

A final issue which affects today's pensioners, and older women in particular, is that of societal attitudes and ageism, and the negative connotations that surround old age are in part reinforced by discussions such as those rehearsed here about loss of capacity and morbidity. But it has been shown (Arber and Ginn 1995) that attitudes are particularly discriminatory and antagonistic to older *women*.

The next section briefly explores inequalities in economic well-being across the middle of the life course, drawing largely on Jenkins (2009b).

5.3 Inequalities in mid-life

Jenkins's (2009b) study investigates how incomes vary for men and women across their own life courses and for different population groups, namely those defined by birth cohort and by level of qualification. His paper stresses the extent to which life courses measured in real time differ from inferences about economic well-being drawn from looking across those of different ages at a single point in time. He also shows the extent of variation in individuals' incomes (the spaghetti of the title) compared with the neat pattern that might be gathered from simply looking at the average. These issues of measuring over time or at a single point in time, and the heterogeneity within groups that is often disguised in simple cross-group comparisons, are recurrent themes for this book.

Figure 5.5 shows how individual earnings trajectories as people age differ from earnings averaged at each age. The contemporary point in time story to the right is one, for men, of a rise over the mid-life period and then a decline with the approach of retirement and, for women, a slower rise, a flatter mid-point and an earlier decline as caring responsibilities impact on earning capacity. But, when looking at the earning trajectories of younger and older men and women, the gentle humpback appears to apply only to the older cohort of men. What is noticeable is the way that the trend for women is generally upwards, though with some fluctuations and clear differences by both cohort and education level. By contrast, the experience of unqualified men from the younger cohort looks close to that of the older cohort of unqualified men. This is because, in the cross-sectional snapshot, the age effects capture women who have different average qualifications levels and do not take account of the way in which qualifications levels and earnings are changing over time for different cohorts. Thus, while the cross-sectional picture is true of all women at different ages at this one time point – on average – it does not tell us how any woman can expect her earnings to change over time, or about the changes she has experienced. These patterns show something of the diversity in lifetime earnings trajectories, which do not follow simple patterns. But they are simplifications of much more varied and complicated actual earnings patterns. Moreover, if income is used instead of earnings (so covering all individuals, not just those in work) the pattern is substantially different again.

The heterogeneity and fluctuation in incomes was also clearly demonstrated in another study using the same data. Rigg and Sefton (2006) developed a sixfold typology to summarize the different patterns of earning experience across a ten-year period. They characterized the types as 'flat, flat with blips, rising, falling, fluctuating and other'. The nature of the terms indicates that only three (flat, rising and falling) could easily be represented in stylized form as a summary of individuals' experiences. Part of the reason for this is that, while a measure at a point in time summarizes people's experience up to that point, including all the positive and negative things that have affected their earnings levels, following their individual life courses incorporates relevant events as they occur. Thus, for women, for example, relatively stable household income trajectories when they are part of a married couple with children may be disrupted by divorce and the consequent high risks of becoming poor in the immediate term, even if some recovery of income is achieved later (Jenkins 2009a).

Other events that can change the direction or cause a blip in income include events such as the birth of a child or a child leaving home, the onset of disability (Burchardt 2000a, 2003; Jenkins and Rigg 2004), or unemployment, redundancy or retirement (Bardasi et al. 2002). Such events can also move people into poverty (Jenkins and

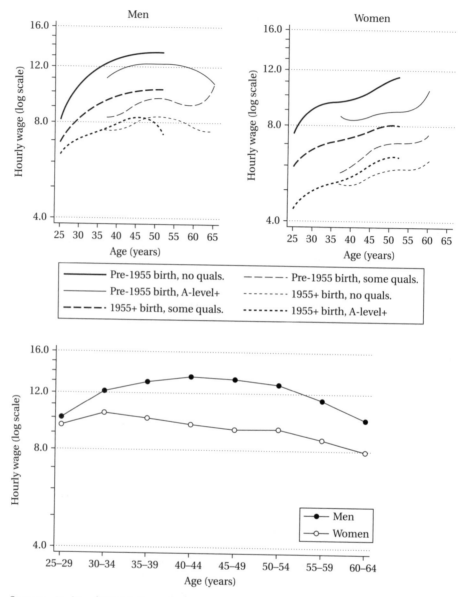

Source: Jenkins (2009b), figure 8.

Figure 5.5 Men's and women's earning trajectories.

Rigg 2001). Thus relative positions and inequalities or advantage and disadvantage in those positions are not fixed; and while there may be systematic differences when aggregating and comparing the experience of groups, an individual life-course trajectory may take a very different and far more varied route than that predicted by its average chances.

Questions for reflection

1 What does a life-course perspective offer that inspecting age-related inequalities cannot?
2 How do people's extended transitions contribute to inequality?
3 If people's work and family trajectories are discontinuous, does it make sense to generalize at all about lifetime inequalities?
4 What are the different factors contributing to heightened inequalities in old age?

Further reading

Mayer (2009) provides a valuable overview of life-course research and developments in the field, while Irwin's (2005) engaging and stimulating account of social life explores changing transitions and life stages. Arber et al.'s (2007) special issue of *Current Sociology* presents international perspectives on the intersection of gender and ageing, while they themselves provide an introduction to the sociology of gender and age. At the other end of the life course, Henderson et al. (2007) reveal youth inequalities through their biographical approach.

6 Education

> Seeing ma dad work from that level, from the bottom, from changing tyres every day to working to become a manager that really . . . does motivate me. Because seeing that he could do that in his position, not having no qualifications, not knowing how to speak English properly, that does really, really motivate me . . . and ma dad always from when I was young, always fed it into me . . . get a good education, achieve at school and go to university.

> There's like more job opportunities for women, parents . . . are . . . encouraging women more . . . there's been an increase in the amount of encouragement a lot of women get . . . I think the boys are more naughty if you know what I mean and I think if they aren't successful in something like their GCSEs then they'll give up more . . . there's a lot of stuff that's going on like violence and stuff and they're getting really influenced by that and they're getting involved in that.

These two quotations both come from a study of social capital and educational aspirations among young Pakistani men and women (Thapar-Bjorkert and Sanghera 2010). The first, from an interview with a young man, describes, as the authors point out, how migrant background can disrupt classed patterns of educational aspirations. Rather than having their outlook constrained by their class position, minority group children aim to fulfil the aspirations that were unavailable to or denied their parents – a trope of the migration literature more generally. This respondent represents his father as intragenerationally upwardly mobile partly through substantial effort, but nevertheless stressing the importance of education and the much more extensive opportunities it brings. Differentiated outcomes and the complex intersections of ethnicity, gender and educational outcome are central themes in the discussion of educational inequalities that follows.

These themes are picked up also in the second quotation, which are the words of a young Pakistani woman. While her position reflects changes of attitude within the Pakistani community, it also resonates with wider shifts in gendered patterns of both educational participation and achievement, with girls now outstripping boys at all levels of qualification. Moreover, her response highlights some of the factors that have been implicated in boys' underachievement more generally, as well as in gendered patterns of achievement within ethnic groups. She rehearses in her own terms dominant discourses regarding boys and education: the 'problem with boys', and with minority group boys in particular. The quotation thus speaks to and for some of the main preoccupations of sociological studies of, and policy concerns relating to, educational inequalities.

6.1 Qualifications and inequality

When thinking about educational inequalities, a major focus is on differences in qualifications. While that is not the only factor that can cause education to be experienced as unequal across groups, it is a particularly salient one. Experiences of bullying and victimization, of teaching styles, of extra-curricular opportunities, can shape engagement with educational institutions and educational outcomes, as well as being important for the qualitative experience of life during the school years. But these are not explicit concerns in this chapter, where the focus is on attainment, and attainment in relation to recognized standards endorsed by a contemporary qualifications framework. This is because qualifications are so heavily implicated in future life chances, and they are an area in which inequalities become evident and are played out. Moreover, as this chapter will show, differences in educational attainment reveal intriguing patterns at the intersection of gender, ethnicity and class, which raise questions for the understanding of processes of educational achievement across individual social groups.

At the same time it is important to recognize that the organization of education is pertinent to the achievement, measurement and meaning of success. What we understand as education – increasingly, as Stephen Ball (2006) has pointed out, constructed in terms of 'outputs', supplied under a regime of 'new managerialism' – is not transparent or self-evident. Qualifications are not innocent markers that distinguish neatly between different levels of capacity or knowledge, but are designed and delivered to differentiate pupils and students in the context of specific policy regimes. Their significance and value is a negotiated process. and they are gained or allocated at the intersection of various systems – school, family, state. Nevertheless, qualifications do provide a simple proxy for variation in educational resources. Moreover, they are significant for other aspects of life and its inequalities, and variation in their impact also illuminates particular group inequalities. Attainment of qualifications, to the – partial – extent that they are independent of family background, provides some possibilities for addressing persistent inequalities associated with certain groups, and thus for changing expectations as well as individual life chances. This is recognized in the strong emphasis among many migrant families on qualifications, as in the opening quotation, even if they are mediated by other social structures. Moreover, qualifications and who gains them provide a thermometer of what is valued and how that value is enabled to be distributed across different social groups. While it is never possible to map them against the counterfactual of what a distribution of 'talent' would look like in the absence of systematic group inequalities, differences in achieved qualifications *between* social groups provide prima facie evidence of systematic inequalities in educational opportunities.

As well as bearing in mind conceptual caveats, there are issues of how we measure differences in qualifications across the population or social groups within it. A distinction needs to be made between the 'stock' of qualifications – what the patterns are across the population as a whole and how they are associated with labour market outcomes – and the qualifications currently being achieved in school and in post-compulsory education. For example, across the population as a whole among those of working age, only 19 per cent had a degree, but among those aged twenty-five to twenty-nine the proportion was nearly 30 per cent. Though current qualifications and trends in their attainment will ultimately affect the profile of qualifications across the population as a whole, the substantial changes that have taken place in educational achievement and the relative rates of success between groups mean that, currently, an examination of the 'stock' reveals quite a different picture to the examination of contemporary school leavers. The stock represents past relationships between social groups and educational achievement, and in the stock of the population women are less well qualified than men. However, nowadays women are more likely than men to achieve post-compulsory qualifications and less likely to have no qualifications, gradually reversing the earlier scenario.

Here we concentrate on educational qualifications for those currently going through school and in post-compulsory education, as these are most relevant to understanding educational inequalities and their operation. But it is important to note that the association between education, employment and social mobility is based on the educational patterns pertaining across the stock, or for the cohorts considered. As rates of qualification both increase and change in their distribution across social groups, their association with other outcomes may also shift. Given the differences in educational systems across the UK, the focus is predominantly on the attainment of qualifications in England.

Educational trends

There are currently around 10 million pupils in schools in the UK, made up of approximately equal proportions of boys and girls. This partly reflects simply the number of young people of compulsory school age (five to sixteen) in the population, but is also a manifestation of the increasing tendency to stay on at school beyond the compulsory age. In England this increased at various points across the last century, to fourteen in 1918, fifteen in 1947 and sixteen in 1972. At that point, it was possible to leave before sitting exams for those who had turned sixteen in the first half of the school year. Since 1997 it has not been possible to leave until after the examination period for the school year in which an individual reaches sixteen, thus attempting to ensure that more pupils sit standard end of school exams (GCSEs). Plans to raise the school leaving age to eighteen to cover two years of post-compulsory education or work-based training have been mooted. This is partly because the majority of young people (around three-quarters) already remain in education and training during these years, but also because those who do not have very limited employment opportunities, which may leave them vulnerable to unemployment in the future.

The trend, therefore, has been for young people to remain in school longer, to complete exams, and to stay on in post-compulsory schooling longer, either to have a second go at school leaving exams or to gain further qualifications. There has also been an increasing trend to go into and complete higher education, discussed in the final section of this chapter. The result over the long term is that the proportion of those who end up with a baseline level of certificated education has risen dramatically: around 14 per cent of 1961/2 school leavers achieved the then equivalent of five GCSEs grades A* to C (level 2), compared with 58 per cent among 2005/6 leavers. Thinking about it another way, three-fifths of those born between 1910 and 1919 gained no qualifications; this proportion fell to just over a third of those born in the 1940s, 13 per cent of those born in the 1960s and only 8 per cent of those born in the 1970s (some of this last group may have gained qualifications since).

There has been a rapid growth in the achievement of level 2 qualifications just in recent years, rising from 49 per cent to 58 per cent over the period 1999–2006. There has also been marked development in post-compulsory education: the proportions achieving two or more A-level qualifications increased from 22 per cent in 1993 to 36 per cent in 2006 (DES 2006b). If we include vocational routes to level 3 qualifications, the proportions rise from 30 per cent to 46 per cent over the period. But the story of substantial increase is the same. These are trends across the cohorts of pupils. Debates have raged in the press and among politicians about the extent to which exams have become easier, and questions are also raised about the value of qualifications over time as increasing proportions of the population obtain more and achieve higher levels. But from the perspective of inequalities across social groups, what is important is whether this increase in qualifications has been consistent across social groups or, indeed, has closed the gap between them. In the next sections we therefore look at qualifications across gender, class and ethnic group, and in combination, to investigate what they can tell us about educational inequalities.

6.2 Education and gender

Girls do better than boys in terms of educational achievement. It is now clear and reasonably well known that girls do better than boys at school, are more likely to go on to tertiary education, and are more likely to get first- or upper second-class degrees. Fewer girls leave school with no qualifications (Hills et al. 2010). Table 6.1 shows the trend in achieving level 2 qualifications among boys and girls reaching the end of compulsory schooling. As we can see, there has been an upward trend for both girls and boys, with an increase in attainment of nine percentage points among girls and ten percentage points among boys. Boys have thus narrowed the gap very slightly, but it is clear that over this period girls have been strongly and consistently outperforming boys at this level. But it was not always this way. Figure 6.1 illustrates the trend in attainment among boys and girls over time.

As we can see from figure 6.1, up to the late 1960s, girls in England were underachieving relative to boys in terms of school leaving exams; though not illustrated, their relative underachievement at higher levels (A levels and in higher education) was much greater and continued for much longer. However, there was a slow equalizing of attainment, and more recently girls started to exceed and then quickly to outstrip boys in the realization of qualifications. This was first evident in GCSE exams from 1988, but subsequently demonstrated in A-levels in 2000 and then in higher, university education. By 2001 a greater *number* of women than men were achieving first-class degrees, as they entered higher education in larger numbers. At most recent figures, the *proportion* of women (12 per cent) has almost equalled the proportion of men achieving first-class degrees (13 per cent), and the proportion of women is markedly higher than the proportion of men gaining either first- or upper second-class degrees (See Higher Education Statistical Agency, www.hesa.ac.uk/).

As DiPrete has pointed out, the reversal of girls' and boys' educational success makes the gender gap in education a fascinating topic for sociological study. And it occurs across a large number of countries. With Claudia Buchmann, DiPrete has

Table 6.1 Achievement of level 2 (five+ GCSEs grades A*–C) among year 11 boys and girls, England

	1999	2001	2003	2006
Boys	44	46	50	54
Girls	54	56	59	63

Source: Adapted from DCSF (2008), table 4.1.1.

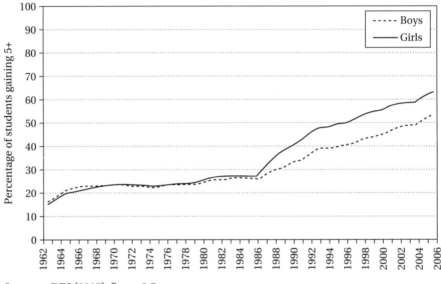

Source: DES (2007), figure 3.7.

Figure 6.1 Percentage of school leavers achieving five+ A–C (or pass) O-levels or A*–C GCSEs, by gender, 1962–2006.

undertaken a number of studies exploring different dimensions of this phenomenon in the US, looking at the role of high-school completion, access to college, completion and success at college, and the role of family background and returns to education for men and women (Buchmann and DiPrete 2006, 2008). However, despite the extensive work on this question, there appear to be no simple answers as to the reason for the change in educational success between boys and girls.

Since girls used to lag behind boys in terms of educational achievement, some effort was dedicated to attempting to explain why. However, now that the tables have been turned, does that render such analysis redundant, or is it still pertinent for understanding the educational experience of boys and girls? As a result of growing recognition in the period up to the 1980s of lower achievement among girls, there was a major feminist focus on trying to understand this and to challenge its apparently complacent acceptance as representing girls' more limited capacity. Part of the problem was that, though it was sensed that girls were not doing so well, there was not a vast amount of information available to demonstrate differential achievement:

figures were neither so readily collected and produced nor as accessible as they are now. It required specific effort to understand what the patterns of achievement were.

Moreover, the figures that implied girls' underachievement were potentially misleading and complicated by differential rates of exam entry. In the 1960s and 1970s, boys were entered for, and therefore took, more O-levels than girls. In the 1960s, of those entered for any O-level, on average 55 per cent were boys and only 45 per cent were girls. By contrast, since the 1980s, entries have become more evenly split between boys and girls. This difference means that boys in the 1960s were slightly more likely to get five or more O-levels, partly because they were also significantly more likely to *take* O-levels in the first place. Adjusting for the fact that fewer girls were entered for the exams would indicate that they were not *performing* as badly as suggested by the unadjusted rates. However, the assumption at that time was that only those who were entered for the exams (which, until 1973, were taken a year after the end of compulsory schooling) had the potential to pass them. Given the degree of uncertainty associated with predicting success, and the ways in which expectations can easily disadvantage those from less privileged backgrounds, this assumption is unlikely to represent an accurate picture of potential success rates. Differential entry rates for exams were also a major factor in class differences in education, with working-class pupils being less likely to be entered for exams. The opportunity to take exams affects average attainment levels for groups in the population. This remained an issue up to 1997, when pupils of school leaving age could no longer leave before the period for sitting GCSEs (Del Bono and Galindo-Rueda 2006).

Moreover, even if girls were not performing so well at the end of compulsory schooling, they appeared to be outperforming boys at younger ages, such that the scores for the 11 plus exam, which controlled entry into selective schooling in the form of grammar schools, tended during the 1960s to be adjusted to be comparable between boys and girls. Girls were scoring higher on average and, without adjustment, would have much greater entitlement to places in grammar schools than boys. Nevertheless, despite this evidence of equal or better 'capacity' at age eleven, the figures showed that, through a mixture of constraints, choices and performance, girls did fail to achieve the same level of qualifications as boys up until the 1980s and fell much further behind in relation to success in post-compulsory and higher education.

There were therefore a series of feminist studies which aimed to draw attention to this issue and attempt to understand the differences in performance rather than accepting them as natural or inevitable. Such a view of the inevitability of gender differences in educational performance was still widespread in the 1950s and 1960s. This was despite the strong challenges to assumptions of women's intellectual inferiority and a movement emphasizing the importance of girls' education that went back at least to Mary Wollstonecraft's *A Vindication of the Rights of Woman* in the late eighteenth century (Wollstonecraft [1792] 1992). Concerted efforts at challenging assumptions of their lower capacity through analysis of what happened in schools, homes and the education system were important for the recognition of girls' ability and the ways in which it was held back.

A significant early impetus to the consideration of girls' attainment was a series of studies by Reginald Dale from the late 1960s that examined the differential achievement of girls in single-sex and in co-educational schools (Dale 1969, 1971, 1974). These studies demonstrated that, in particular contexts, girls *could* achieve, and that it was not simply that single-sex schools were selective and choosing the more academically able children. If girls could do well, then that suggested there was nothing 'natural' about their lower performance, as was frequently maintained. The spotlight that feminists then focused on girls' educational experience acknowledged that it was neither acceptable nor sufficient to assume that they would do less well or to expect that schools were spontaneously meeting the educational needs of both boys and girls. They attempted to investigate the gendering that took place in the classroom (in addition to that which could be assumed to be occurring in the home). One line of study looked at classroom interaction and the role of teachers. Stanworth studied the different responses of teachers to girls and boys. She revealed how boys both demanded and received more attention, that they were expected to succeed more, and that they were therefore rewarded to a certain extent in line with expectations (Stanworth 1983). Spender also noted the disappearance of girls in classroom interactions in her work *Invisible Women* (1982).

Subject steering was also researched – that is, where girls were guided via the 'hidden curriculum' into subjects that not only were regarded as more suitable to their 'nature' in a biological perspective but also fitted their future roles as wives and mothers. These subjects, such as home economics, were ones that did not necessarily make women especially employable, particularly in 'better' jobs, and commanded less prestige. There remain clear differences in the choice of subjects between boys and girls, particularly at post-compulsory level. But whether this is as a result of teacher (or parental) expectations, genuine preferences or an understanding of the gendered nature of the employment context, which may make some options less appealing, is hard to disentangle. Gendered preferences for the future and for specific occupational and family trajectories begin early, but sociological research unravelling the mechanisms by which they develop has not as yet come to any clear conclusions (Marini and Greenberger 1978; Polavieja and Platt 2010).

The National Curriculum has evened out subject choices to a large extent at GCSE, though there is still some variation in choice across optional subjects. At A-level, however, with the greater options for choice, there is much greater differentiation by subject, and choices really do appear gendered, with big differences in the numbers taking physics, maths, computer science, design and technology (more boys) and in those taking biological sciences, art and design, social studies, English and English literature, communication studies and languages (more girls). Girls do better in all subjects (whether they are in the majority or minority), except, it seems, modern languages (where they are the majority), and the idea that girls who take minority subjects are sidelined does not seem to be supported. At the same time, the evidence does not comprehensively support the suggestion that those who take boys' subjects are particularly well placed to succeed (by motivation, interest or ability), since the corollary of that should be less marked success when they take so-called girls' subjects.

Another part of the investigation of girls' underachievement in schools suggested that what were defined as boys' subjects, and the way they were or are taught, actually represented gendered processes. For example, the conception and promotion of science as 'hard' science fitted with both ideas of masculinity and the challenges (it being hard as in difficult) that were seen as appropriate to boys' study and achievement. By contrast, subjects designated for girls were coded as soft. A similar process was noted with the gendering of occupations in which women are concentrated, whereby jobs take on new meanings as their composition changes, and specifically become less valued as the proportion of women increases (Lewis 1984). The argument about subject choices was therefore reversed in this scrutiny, to suggest that the valuation of particular subjects was related to who took them rather than that girls failed to take highly valued (and demanding) subjects. This was then reinforced, it was suggested, by the style of teaching associated with different subjects, which mapped on to models of masculinity and femininity and masculine and feminine learning.

Other issues impeding girls' success related to the lack of high-flying role models, and the fact that within schools women were concentrated in the lower echelons of the teaching profession, while men were more likely to be found in senior positions and as heads. There was, moreover, evidence that girls' own aspirations did not predominantly require them to be successful in education. Sharpe carried out a study of schoolgirls in the 1970s and found that they tended to view their future in terms of being a wife and mother, with work being regarded as an interim or supplementary activity (Sharpe 1976). The interplay of preferences and structural constraints in determining particular choices can be observed here. At what point preferences develop and how they relate to perceived possibilities, as well as the triggers to generational shifts, remain core questions for analysis of gendered outcomes.

There have been arguments that forms of assessment affect success rates. In particular, it has been argued that, at GCSE, the advent of more continuous assessment and coursework favoured girls, who are regarded – or stereotyped – as more hardworking, assiduous and consistent in their approach to schoolwork. While it does seem to be true that girls do better in coursework – and we saw in figure 6.1 how the attainment of girls did seem to break away from that of boys following the introduction of GCSEs in 1988 – nevertheless, to succeed at GCSE, girls also have to be good at exams. The discussion of gendered differences in capacity for different types of exercise is also close to a discourse that sees girls' talent as being more limited, to do with hard work rather than the talent, imagination and spontaneous flair associated with boys' learning. This is a discourse that has continued to impact on patterns of success in higher education. Interestingly, despite the construction of 'merit' as talent *plus* effort that is the basis of arguments about the structure of a meritocracy, there is a perceived tendency to regard easy or 'natural' achievement as of higher value than that which involves hard work.

So there seemed a good array of reasons to explain the underachievement of girls relative to boys without naturalizing it. But what are then the implications of the switch in relative performance? Does that mean that these gendered structures and assumptions have reversed? Has everything changed for girls? Some would argue that in fact very little has changed in terms of gendered practices in education, and that girls' achievement comes despite the persistence of practices that used to favour boys. For example, Smith has maintained that 'Research on gender and schooling shows a persistent replication of gender relations that develop over time as exclusive gender groupings marked by the privileging of male voices and male activity in the classroom, playground, sportsfield and hallway' (2000, p. 1149). There does not seem to be substantial evidence that classroom practices *have* changed. Instead, similar arguments to those that were used to explain female failure are now used to explain male failure. For example, the dominance of male voices in the classroom is now interpreted as part of what is seen as a problem of boys' underachievement, though, as we saw above, it is not that boys are failing to improve their performance, just that they are not catching up with girls. Boys' attention-seeking in classrooms has become viewed as 'playing up', which both antagonizes the teacher and can lead, at the extreme, to exclusion. Boys, then, are regarded as disrupting their own and others' (particularly other boys') learning.

This is sometimes linked to a wider discussion about the crisis of masculinity which sees boys as lacking clear trajectories (particularly in relation to employment), understanding of where they belong and confidence in themselves and their futures – and so behaving badly. It is argued that today's boys have difficulty knowing how they can be both men and new men. As working-class jobs become more scarce, those for whom school was a place in which they learnt 'to labour', in Paul Willis's famous phrase, now have to learn how to become educated.

Moreover, expectations have changed. Since teachers know that girls do better than boys, they may have higher expectations of them (on average), with reinforcing effects. This may not come in the form of greater classroom attention but rather in such actions as setting girls tasks and assuming that they will carry them out, thereby developing self-direction. And in this regard, the introduction of project work and some form of continuous assessment in addition to exams has proved beneficial to girls, as it requires that they demonstrate their aptitude in study time rather than through display within the classroom. A change in the emphasis on which skills should be tested may also have complemented coursework in mode of assessment (Machin and McNally 2006). It is not plausible, however, that this should account for the whole or even the main part of the gap: exams still have to be sat and a shift in the valuation of skills at GCSE does not account for why boys should experience relative underattainment at all levels.

In addition, the aspirations of students have changed. When Sue Sharpe repeated her study of schoolgirls' attitudes to the future in the 1990s, she found that they were now aspiring to be successful women and have careers. Motherhood remained a goal but often at a later stage, following a career. This links to arguments about socialization and role models – girls can now see successful women 'out there' and are also much more likely themselves to have been brought up by professional women. With the increase in information on and discussion of women in the labour market, they can perceive girls' success and see more future possibilities (Polavieja 2009). Linked to the 'crisis of masculinity' thesis, it has been argued that boys now need male teachers as role models to help show them the value of education and opportunities, and this is argued to be of particular importance given the growth in lone-parent families. But there is no good evidence for different school characteristics or concentration on single-sex teaching in influencing the gender gap (Arnot et al. 1998).

A persistent difficulty with employing arguments around changes in aspirations and expectations is the question of what initiated the change. Now that girls are known to achieve highly in education, this can become a clear aspiration for them and an expectation from their teachers (and parents). But since this was a *change*, there must have been some point at which it started. The increase in women's labour market participation can have been part of the story, though what actually drove that particular shift is also not clear cut. Girls can have been influenced by their mothers having gained more qualifications, but that would involve a generational delay.

As men still experience substantial labour market advantage and political and

Table 6.2   Percentage of children obtaining five+ GCSEs grades A*–C, by social class of parents, England

NS-SEC of parents	1999	2001	2003	2006	Has achieved level 3 by age 18
Higher professional	75	77	76	81	69
Lower professional	62	64	65	73	62
Intermediate	49	51	53	59	47
Lower supervisory	34	34	41	46	33
Routine	26	31	33	42	28
Other/not classified	24	26	34	34	26

Source: Adapted from DCSF (2008), table 4.1.1, and DCSF (2009), table A.

social dominance, are over-represented in positions of power and authority, and get better returns to their qualifications than women, it is not clear why boys' aspirations should be so dented. On one level, perhaps, they see that they need to do less educationally to stay still, and thus we see an upward trend but at a lower level. However, such inferences are largely speculative.

Some discussion has focused on the class aspects of achievement and located the understanding of educational differentials between boys and girls in the lack of jobs for working-class men and the lack of congruence between educational ideals and aspirations with backgrounds and modes of behaviour of working-class boys. There are certainly differences in attainment by social class, as I go on to show; but inferring the extent to which class can help us to understand gendered patterns in educational qualifications is complex.

Gender and class

Overall, there are clear class differences in education achievement (see table 6.2). While there has been an upward trend since 1999 for all classes in rates of attainment at the standard level 2, and while the increase has been greatest for those with parents in routine occupations, huge class disparities remain. Children whose parents are classified as in the higher of the professional/managerial groups have nearly twice the chance of achieving at this level as those from routine social class backgrounds. Moreover, among those who do achieve at this level, a smaller proportion from lower social class origins apply for higher education (65 per cent) compared with those from higher social class backgrounds (78 per cent). Class thus continues to act on educational experience, even at higher levels. Table 6.2 also shows the net effect of differences in GCSE achievement and in completing post-compulsory education up to the age of eighteen on the chances of achieving level 3 (equivalent to two A-levels) by social class, with a gap of over 40 percentage points between those with parents in the higher professional classes and those whose parents are in routine occupations.

Receipt of free school meals (FSM) is a commonly used measure of disadvantaged background, since it can be assessed directly at the pupil level. This again shows a similar picture of the strong relationship between background and attainment. Employing a continuous measure of educational attainment, boys receiving FSM

Table 6.3   Boys and girls achieving five+ GCSEs grades A*–C, by receipt of free school meals, England, 2006/7

	Not FSM	FSM
Boys	45	31
Girls	68	40

Source: DCSF (2007).

were disproportionately represented at the bottom end of qualifications: half were in the bottom quarter of the distribution, twice as many as you would expect if qualifications were equally distributed (Hills et al. 2010). Moreover, advantage can also find expression in qualifications through the use of the independent sector. In England, the vast majority of children are in maintained schools when they are taking their GCSEs (93 per cent), but those in the independent sector perform, on average, better.

These differences in educational attainment as a consequence of parental occupation or class background are startling. They have been explained in terms of lack of practical support for education in less advantaged homes, such as the availability of books (DES 2006a), resources for extra tuition, extra-curricular activities that appear to support learning (DCSF 2009), and even factors such as available or dedicated space for carrying out homework. The ability of parents to contribute direct support is clearly important, and their own educational level and competence will influence this, as well as the networks of support to which they have access. A mother's level of education can be a particularly important factor in her children's educational and occupational success. The language of the classroom, and the fact that it is more accessible to those raised in middle-class homes than to those from working-class homes, was the subject of Bernstein's influential analysis of the spoken 'codes' used in teaching (Bernstein 1971). This, he argued, could go some way towards explaining differences in performance in language-related subjects in particular. It is also clear, as described in chapter 5, that class influences on education start early.

Class clearly does have a very significant role to play in educational outcomes, and it affects both girls and boys. However, what it cannot do well is to help explain gender inequalities. As we can see from table 6.3, girls on free school meals perform substantially better than working-class boys. But the arguments relating to class differences in education might well suggest that, if class dominates outcomes, then there should be no difference between disadvantaged boys and girls, or even that girls should be performing worse.

We might think that working-class girls should do at least as badly as working-class boys because occupational opportunities are constrained for both. Moreover, if there are limited resources for investment in education, it is not clear why parents would prioritize girls. In fact, we might expect the opposite to be the case, given the traditional patterns of investment in girls' education and women's expected earnings. Studies have shown that access to homework space may be particularly constrained for working-class girls. Additionally, since languages are an area in which girls are more likely to concentrate and do well – indeed, it is differences in language and literacy skills that drive the gender qualifications gap – working-class girls may suffer particularly from lack of access to Bernstein's 'elaborated codes'. Moreover, Willis

(1977) showed how part of working-class boys' school identity was strong derogation of girls, which might be expected to impact on girls' performance.

Class also does not explain the particularly strong performance of girls from professional backgrounds. If working-class boys have a lot to lose from changes in the class structure, then middle-class boys have a lot to gain. To maintain their class position, some emphasis on educational achievement might be expected (Breen and Goldthorpe 1997), even if educational success is clearly not the only component of their heightened opportunities. By contrast, the future class position of women is influenced by their partner to a much greater extent than it is for men. Understanding differences in educational qualifications by gender, then, remains something of a puzzle. While much attention has been paid to boys' underachievement relative to girls and how to correct it (Weiner et al. 1997), attempts to explain the factors underlying it still beg as many questions as they answer (Machin and McNally 2006). Just assuming that there is no scope for boys to achieve further does not seem plausible – it is clear that gains have been made, and that they can continue to be made. However, since strategies to improve boys' performance are also likely to be positive for girls, they may not reduce the gap between the sexes (DES 2007). Perhaps what is more important is to understand what it is that has enabled the improvement in boys' as well as girls' performance rather than focusing primarily on the gap between the two. This takes us back to the recurrent theme of this book, on absolute versus relative differences, as well as the changing nature of opportunities and distributions of rewards.

It may also be that class operates in different ways at different levels of social class origins. One issue that has been highlighted in the otherwise somewhat equivocal summary of 'what works' is addressing laddish behaviour (DES 2007). This may take different forms but still be pertinent for those from different class backgrounds. It could be that it is induced by complacency among boys from professional backgrounds, since they have a range of resources for maintaining their class advantage (Savage and Egerton 1997), while the disjuncture with their opportunities and experience may be felt most clearly by boys from working-class backgrounds and find expression – among some – in rejection of normative behaviours. While girls have adjusted to the new occupational structure, including expectations of their own employment, this can prove harder for boys holding a particular notion of the nature of masculine work and its rewards.

If class does not make a particularly effective framework for explaining gender differences, it has been used more comprehensively in discussions of ethnic group differences in educational outcomes. On the other hand, the intersection between class, gender and ethnicity complicates yet further our understanding of how educational inequalities come about and are maintained. It is to these areas that I turn next.

6.3 Education, ethnicity and intersections

We start by examining how qualifications are distributed across the population according to ethnic group. First we look at the overall stock, then we break down according to 'generation', since those born and brought up in the UK represent a better comparison with each other. Those brought up in different education systems will have different qualifications, and, perhaps more importantly, migrants

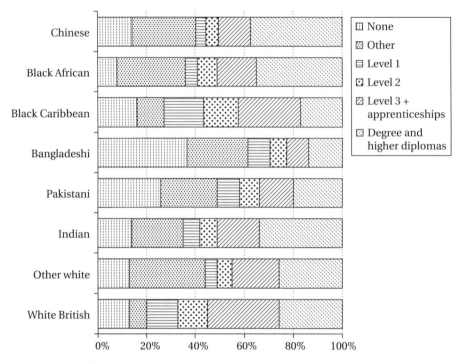

Source: Pooled Labour Force Survey 2002–5, author's analysis.

Figure 6.2   Stock of qualifications by ethnic group: men.

can be expected to have particular characteristics (which may include higher or lower educational levels) that caused them to choose to migrate in the first place. The breakdown by generation is carried out in two ways, first by describing the contemporary profile of those who are and those who are not UK born. An alternative comparison is provided by drawing on Heath and Yu's (2005) distinction between an earlier generation (the migrant first generation among minorities) and those from the 1990s who represented the second generation.

Starting with the total stock of qualifications, figure 6.2 shows the distributions for men and figure 6.3 for women. We can see that there are distinctive patterns across ethnic groups. There are greater proportions of those with higher qualifications and relatively low proportions with no qualifications among black African and Chinese men, while Pakistanis and Bangladeshis show more or less the reverse pattern. White British and other white men lie somewhere in between, while Indian and black Caribbean men demonstrate some similarities with this group, but with slightly larger proportions of Indians holding higher qualifications and slightly lower proportions of black Caribbean men holding higher qualifications. We see that there are distinctively high proportions of minorities with 'other' qualifications, which will tend to refer to overseas qualifications that are not easily coded within the UK framework. These stock figures combine UK and non-UK born and raised and also fail to distinguish the different demographic profiles of various groups: as qualifications are generally improving, we might expect 'younger' groups to have better educational profiles. Turning to

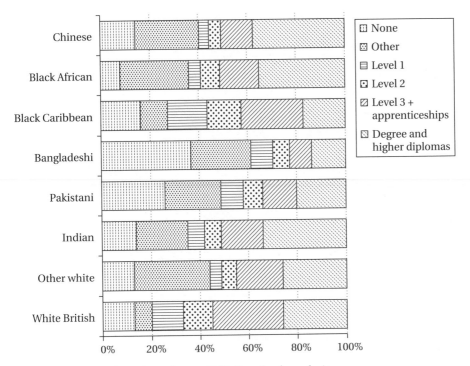

Source: Pooled Labour Force Survey 2002–5, author's analysis.

Figure 6.3 Stock of qualifications by ethnic group: women.

women, it is interesting to note the extent to which the patterns parallel those of men across the groups. It appears that gender differences are, perhaps, less significant than ethnic differences in education. This is an issue we return to later in this section.

Given that figures 6.2 and 6.3 group those of different migration generations (UK born and non-UK born) together, it is worth distinguishing across groups according to whether they obtained their education predominantly in the UK or in another country, as that could be argued to be more informative about educational inequalities within the UK. Moreover, whether it is right or not, it is clear that qualifications obtained abroad are less salient in the labour market than those obtained in Britain (Bell 1997; Blackaby et al. 2002; Cheng and Heath 1993; Shields and Wheatley Price 1998), and therefore it has been argued that it is only when comparing those with qualifications gained in the UK that we can understand the extent to which minorities are penalized in relation to their qualifications.

Figures 6.4 (men) and 6.5 (women) break down qualifications by ethnic group and according to whether or not they were born in the UK. Unsurprisingly, we can see that 'other' qualifications are much more dominant in the first than in the second generation. Moreover, among the latter there has been a strong shift away from holding no qualifications (particularly among Pakistani and Bangladeshi men) and towards higher qualifications. The patterns seem to equalize a bit across groups, but there are still some substantial differences, particularly in the proportions with degrees, which are highest for Indian and lowest for black Caribbean men.

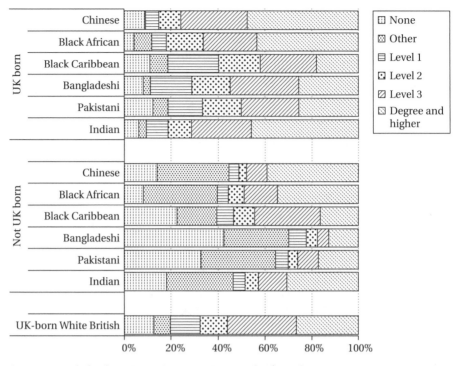

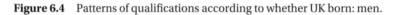

Source: Pooled Labour Force Survey 2002–5, author's analysis.

Figure 6.4 Patterns of qualifications according to whether UK born: men.

Turning to women, we can see a similar story of a strong reduction in those with no qualifications (particularly among the three South Asian groups) and in those with 'other' qualifications, particularly among Chinese, black African and Indian women. Figure 6.5 reveals much greater levels of higher qualifications among those born in the UK, the differences being dramatic for Pakistani and Bangladeshi women. We can also see that rates of higher qualifications among the UK-born white majority are comparable to or somewhat lower than those from the minority groups. And, once again, there are striking similarities in the patterns for men and women from the same ethnic group.

What these figures do not take into account, though, is the shift in educational qualifications that has occurred over time, so that younger generations are more likely to be qualified than older generations. Since ethnic groups vary in their age profile, this change over time will affect the comparison between groups. To address this particular problem, Heath and Yu (2005) use an alternative approach which constructs generations at separate time points when they are more of a comparable age: thus the first generation is measured in the 1970s and the second generation in the 1990s. Their distributions are summarized in figures 6.6 and 6.7. This does not tell us about the contemporary stock of qualifications in the working-age population, as many of those who were entering the labour market in or before the 1970s will now have retired. It does, though, give us a clear illustration of the qualifications shift over

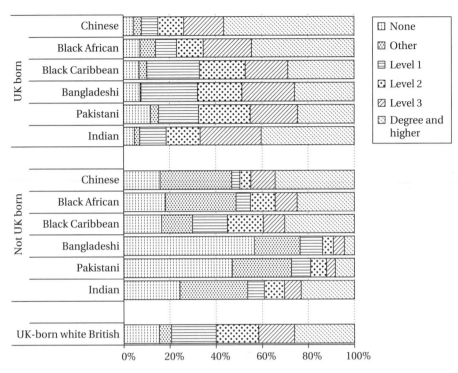

Source: Pooled Labour Force Survey 2002–5, author's analysis.

Figure 6.5 Patterns of qualifications according to whether UK born: women.

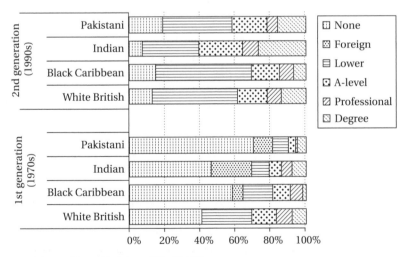

Source: Adapted from Heath and Yu (2005).

Figure 6.6 Educational qualifications across ethnic groups and by generation: men.

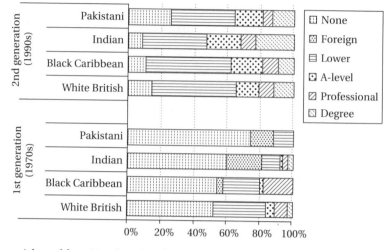

Source: Adapted from Heath and Yu (2005).

Figure 6.7   Educational qualifications across ethnic groups and by generation: women.

generations. There is a major move away from no qualifications between the earlier generation and the later generation and for all groups. Compared with the contemporary distributions we saw in figures 6.4 and 6.5, we can also see how this shift in the attainment of higher qualifications is continuing. There nevertheless remain distinctive distributions of qualifications across these four groups, and some continuities in their relative positions across generations: for example, Caribbean men increased their proportion of higher qualifications but remained the group with the lowest proportion of the four, while Indian men showed quite a dramatic increase in higher qualifications and an equally dramatic decline in those with no qualifications.

Figure 6.7 shows an even more dramatic transformation in qualifications between the generations among women. Again, Indian women appear to have made the most substantial gains, but the increase in higher qualifications among Pakistani women is also very striking. At this point we can see that, though women appear to have made greater gains across the generations than men, in this cohort at least, Pakistani women have not yet overtaken Pakistani men. Once again there are similarities in the experience within groups between men and women, both in terms of the changes made between generations and in the pattern of qualifications of the 1990s generation.

These differences between groups and the substantial shifts between generations can be understood in part in terms of patterns of migration and migration histories and by typically high investment among migrants in education of the next generation. This has received substantial sociological attention, particularly in the US literature but also in European studies (Card 2005; Lauglo 2000; Zhou and Xiong 2005). Accounts attempting to explain the situation of what are commonly regarded as the more successful of the UK's minority ethnic groups (Indian or East African Asian and Chinese) have often stressed a particular group-specific attachment to education (Modood 2004; Francis and Archer 2005). However, commitment to education is also well attested among groups that achieve less success. The higher rates

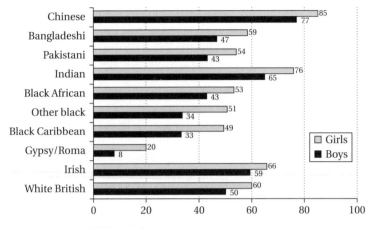

Source: Adapted from DES (2006a).

Figure 6.8 Percentage of children achieving level 2 qualification, by ethnic group and sex, England, 2005.

of staying on in school among minority groups, including 'less successful' minority groups such as Caribbeans and Pakistanis, suggest that minority group members are well aware of the importance of education as a necessary (if not sufficient) route to success, and that they are highly motivated (DES 2004; Heath and Yu 2005). Drew, Gray and Sporton (1997) pointed out that constraints, in terms of limited employment opportunities for young people of minority ethnicity, are also likely to be playing a role in extended periods in education, encouraging continued participation among those who would normally expect to leave and obtain work. Qualifications may not bring the same returns to all ethnic groups, as illustrated in the discussion in chapter 4, but there do not seem to be distinct differences in their valuation among minority groups. The question of orientation to education is pertinent when considering the outcomes among the current cohort of school leavers, which is what this section turns to next.

Figure 6.8 shows the proportions of the cohort of children at the end of compulsory schooling who achieved level 2 qualifications in 2005. The pattern has remained relatively constant since. There is substantial variation across ethnic groups, with Chinese pupils performing best and Gypsy and Roma children achieving at a very low level, far behind that of any other group. The situation of the latter in terms not only of education but also in material deprivation and poverty is a source of some concern (Cemlyn and Clark 2005; Hills et al. 2010). However, there is far less information about this group, and for consistency with the rest of this book we will focus on disparities between the other groups. In all groups, girls are performing better than boys from the same groups. This is a relatively new switch for some groups, such as Gypsy and Bangladeshi children, among whom in previous years girls still underachieved relative to boys. Girls from most groups are also performing better than majority group boys. After Chinese pupils, high proportions of Indian children achieve level 2, with Bangladeshi boys and girls and white boys and girls in a similar position somewhat below this, and black African and Pakistani girls somewhat further behind. What many have drawn attention to, however, is the singularly poor position of black Caribbean boys in terms of average levels of attainment. Indeed, within the discussion of boys' underachievement, the situation of black boys has taken a particular place.

The factors that are held up as having a potential explanatory role for boys' under-achievement in general are also used to explain the underachievement of black boys, though with a particular, often cultural focus. Thus arguments that attribute under-achievement in part to the lack of role models have led to a focus not only on how to recruit black male teachers into schools but also on home life and family structure, picking up on the greater proportion of lone-parent families among Caribbeans compared with the average. There have been discussions about particular models of masculinity that prevail within different groups – arguments that have been used to discuss Pakistani boys' orientation towards education. Black gang culture has been invoked as part of the context within which Caribbean boys' underachievement should be understood (McMahon and Roberts 2008). The tendency, then, has been to resort to assumed 'cultural' differences that operate within groups to understand differential patterns of achievement, even though the evidence to support these explanations is thin. The boys' underachievement agenda has also allowed the situ-ation of girls to go relatively unremarked, and thus the poor position of Caribbean girls on average, relative to other *girls*, has not been the focus of such debate, even though even when the average is not a cause for concern, it is hard to see how it could be accounted for within the same framework. Moreover, within groups there remain substantial proportions of 'poor performers', for whom 'underachievement' at the individual level warrants consideration.

Another issue that has been linked to underachievement among Caribbean boys is the relatively high levels of exclusions they experience. This has long been recognized as a cause for concern, since a series of investigations in the 1980s by the Commission for Racial Equality highlighted it as a systematic problem within the education system and one that disadvantaged Caribbean boys. Exclusions still remain rela-tively high for this group, though the differential has declined over the years. Even if exclusions on their own do not occur in sufficient numbers to account for gaps in attainment, they may be indicative of wider problems within schools that are impacting negatively on the overall performance of black boys. Interestingly, in their study of attainment and ethnicity over time using administrative data from schools across England, Wilson et al. (2005) found that it was only for the Caribbean group that the particular school seemed to matter. That is, for Caribbean pupils the school they attended could make a difference to levels of attainment, over and above other relevant factors such as previous attainment, receipt of free school meals, and the overall composition of the school. This may imply that styles of teaching and school cultures and stereotypes are pertinent for the success or failure of Caribbean girls and boys, where they do not impact on those from other groups. There is also evidence of teacher stereotyping of pupils with differential expectations across ethnic groups, which could impact on actual performance (Burgess and Greaves 2009).

Discussions about orientation towards education have led some researchers to suggest that processes of 'segmented' assimilation' can help us to understand differential achievement between groups (Portes et al. 2005; Zhou and Xiong 2005). That is, it matters who the reference category is to what counts as educa-tional success or appropriate level of attainment. This has been used to suggest

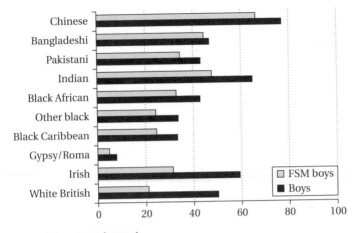

Source: Adapted from DES (2006a).

Figure 6.9   Percentage of boys achieving level 2 qualifications, by receipt of free school meals, England, 2005.

that the 'underachievement' of black Caribbeans may stem in part from having a working-class reference point and a measure of success based in non-professional employment both from previous generations and from current comparators (Heath and Yu 2005; Peach 2005; Platt and Thompson 2007). However, empirical investigation testing motivation finds that there is little support for the theory of 'adaptation' to lower expectations (Thomas 1998). And, as Heath and Yu (2005) have pointed out, the evidence on differences in retention in education, discussed above, suggest high levels of motivation across minority ethnic groups. Perhaps most importantly, when we break down attainment by receipt of free school meals, we find that it is white boys who actually perform worst. The intersection between ethnicity and receipt of free school meals is therefore worth some further consideration.

Ethnicity, gender and class

Figure 6.9 shows attainment of level 2 within a recent cohort of schoolchildren broken down by receipt of free school meals (FSM) and ethnic group. For simplicity it gives the results just for boys. As we saw before, FSM receipt also impacts on girls and lowers their results relative to those not on FSM; but, given the focus on boys' underachievement, it is particularly instructive to concentrate here just on the results for boys. It is clear that being on FSM makes a difference across all groups, from those performing best to those performing worst. But the gap is much greater for some groups than others. It is low for Pakistanis and Bangladeshis, where rates of FSM are high, and it is higher for Indians, and especially, for white British and Irish boys. The result is that, while white boys not on FSM perform better than all other groups not on FSM except Irish, Chinese and Indian boys, white British boys on FSM perform worse than all other groups, with the exception only of the outlier group of Gypsy/Roma. This can be seen even more clearly in figure 6.10, which gives the attainment for just a few groups divided between FSM and all boys.

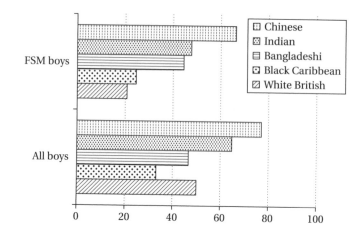

Source: Adapted from DES (2006a).

Figure 6.10   Percentage of boys of selected ethnic groups achieving level 2 qualifications, by FSM receipt, England, 2005.

We can see from figure 6.10 that rankings within those on FSM are different to the rankings for all boys. In particular, white British boys perform worse than all other disadvantaged boys and, though Caribbean boys on FSM also show low levels of level 2 attainment, they are not that much lower than those for all Caribbean boys. The class story for Caribbean boys is therefore not self-evident, while it is very strong for white British boys. Looking for the sources of 'underachievement' in similar processes across groups may not therefore be highly fruitful. Instead we are faced with a picture of complexity at the point where gender, ethnicity and class intersect.

Gillborn and Mirza (2000), reviewing the research on educational inequalities across England and Wales, identified the complexity of achievement patterns. Thus, every one of the ethnic minority groups considered (white, black Caribbean, black African, black other, Indian, Pakistani and Bangladeshi) was the best performing in at least one of the 118 local education authorities considered. But the general picture for those passing through the system currently is one of divergent outcomes between the most and the least successful. This is particularly clear from work by Simon Burgess and others (Burgess et al. 2009), which has charted individual trajectories through school. This makes it possible to see how attainment at one point builds on or diverges from attainment at other points. Their illustrations make it clear that, for white British girls and boys, attainment is relatively flat over time. By contrast, many minorities appear to improve their attainment over the school period. A particular 'lift' is evident for many groups on average in the final two years of schooling. This enables those that started off somewhat behind, such as Pakistani and Bangladeshi pupils, to catch up, while Indian and Chinese pupils move further ahead. However, Caribbeans as a whole experience a much flatter pattern of attainment and do not experience such an evident lift.

Among those on free school meals, white British pupils appear to experience a decline in relative attainment across the school years; Caribbean pupils experience

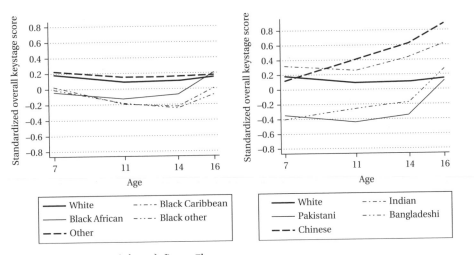

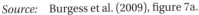

Source: Burgess et al. (2009), figure 7b.

Figure 6.11   Standardized test scores for a panel of non-FSM girls passing through school.

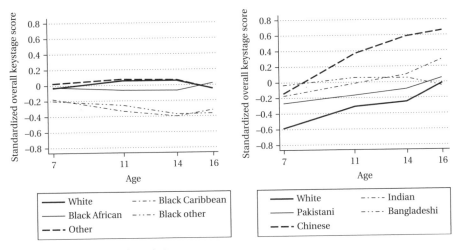

Source: Burgess et al. (2009), figure 7a.

Figure 6.12   Standardized test scores for a panel of non-FSM boys passing through school.

a decline, though some small recovery towards the end; and others show a pattern of improvement from lower starting positions. Unlike white British boys, white British girls on FSM show some degree of improvement towards the end of compulsory schooling, but their overall relative position remains low. These patterns are also consistent with research by Plewis (2009), who looked at the outcomes for younger age groups. Figures 6.11 to 6.14 show these cohort educational patterns for non-FSM girls, non-FSM boys, FSM girls and FSM boys, respectively, for selected ethnic

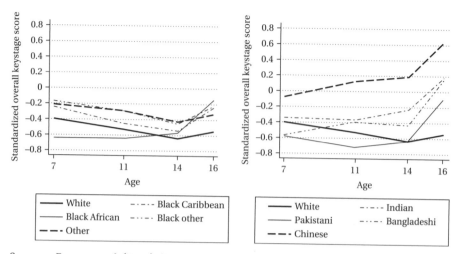

Source: Burgess et al. (2009), figure 6b.

Figure 6.13   Standardized test scores for a panel of FSM girls passing through school.

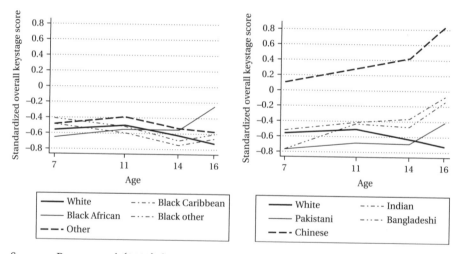

Source: Burgess et al. (2009), figure 6a.

Figure 6.14   Standardized test scores for a panel of FSM boys passing through school.

groups, and reveal something of the different pathways through school of the different groups when all three dimensions are taken into account.

Attainment at GCSE level is important for subsequent outcomes, including remaining in education and obtaining higher qualifications with greater returns in the labour market. Patterns of university attendance vary substantially according to attainment at this point. We therefore turn to look at inequalities in higher education.

6.4 Higher education and inequality

Higher education is clearly related to past attainment. This is perhaps unsurprising given that there are entry requirements to undertake higher education. But attendance is not just to do with academic success. Among recent cohorts, the majority of those who were most successful at GCSE were likely to continue their studies. For those with middle levels of qualifications, those from minority ethnic groups were more likely to move into higher education, while those who were on FSM, even if they had done well – and that against the odds – were less likely to go to university (Hills et al. 2010).

There are also differences in the particular institution selected. Shiner and Modood (2002) have shown that there are distinct variations by ethnic group in the type of university attended, with minorities more likely to go to a new university, with potential subsequent consequences for their occupational success relative to other graduates. Those from working-class backgrounds remain under-represented at 'elite' institutions, and there are differences in institute attended by sex and whether students have or have not been privately educated (Machin et al. 2009). Machin et al. also noted variations in degree class according to social background, sex and ethnicity. When comparing otherwise similar candidates in terms of prior success, subject, and so on, they found that minority ethnic group candidates were relatively less likely to get first- or upper second-class degrees compared with white candidates. Once the institution was taken into account, those who had been privately educated were less likely to get a higher degree than those who had been through the state system, since those who were privately educated were more likely to attend a more prestigious Russell Group university. Men also performed relatively worse than women. Among women, those from an advantaged background were more likely to get a 'good degree'.

Machin et al. (2009) found that, comparing like with like, all minority ethnicities were less likely to be in employment six months after graduating than white graduates. There was some reduction in the gap over time, with Indian employment rates overtaking those of the white majority. But the other groups remained well behind in employment chances, and this was the case for both men and women. Moreover, despite the fact that those who were privately educated were less likely to get a good degree, other things being equal, six months after graduation these privately educated graduates could expect to be earning more than state-educated graduates.

These findings of differential success indicate that higher education, though it opens up job opportunities, continues to reflect stratifying influences. Even when those from less advantaged circumstances manage to navigate particular hurdles, there remain obstacles to success which are strongly embedded in social structures. Glass's analysis of the grammar system fifty years ago seems to hold some parallels in the contemporary analysis of the higher education sector.

When discussing the French educational system, Bourdieu (1977; Bourdieu and Passeron 1977) drew attention to the ways in which privilege is maintained through an apparently equalizing or fair system of qualifications that is nevertheless really accessible only to those who can use their advantaged position. By these means, qualifications – or particular qualifications which allow access to privileged employment positions, such as in the civil service – become not measures of ability but a form of credentialism. That is, they form a justification for the maintenance of a system of advantage embedded in relatively rigid class structures. The illusion that success is open to anyone if they can only achieve remains just that, an illusion. Achievement is in fact conditional on having the cultural capital of the privileged classes. As Bourdieu himself expressed it:

> Academic qualifications, like money, have conventional, fixed value, which, being guaranteed by law, is freed from local limitations (in contrast to scholastically uncertified cultural capital) and temporal fluctuations: the cultural capital which they in a sense guarantee once and for all does not constantly need to be proved. The objectification accomplished by academic degrees and diplomas and, in a more general way, by all forms of credentials is inseparable from the objectification which the law guarantees by defining *permanent positions* which are distinct from the biological individuals holding them, and may be occupied by agents who are biologically different but interchangeable in terms of the qualifications required. Once this state of affairs is established, relations of power and domination no longer exist directly between individuals; they are set up in pure objectivity between institutions, i.e. between socially guaranteed qualifications and socially defined positions . . . .
>
> The educational system helps to provide the dominant class with what Max Weber terms 'a theodicy of its own privilege', not so much through the ideologies it produces or inculcates . . . but rather through the practical justification of the established order which it achieves by using the overt connection between qualifications and jobs as a smokescreen for the connection – which it *records surreptitiously*, under cover of formal equality – between the qualifications people obtain and the cultural capital they have inherited – in other words through the legitimacy it confers on this form of heritage. (Bourdieu 1977, pp. 187–8)

A similar point was made by Bauman when describing the elision that takes place between the possession of credentials and the actual knowledge they are intended to signal. He also highlighted how qualifications act to restrict access to privileged positions to those who can demonstrate that they have the relevant attributes:

> we believe that people become members of the institutionalized 'knowledgeable' communities because they are learned scholars in their own right – while in practice we assume that X is a learned scholar when told that he is a member of the above-mentioned community. Moreover, we meticulously observe a complicated procedure of apprenticeship, whose real function consists in decisions by the institutionalized communities themselves on who does and who does not deserve to become one of their number. (Bauman 1973, p. 16)

While Bourdieu's account was particularly relevant to some specific features of the French qualifications system, it has been highly influential in descriptions of limitations of access to higher qualifications and, within higher education, to elite institutions in particular. Narratives that use a Bourdieuian perspective to describe and interpret systematic inequalities in achievement are prevalent. At the same time, Bourdieu's perspective has been critiqued as overly deterministic: that it implies that individuals are tied by their class location and that, in one way or another, through the fungibility of cultural, social and economic capital, advantage will necessarily reinforce itself (Bourdieu 1997). His account of the specific role of cultural capital in creating intergenerational advantage has been extensively tested and found wanting (Irwin 2009). Additionally, it has been argued that emphasizing the need for individuals to create a fit between the experience of a privileged setting and taking on the dominant cultural practices can ignore the ways in which, at the individual level, achievement by those from less privileged backgrounds can be experienced without either alienation from their background or feeling their success as partial and uncomfortable. For successful individuals from less advantaged backgrounds, education can truly be experienced as a route to realize their ambitions and reinforce a sense of self-worth without needing to adopt the cultural practices and expectations of more privileged counterparts. For example, Reay, Crozier and Clayton (2009) draw heavily on Bourdieu's work in their discussion of the experience of working-class students in an elite institution. However, while their students recognize the privilege and confidence in belonging that marks their fellow students from middle-class and, especially, privately educated backgrounds, they nevertheless endorse meritocratic principles. They manage the dislocation between their backgrounds and those of the majority of their fellow students not by acquiring or cultivating dominant social capital, but through academic success and hard work.

Even if the price of success does not have to be high in terms of dislocation from origins, the reality of the differential chances of academic success across social backgrounds remains startlingly true, even at the level of higher education, where, as we have seen, those who enter from less privileged backgrounds are highly selected: such individuals are less likely to achieve the minimum requirements for university in the first place and, having achieved them, are less likely to enter higher education.

The cumulative impacts of background in early years continue to operate even as those from less advantaged or more marginalized backgrounds have negotiated various hurdles and achieved academic success. The relevance of social group is felt not just in early childhood but throughout youth and into occupational choices and careers. It is clear there is no single point at which the breakthrough into an alternative upwardly mobile trajectory is made that puts individuals from different backgrounds on a par with each other, and this analysis of transitions into working life among those recent graduates is highly indicative of continuing social stratification. Nevertheless, the incremental gains in terms of educational success and the possibilities of different occupational futures dependent on them are themselves likely to be cumulative, even if the pace of change is slow.

Questions for reflection

1 What do qualifications measure?
2 Why do girls perform better than boys in terms of education?
3 Do qualifications matter for success?
4 Is education the route to a more equal society

Further reading

Halsey et al.'s (1997) edited volume brings together a large collection of key papers in the sociology of education. The report by Gillborn and Mirza (2000) continues to provide a useful reference point for intersections of educational inequality, while that by the Department for Education and Skills (DES 2007) offers a comprehensive overview of the underachievement debate and literature. For international comparisons, Shavit et al. (2007) provide an account of inequalities in higher education across fifteen countries.

7 Income, Wealth and Poverty

Among the rich developed countries . . . most of the important health and social problems of the rich world are more common in more unequal societies. . . . You can predict a country's performance on one outcome from a knowledge of others. If – for instance – a country does badly on health, you can predict with some confidence that it will also imprison a larger proportion of its population, have more teenage pregnancies, lower literacy scores, more obesity, worse mental health, and so on. Inequality seems to make countries socially dysfunctional across a wide range of outcomes.

(Wilkinson and Pickett 2009, pp.173–4)

Poverty strips your dignity. You can't have dignity with poverty. Where I come from you've people, like they go to the supermarket, they haven't got enough money to pay for what they need. And how does that person go home and say to the children that they haven't got enough money to feed them?

(Beresford et al. 1999, p. 90)

It means we don't have choices. We don't have the option to do what we want to do. We're very limited both in what you actually do and when you do it. If you don't have money you can't get anywhere, so I mean that can be down to a thing like it's difficult to choose where your children can go to school. You don't have options like people who have more money, or like getting out of the area.

(Ibid., p.106)

Wilkinson and Pickett (2009), in the quotation that starts this chapter, are putting forward the central argument of *The Spirit Level*, that economic inequality – large differences in income across societies – is bad for societies and damages everyone. It is not just that there are more 'poor' people who suffer from imprisonment, low literacy, and so on; these social ills are more common across populations where the gap between poorest and the middle and that between the middle and the richest are larger. Nevertheless, while it is the scale of inequality that is damaging at the societal level, it is inequality between better off and worse off, and particularly the difference between being poor or not being poor, that matters for individual outcomes. Economic inequalities are unevenly distributed across populations. Some groups are much more vulnerable to poverty or experience more of the consequences of an unequal distribution of income and wealth. This chapter outlines some of those differences in income and poverty.

The negative consequences of income inequality are partly illustrated in the second two quotations, taken from groups of low-income respondents who were asked about their experience of poverty (Beresford et al. 1999). They highlight not only the material aspects of poverty but also the stigma associated with it and the absence of choice, issues which recur throughout these chapters. Is it realistic to talk about equal opportunities in an unequal society, when people's ability to choose and exercise their agency, and their capability and motivation is so constrained by structural inequality? And one of the most fundamental constraints is lack of income.

Income – or poverty – cannot be considered a form of social grouping in any meaningful sense, despite the common assumption in the past that the poor constituted a specific 'class' of people. Nevertheless, lifetime income can be considered perhaps the most crucial determinant of life chances, and its distribution across social groups, or at their intersection, can be very informative about their overall chances and constraints and how they fit into the social structure. While income inequality, its growth and stabilization over time, and its relationship to the structure and fiscal policies of states has been subject to extensive research (Atkinson 1995, 2000; Cappellari and Jenkins 2007; Hills et al. 2010; Jenkins and Micklewright 2007), there has been little that links it explicitly to other inequalities, though Jenkins (1995), Gardiner ([1993] 1997) and Brewer et al. (2009) do evaluate the contribution of the composition of the population and thus income of different social groups to inequality trends over a number of decades. However, the interest in income inequality across social groups is largely to identify the extent to which particular groups tend to be clustered in one part or another of the income distribution and, more specifically, what the chances are of having wealth or of being poor. Different risks of poverty between groups remain a fundamental inequality and one that has consequences for shaping experience in other areas, including even in the constitution of the group itself.

Poverty and income inequality are conceptually distinct and, as Atkinson (1987) has pointed out, it is perfectly possible to be concerned about one without being concerned about the other. Concern with the situation of the most disadvantaged is not incompatible with a belief in a system of differential rewards and thus in the necessity of inequality. Nevertheless, analysis of the two tends in practice to go together, since poverty can be regarded as a form of income inequality deriving from dispersed incomes. A number of studies have therefore linked the discussion of inequality and poverty, moving from looking at differences across incomes, and specifically at the gap between the best off and the worst off, to exploring how those who are worst off form a group that enjoys sufficiently less than 'average' incomes or living standards that they can be considered poor (Atkinson 1995; Brewer et al. 2008; Gardiner [1993] 1997; Jenkins and Micklewright 2007). At the opposite end, the accumulation of wealth is also distinct from the distribution of incomes, though how incomes do or do not cumulate across the life course has an important role to play in later-life wealth. But wealth is much more unevenly distributed than income. Wealth is liable to become increasingly concentrated and has a powerful impact on life chances and other outcomes, including mortality risks. The implication is that to focus solely on poverty when considering income inequalities misses the extent to which disparities in wealth may make a profound difference over and above low income risks.

Investigation of the distribution of wealth and studies of wealth across social groups are, however, not nearly so well developed at the current time as studies of poverty (Dorling et al. 2007). Moreover, longstanding traditions of poverty research have tended to bring with them the implication of normative requirements about the need to address poverty where it is found, and have resulted in intense debates around concept and measurement. These debates have been central to the formulation and reformulation of poverty in sociological analysis, and it is thus worth paying some attention to them. This chapter therefore reflects the emphasis in the literature and pays greater attention to poverty than to wealth or income distribution.

Even so, while there are extensive studies of poverty in relation to some demographic groups, such as lone parents, children and, to a certain extent, disabled people, the relative poverty risks of other social groups have received much less attention, from either analysts or policy makers. For example, despite a few important studies on poverty among ethnic minorities (Berthoud 1997, 1998; Platt 2009a), which have revealed both the stark differences between and the diversity across groups, these come nowhere close to the attention that has been paid to labour market participation and job experiences and chances across minorities, while they are exceptions in the literature on poverty. The claim that Glenn Loury made in relation to the US, when attending a conference on poverty, that 'one encounters the disturbing evidence that racial differences in the experience of poverty are large, intractable and poorly understood' (Loury 2000, p.59), can also be said to apply to the UK. While Loury's claim might be surprising, scrutiny shows that transatlantic debates on 'underclass' or 'social exclusion' are not actually about poverty but predominantly about areas, geography or employment.

Part of the reason can be found in the tendency to focus on an individualized model for certain social groups, which fits ill with attention to poverty. This individualized model emphasizes agency – and responsibility – in relation to less advantageous outcomes, rather than concentrating on the structural position of groups or their economic well-being. Minorities are thus constructed and scrutinized as agents responsible for their own welfare. By contrast, poverty measurement and analysis emphasizes the responsibility of society and social structures and leaves questions of individual action largely to one side. Thus, it has been argued (Platt 2007c) that a cautious approach to analysing and addressing minority group poverty stems from a reluctance fully to acknowledge minority groups as having claims on the state on a par with majority groups. It is part of the way in which minorities continue to be excluded from the norms, practices and expectations of the wider society. The emphasis instead tends to be on minorities 'earning' rights through labour market participation.

I have argued that we can call the individualized approach the 'immigrant paradigm'. This focuses on individuals, locates their differences in experience in their different (individual) histories, and links them neither to social structures nor to family household context. This paradigm conflicts with the underlying assumptions of poverty analysis, which tend to bring a normative demand for attention and a distancing of the experience from individual responsibility. The normative role of poverty analysis in focusing on consequences rather than individual characteristics is particularly evident in discussions of child poverty. Child poverty has become a point of mobilization for those concerned with poverty and with wider inequalities on account of its ability to command interest and expectations of action (Walker 1999), as poverty campaigners have long recognized (Platt 2005c). It has been intensively researched for many decades and has been high on the UK policy agenda since 1999, as well as featuring increasingly on the agendas of other European countries and more widely (UNICEF 2000). The well-being of children is an apparently uncontroversial inequality that begs attention and amelioration.

I would argue that we should move towards an 'ethnicity ' paradigm which incorporates into the understanding of minorities the ways in which ethnic difference is socially constructed and the ways in which ethnicity is reproduced at a family and society level, which can also bring in relation aspects in outcomes and difference. Such a paradigm pays more attention to the experience of households and to the various ways in which state systems interact with individual positions and characteristics to exacerbate or mitigate poverty risks. Paying more attention to the poverty risks of marginalized groups, and particularly those rendered largely invisible in relation to their economic well-being, could help to move us from conceptions of inequality and its causes based in the individualized immigrant paradigm and towards a more integrated understanding of minority groups' well-being.

For this reason, the discussion of empirical findings relating to poverty will hone in on an area that is marked by the absence of research, specifically the poverty (and income inequalities) of ethnic minority women. Research on ethnicity and poverty is not extensive, particularly in comparison with that of other groups, and this is even more the case when we look specifically at the poverty of ethnic minority women. A notable exception is the study that I draw on in this chapter (Nandi and Platt 2010). Processes of simultaneous visibility and invisibility seem to be at work in relation to ethnic minority women (Crenshawe 1991; Mirza 2008) – that is, attention is drawn to them on certain dimensions and as the visible carriers of 'culture', but direct considerations of their economic welfare are written out of the construction. Their disadvantage is of interest in so far as it reflects on the group – or on the perceived problematic of minority integration – but not so far as it reflects the way social structures lead to inequality, where the impacts of gender and ethnicity are liable to compound one another.

By contrasting the lack of treatment of ethnic minority women's poverty with the extensive attention paid to child poverty, we can see how poverty is used to construct groups in policy terms. On the one hand, we see a group where issues of responsibility or identification are not considered relevant to the demands they make to have inequalities addressed. At the same time, to maintain that position they must remain relatively homogeneous and undifferentiated (Platt 2007a). On the other hand, we see a group that is excluded from policy attention, partly through a focus on distinctiveness and difference.

This discussion will follow a brief review of wealth inequalities and general consideration of poverty risks and income inequalities across subpopulations. I start, however, with a discussion of concepts and then briefly outline the measures used.

7.1 Concepts and measures

Income is relatively unproblematic conceptually even if its measurement raises some complications, as discussed in the next section. And while there is an extensive literature on the distribution of wealth and comparisons over time and over countries, there has been little attention to defining wealth in relation to a specific upper threshold in the way that poverty is deemed to represent a lower threshold below which people are poor. An exception is Atkinson (2006). Conceptual debates on the nature of wealth or what constitutes it are, therefore, not extensive, even if, again, there are specific issues of measurement that it raises. By contrast, there has been extensive debate for many centuries, and at least since Adam Smith ([1776] 1976), on how poverty should be conceived and recognized. I rehearse some of these conceptual debates here before addressing questions of measurement in which the conceptual issues are necessarily implicated. Two important debates have concerned the relationship between poverty and income: first, whether poverty does indeed stem and should be evaluated in terms of low income and, second, whether an absolute or relative conception of poverty should prevail.

While it would appear to be a truism that poverty stems from lack of or insufficient income – and there are a wide range of operationalizations of this concept, including the 'dollar a day' measure often used in the developing world – it is not uncontested. In previous eras, poverty was regarded as a state or condition of individuals, and that it was management rather than lack of income that was at issue. It was this understanding of poverty that Rowntree's early survey set out to refute (Rowntree 1902).

It has also been argued that, conceptually, it makes no sense to extrapolate poverty from an income measure, since that ignores the ways in which people may be constrained or prefer to spend their income; and that poverty is about actual experience, or living standards (Ringen 1987). Many people suggest that it is what people enjoy or consume or how they live that is relevant to their well-being, and that this may have only an oblique relationship to the income at their disposal at any point in time (Atkinson et al. 2002; Callan et al. 1993; Nolan and Whelan 1996). However, this raises the question of what level of experience is appropriate for a member of society and what standard of living falls below that and creates poverty. What should a minimum standard of living look like? If poverty is to be defined in terms of consumption or living standards, who should decide and how should we determine the elements of that living standard? In order to identify such a minimum standard there have been a number of attempts to use 'democratic' measures to ascertain those things that nobody in a given society or a 'civilized' society should be without. But these are only very loosely conceptually framed (Gordon et al. 2000; Gordon and Pantazis 1997; Mack and Lansley 1985). Moreover, they do not get round the problems that what constitutes a majority of views on necessity does not necessarily define a consensus on what constitutes poverty. These studies also do not satisfactorily get round the problem of who should determine the list from which people choose the essentials, nor what they might be prepared to do or contribute in terms of taxes to ensure that all the people in a given population could enjoy such a standard of living (Walker 1987; Veit-Wilson 1987; Piachaud 1987).

These more recent developments both were influenced by and share many of their difficulties with the earlier study carried out by Peter Townsend with the aim of improving the conception, measurement and understanding of poverty in the UK. Following work in the 1950s with Brian Abel-Smith on developing measures of poverty (Abel-Smith and Townsend 1965), Townsend embarked on a major project that he believed would give a true measure of the extent and contours of poverty in the United Kingdom (Townsend 1979). He explicitly set out his approach as relative and relating to typical – or, rather, 'ordinary' – ways of life and argued that poverty measurement needed to move away from an absolute subsistence-based approach:

> Poverty can be defined objectively and applied consistently only in terms of the concept of relative deprivation. . . . The term is understood objectively rather than subjectively. Individuals, families and groups in the population can be said to be in poverty when they lack the resources to obtain the types of diet, participate in the activities and have the living conditions and amenities which are customary or are,

at least widely encouraged or approved, in the societies to which they belong. Their resources are so seriously below those commanded by the average individual or family that they are, in effect, excluded from ordinary living patterns, customs and activities. (Townsend 1979, p. 31)

In fact, as has been noted, in opposing absolute measures in general and Rowntree's studies in particular, Townsend was setting up something of a straw man (Hennock 1991; Veit-Wilson 1986a, 1986b). Rowntree had himself acknowledged that poverty had a context and that expecting people just to consume the minimum to survive was not meaningful. He recognized that people would prioritize expenditure that gave them dignity (such as funeral insurance), even if it did nothing to increase their 'physical efficiency', and he also perceived the social context within which people lived, as well as the fact that, for some expenses, such as housing, options were relatively constrained and actual expenditure was the best guide to the minimum that could be afforded.

If Townsend's starting point from a critique of Rowntree was somewhat misplaced, in that the two men shared more than separated them, his own study was extensively critiqued by other poverty researchers for both his method and his findings (Piachaud 1981). Despite this, Townsend's work was conceptually important in establishing the idea that (in)ability to participate as a citizen should be key to the way poverty was conceived and measured.

However, the relative nature of his definition has created some confusion, given that all proposed poverty measures have related in some way to contemporary society rather than to a notional minimum. His insistence on the specific importance of a relative measure has also resulted in some rather circular arguments with Amartya Sen. Sen (1983), drawing on the tradition of Adam Smith, recognized that avoidance of poverty was temporally and culturally specific, but asserted that it was important to retain a concept of the absolute needs, or rather the capabilities, that underlay the specificities of its expression. He expanded this position in the following terms.

> Some capabilities, such as being well nourished, may have more or less similar demands on commodities (such as food and health services) irrespective of the average opulence of the community in which the person lives. Other capabilities . . . have commodity demands that vary a good deal with average opulence. To lead a life without shame, to be able to visit and entertain one's friends, to keep track of what is going on and what others are talking about, and so on, requires a more expensive bundle of goods and services in a society that is generally richer, and in which most people have, say, means of transport, affluent clothing, radios or television sets, etc. Thus, some of the same capabilities (relevant for a 'minimum' level of living) require more real income and opulence in the form of commodity possession in a richer society than in poorer ones. . . . There is thus no mystery in the necessity of having a 'relativist' view on the space of incomes even when poverty is defined in terms of the same *absolute* levels of basic capabilities. (Sen 1987, p. 18)

The dispute between Sen and Townsend was not resolved, however, despite distinct similarities in their practical position, and perhaps indicates that a conceptual distinction between absolute and relative poverty is not a fruitful one – indeed, it may even be spurious (Ringen 1987).

Townsend (1979) also stressed inability to participate in society as a key defining element of poverty, and this extends to social activity itself. The issue of participation raises the question of whether it is an indicator or an outcome of poverty. That is, does lack of social activity constitute poverty or is it a consequence of poverty? There is clearly a case that lack of participation in its own right is part of what makes someone poor or deprived, and this is acknowledged, for example, in the UK deprivation measures that are linked to the monitoring of child poverty. They include measures of social interaction at the level of both child and parents, as well as material measures (Brewer et al. 2008; DWP 2008). Opportunities for 'normal' social interaction and the enjoyment of communal activity, including such things as celebrations of significant religious events and being able to extend hospitality to children's friends, neighbours and family, are therefore seen as key to inclusion and well-being, and their absence constitutes a form of exclusion. Opportunities for participation also link concepts of poverty and the rather less coherent concept of social exclusion, and in defining social exclusion analysts have highlighted the centrality of social relations to inclusion (Burchardt 2000b; Hills et al. 2002; Levitas 2006).

Social participation is central to the possession or lack of social capital, which can also be regarded as a form of resource and – in Bourdieu's formulation – is fungible, being able to be transformed into economic or cultural capital. Though the instrumental role of social capital is emphasized in many discussions, where networks are regarded as the means to maintenance or improvement of social position (Coleman 1988; Franzen and Hangartner 2006; Putnam 1995, 2000), it is possible to conceive of social capital, and hence forms of social participation, as an end in itself and hence an aspect of welfare.

The key insights from both Sen's and Townsend's discussions are, then, that avoiding poverty is as much about what you do as what you have. Whether income is a sufficiently good measure of whether or not you can avoid shame, engage in social interaction, or keep your children safe remains unresolved. Income clearly has an important role in enabling a range of forms of activity as well as of ensuring material comfort and avoiding unhealthy or dangerous environments. There continues to be a strong strand of analysis which is resistant to conceiving of poverty in income terms (Ringen 1987; Callan et al. 1993; Nolan and Whelan 1996). However, if addressing poverty needs to find some compensation (Piachaud 1987), it seems likely that this is best conceived in money terms and that therefore finding some way to translate a minimum standard of living into money terms is likely to be a necessary first step. The value of that minimum income standard seems the critical question, then. Setting a specific value on poverty – or its avoidance – requires a formula or definition that both commands some degree of acceptance (or at least transparency) and is practical to implement.

Given that the perception of essentials (as measured by Mack and Lansley) and what is actually essential for participation (in Townsend's formulation) or the realization of absolute capabilities (in Sen's definition) changes with time, both the ongoing measurement of poverty and analysis of changes or trends becomes highly problematic. Yet it is both practical measurement and a measurement which provides a notion of whether things are getting better or worse in terms of amounts and nature of poverty that is of interest to policy makers and of concern to analysts. Therefore, in practice, measures which are relatively easy to obtain and that are repeatable are regularly used to assess poverty levels, however unsatisfactory they may be in some respects. Thresholds represented by proportions of average income seem to meet these requirements, and relate to changing living standards and the expectation that poverty is about being excluded from what is normal, expected or 'ordinary'. Such measures are discussed further in the next section.

However, the relevance of change over time also introduces the question of the extent to which poverty itself is a temporal phenomenon. Part of understanding the influence of poverty and wealth is to regard them in a temporal dimension. As Walker and Ashworth put it, 'without taking time into account it is impossible fully to appreciate the nature and experience of poverty or truly to understand the level of suffering involved' (1994, p. 1). The same could be said of wealth, though in this case it is the protective and beneficial nature of wealth accumulation that needs to be understood. While there has been little longitudinal analysis of wealth, there is substantial and growing literature on longitudinal poverty measurement, which has amplified the conceptual and measurement issues and revealed the impacts of poverty experienced in a temporal perspective. As chapter 5 describes, Rowntree conceptualized the life course in terms of periods of alternating poverty and subsistence (see figure 5.1). His insights are as important today, when the claims about the numbers in poverty, based on a measure at a single point in time, underestimate those who will ever be poor, while possibly overestimating the number for whom it is a critical issue: a low income today but not tomorrow may not introduce great hardship, but several years on a low income will bear heavily on a person's ability to manage. Increasingly, therefore, as techniques and data have allowed, investigation has turned towards looking at how poverty is experienced over time in terms of both duration and movements in and out of poverty. Smith and Middleton (2007), in their review of this literature, noted the importance of making distinctions between transient, recurrent and persistent poverty, with persistent poverty being most seriously implicated in negative consequences both for the individuals and the families concerned and for future generations.

While many of the illustrations in this chapter will reflect only incomes and poverty at single points in time, it is important to complement such versions of income inequality with a longitudinal perspective as far as is possible, to develop a more complete understanding of income inequalities and poverty variation across groups.

Measurement of income, wealth and poverty

Income refers to the flows of resources that are available for spending or saving. A standard assumption is that all members of a household benefit from the combined income from all sources from all members. It is also possible to look at the incomes that accrue just to individuals, which represent the income over which they potentially have control – or control to distribute – though this is less likely to be a good measure of household income. If all individuals in a household benefit from total household income, the extent to which they benefit will still be dependent on the number of people. Net income is therefore adjusted for the numbers of adults and children it has to support and takes account of economies of scale within the household. Once every member of the household has been allocated the same adjusted (equivalent) income, they can all be ranked in terms of their income.

It then becomes possible to estimate the degree of inequality across the whole distribution of that income – or to look at various points in the distribution, such as the midpoint – and show who falls above or below it. The distribution can be compared over time to calculate trends in overall income inequality, and the proportions of various population groups falling below different points on the distribution can also be measured. A common measure used to calculate the distribution of income across the population as a whole is the gini coefficient, which gives a single value that summarizes how close incomes are to total equality. If everyone had the same income, the gini would have a value of 0; if, on the other hand, one person had all the income, the gini would have a value of 1 (Goodman et al. 1997). The annual *Households Below Average Income* publications (HBAI) measure the points between which various fifths of the income distribution lie, so that 20 per cent of the population is in the bottom fifth, 20 per cent in the second fifth, and so on. This allows us to see the extent of the gap over the distribution as a whole, and also to look at whether different subpopulations are over- or under-represented at the top or bottom, since in a situation of equality *between* groups all subpopulations would have 20 per cent in each of the fifths. For example, if children make up 20 per cent of the population but 30 per cent have their incomes in the bottom fifth of incomes, then we can see that they are over-represented at the bottom – they are more likely to be poor.

As noted, measuring equivalent income in this way to imply the income (and economic well-being deriving from that income) of individuals is strongly dependent on the assumption that there is equal sharing of income within the household. However, this is unlikely to be fully the case. There has been substantial attention drawn to issues of gender and sharing within the household (Phipps and Burton 1998). As Glendinning and Millar have pointed out, 'treating the family as a single unit clearly does not reflect the reality of the way resources are actually distributed within families' (Glendinning and Millar 1992, p. 9). Poverty measures applied to families, it is argued, tend where cohabitation occurs to overestimate the incomes of women and correspondingly to underestimate the incomes of men. Sharing within the household is likely to be related to control of income, so that those who actually receive the pay, benefit income or pension are likely to get more use of it than other members of the household. On the other hand, even when women have control of income, there is some evidence that they may prioritize the needs of members of the family other than themselves (Dooley et al. 2005). This was the justification for paying family benefits (such as child benefit and its precursors) to the mother specifically. The overall level of income within a household is, nevertheless, clearly important. Gregg, Harkness and Machin (1999) found that expenditure on children mirrored income, with lower expenditure on children in poor households; and Gregg, Waldfogel and Washbrook (2005) showed that, as low-income family incomes increased, spending on children also increased.

Appropriate assumptions about within-household sharing remain a perennial problem for analysis of incomes and inferences about economic well-being. An alternative is to use individual incomes, disregarding what is happening in the rest of the household. If the assumptions about shared income do not fully reflect the power relationships and distributions within households, it is also the case that assumptions about individual income will be a distortion, since households engage in sharing of resources even if not exactly equally, and children, who typically have no income, are not neglected on that account. Examining individual incomes can nevertheless be illuminating in illustrating inequalities between men and women, as the Women and Equality Unit (2005) demonstrated.

Assessing income over time requires repeat measures of the same individuals to ascertain how much their individual incomes are changing. This is a different issue from exploring how the pattern of incomes is changing – for example, becoming more polarized and unequal overall. It is not necessarily the case that increases in inequality affect the same people. The bottom 10 per cent, for example, may be falling further and further behind middle incomes, but it may be different people over time who are in that bottom 10 per cent. An increasing number of studies have made use of data which survey people repeatedly to analyse the 'dynamics' of income. Such studies have shown how much movement there is in incomes, but also how much of it is short-range (Jenkins 2011). Nevertheless, certain groups, such as children or lone parents, are more likely to be persistently poor.

Wealth

Wealth refers to resources held at a particular point that may be able to provide income – for example, through interest on savings – but wealth is not the same as income. Wealth clearly provides security to draw on should income be insufficient to maintain a standard of living or should emergencies arise. It can be broken down to resources held in the form of property, such as owner-occupied homes; resources held in the form of financial investments or savings; resources held in the form of moveable physical property, such as furniture, cars or collectables; or resources held in the form of private pension assets. Together these four types can be designated as total wealth (Daffin 2009).

Wealth is much more unevenly distributed than income. Many people will have little or none of the four different types of wealth, and a few will have huge amounts. In some cases, where, for example, they owe more than their assets are worth, people have negative wealth.

Poverty

Poverty is here measured in terms of income, since, as discussed, this provides the most logical, transparent and practical measure, particularly for comparisons across subpopulations. Income poverty is typically measured through ascertaining a particular threshold relative to the average. Once individuals have been allocated the adjusted income of their household, they are lined up, and cut-off is taken at 60 per cent of the median – or mid-point. Though this is arbitrary, it does link to 'normal expectations' to the extent that the average – or mid-point – of income summarizes normal experience and expectations in a particular society. Thus those who are poor are substantially below this mid-point.

This measure is widely used throughout Europe and is the basis of the UK's particular monitoring of income and poverty as published annually in the *Households Below Average Income* (HBAI) series. As long as income data are collected on a representative sample of the population, it is possible to produce an annual account of the extent of poverty on this measure and its variation across subgroups of the population. Recent figures from HBAI are given below in the discussion of poverty risks across subpopulations.

Poverty is particularly meaningful conceptually when it is considered over a longer period than at a single point in time. It has larger impacts on living standards and converges more closely with alternative deprivation measures (Gordon 2006) when considered as a experience that endures (or recurs) rather than as one which is purely transient (Smith and Middleton 2007). There is now extensive research drawing on a variety of longitudinal sources to explore the ways in which individuals remain, escape from, or fall into poverty over time. Measuring poverty persistence in income terms requires having good measures of income repeated on the same individuals. Low-income statistics are reported in the annual British Household Panel Survey, where 'persistent poverty' is defined as being below 60 per cent of the median for three years out of four (with an alternative measure of below 70 per cent of the median for three years out of four). However, these persistence measures cannot easily capture differences between smaller subpopulations, such as disabled people or those from ethnic minority groups.

7.2 Illustrating inequalities in income, wealth and poverty

Income inequalities

Figure 7.1 shows how those in the bottom 20 per cent of the income distribution have only 7 per cent of overall incomes and those in the top 20 per cent have over 40 per cent. Income is highly unevenly distributed. Those in the top quintile had incomes that were six times those of the bottom quintile (an 80:20 ratio).

Looking at individuals according to their particular circumstances, figure 7.2 shows the distributions across quintiles by family type, figure 7.3 shows them for those with specific characteristics, and figure 7.4 shows them according to level of savings. In each case, for a situation of complete equality we would expect to find 20 per cent in each fifth of the distribution.

We can see from figure 7.2 that those who are living in working households tend to be concentrated more at the top of the income distribution while those who are in workless households are concentrated towards the bottom. However, there are some clear differences. Those who are workless in unemployed families are concentrated more heavily at the very bottom of incomes than those who are workless in retired or older families. Couples with one full-time worker are relatively evenly spread across the distribution, as are those where there is a self-employed worker, though among the self-employed there is a small concentration at the top. The best-off individuals unsurprisingly tend to be those where all adults in the family are in full-time work: very few are in the bottom two-fifths and almost 40 per cent are in the top fifth.

Figure 7.3 shows how income is distributed across those with particular characteristics, including gender, disability and housing tenure. Linking to the discussion of wealth that follows, figure 7.4 additionally shows the distribution according to savings accrued – though savings represent only one aspect of financial resources.

In relation to gender, figure 7.3 shows that single men are distributed evenly and therefore face no inequality relative to the population as a whole. Single women are similarly distributed, though there is a slightly lower proportion at the bottom and a higher proportion at the top. However, most men and women live with others and/or with children. The figures for adult women and men reflect the household equivalent income position by sex in all their different family circumstances. We see here that,

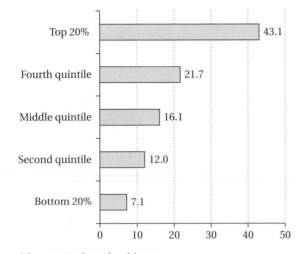

Source: Adapted from DWP (2009), table 2.2ts.

Figure 7.1   Distribution of incomes, UK, 2007/8.

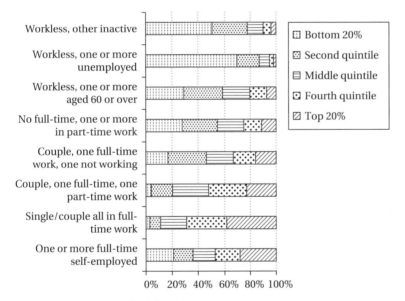

Source: Adapted from DWP (2009), table 3.1.

Figure 7.2   Distribution of individual income by family type, UK, 2007/8.

even though many men share households with women, the distribution of household income overall is substantially more in their favour. This is partly because women are more likely to be lone parents, who tend to fall much lower down the income distribution, and this will depress their situation. Single women pensioners are also poorer than single male or couple pensioners. We can see that children are also

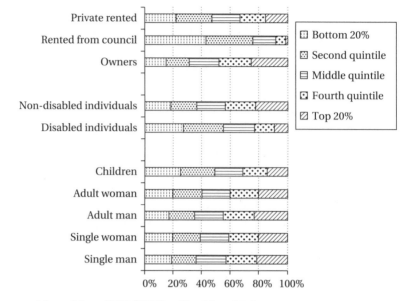

Source: Adapted from DWP (2009), tables 3.1 and 3.2.

Figure 7.3   Distribution of individual income by selected characteristics, UK, 2007/8.

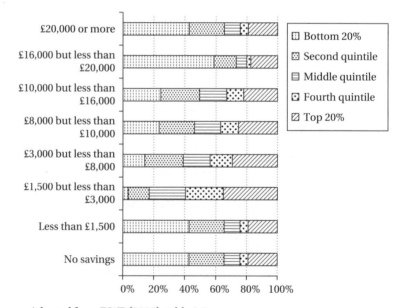

Source: Adapted from DWP (2009), table 3.2.

Figure 7.4   Distribution of individual income according to savings, UK, 2007/8.

more concentrated towards the bottom. Though many live in well-off families, there is a slightly greater tendency for them to live in households with lower equivalent income. The situation for disabled people is worse than that of children in terms of their over-representation in the lower fifths and under representation in the higher fifths.

Particularly striking, however, are the differences in income distribution according to housing tenure. Despite the fact that over two-thirds of households own their home, low-income individuals are under-represented in this category and are dramatically over-represented in local authority housing.

Given the difficulty of saving on a low income, it is perhaps not surprising that those with no savings are over-represented in the bottom fifth and under-represented in the top fifth of the distribution. But it is nevertheless interesting to see the extent to which those with higher levels of savings are increasingly represented at the top, while under-representation in the bottom fifth declines less steadily, partly because pensioners may have low incomes but still retain some savings. It is also perhaps surprising that savings do not buffer further against low income, with around 10 per cent of those with savings of £20, 000 or more still being in the lowest fifth of incomes. The relationship between incomes and assets is by no means exact.

These variations have all been based on equivalent household income. However, as noted, individual incomes can be informative about differences in command over resources between the sexes. Hills et al. (2010) showed that, for individual incomes, inequality within the sexes was similar for men and women and was even slightly larger for women. However, there were big differences in the values at the top, at the bottom and at the mid-points of incomes. For example, the median individual income for women was £180 per week and for men it was £281. The bottom decile, or value above which 90 per cent have their incomes, was £49 for women and £84 for men; and the top decile, or value below which 90 per cent have their incomes, was £435 for women and £649 for men. There were some variations with age, but a lower median individual income for women compared with men at all ages. Individual incomes may not directly reflect welfare, since women may benefit from household as well as individual resources, but the large disparities in individual income do indicate that the control and independence associated with economic security is much more contingent for women than it is likely to be for men. Women may have lower average incomes because of the way that household welfare is managed – for example, by couples engaging in a division of labour between the public and private sphere, as part of which women forego some of their earning power (and individual pension entitlements). Alternatively, their lower average command over resources may make them more likely to live with others. Either way, they are potentially economically vulnerable, which may translate into poverty if they find themselves living on their own without other adults, as we see for lone parents or single women pensioners. (See also the discussion in chapters 3 and 5.)

Inequalities in wealth

Wealth is far more unequally distributed than income. As figure 7.5 shows, those at the bottom end hold nothing or negative wealth, while the top 10 per cent hold over

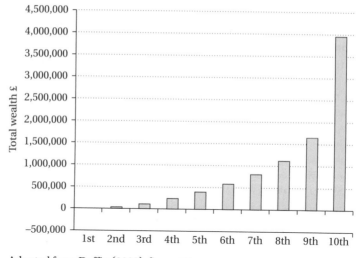

Source: Adapted from Daffin (2009), figure 2.1.

Figure 7.5 Distribution of wealth, Great Britain, 2006/8.

two times as much as the next wealthiest 10 per cent and nearly five times the amount held by the bottom 50 per cent (Daffin 2009). The top 1 per cent of households hold around 20 per cent of total wealth. Wealth is very unevenly distributed in many countries, particularly the USA but also Germany and Sweden, where incomes are more equal than in the UK (Hills et al 2010). The gini coefficient for the distribution of wealth was 0.61 in the period 2006–8, whereas the gini for equivalent income was 0.36 (DWP 2009).

Wealth tends to be accumulated both across the life cycle and across generations, before decreasing to a certain extent in older age. Therefore it is no surprise to find that there is variation in wealth holdings by age. In fact, while the wealthiest subgroup of households in the recent report of the Wealth and Assets Survey was found to be those headed by a self-employed person, the next wealthiest was retired households, which had median wealth of £268,600. Figure 7.6 shows median and mean (average) wealth by age and how it rises to the pre-retirement period before starting to decline. We should be aware that these age bands combine age and cohort effects. That is, it is likely that those who are currently at pre-retirement ages will have accumulated greater resources than did those who are substantially older, and therefore may not see quite such a strong decline in old age.

Wealth is also associated with qualifications, and figure 7.7 shows how it is very unevenly distributed across social classes, bringing into question the ability of those from less privileged backgrounds to provide resources to equalize opportunities for their children. It has been shown that even a modest level of savings can act as a buffer against poor outcomes as children grow up. Thus differences in wealth can affect whether children are set on positive future tracks, with the consequent potential for high incomes and accumulation that those imply. And, at the other end of the life course, wealth and life expectancy among older adults are strongly connected (Hills et al. 2010).

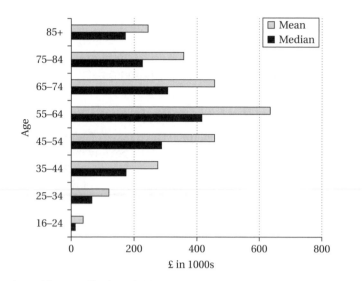

Source: Adapted from Daffin (2009), figure 2.7.

Figure 7.6   Wealth by age, Great Britain, 2006/8.

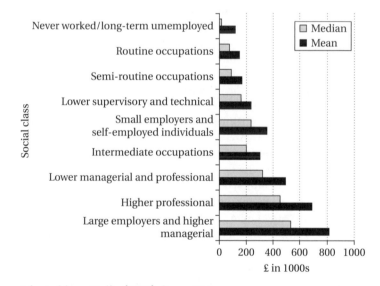

Source: Adapted from Daffin (2009), figure 2.10.

Figure 7.7   Wealth and social class, Great Britain, 2006/8.

This gives some indication of the very uneven and unequal distribution of wealth across social groups, with striking social class differences. Given the connection of wealth with life chances over and above the impact of income, if wealth remains so unequally distributed it means that equalizing median incomes between groups, even if demanded by 'social justice', will not on its own remove overall inequality. Yet wealth, particularly housing wealth, is often regarded, even more than income, which rises and falls and comes and goes, as something over which individuals have rights, and which they also have rights to bequeath to the next generation (Rowlingson 2006), even if this forms a clearly unmeritocratic transfer.

Poverty risks and inequalities between social groups

Differences in poverty risks can be identified for a range of population subgroups. As discussed, we are using an income measure of the poverty threshold that is set at 60 per cent of median equivalent combined household income. This forms a standard measure for point in time comparisons and for analysis of trends. Overall, the risk of poverty in 2007/8 was 18 per cent. That is, among any 100 individuals we would expect to find eighteen poor. But the risks are not evenly distributed across all people in the population. Table 7.1 shows the risks of poverty for a range of subpopulations and the extent to which they contribute to the total population of the poor. Note that the composition is not exclusive, so that the 25 per cent of poor people who are disabled will include those poor disabled people who are also pensioners, lone parents or of minority ethnicity. Those groups that are more common will make up a larger share of those poor, even if their risks are relatively low. Thus, for example, the poverty risks of single women pensioners are high, at 30 per cent: nearly one in three of such women lives in poverty. But single women pensioners make up less than one-tenth of those poor, because there are relatively few of them. The different chances of poverty are striking. In addition, those who have a higher risk of poverty will also tend to have a higher risk of long-term poverty, of deprivation and of lack of opportunities to participate in society.

While the proportion poor in the most recent year was 18 per cent, at most recent estimates half this proportion, 9 per cent of individuals, risked being in poverty for three out of any four years. This risk was higher for children (10 per cent) and pensioners (16 per cent) and lower for working age adults (6 per cent) (DWP 2009). Those who are at greater risk of persistent poverty are those who are more likely to suffer hardship or to get into debt, with the wearing down of resources. Daffin (2009) showed that the chances of falling into arrears and owing money varied across household and family circumstances. Lone parents and those households where the head was unemployed or looking after home and family were most likely to be in this position.

The UK income distribution, then, is not only unequal, with some people much better off than others, but the chances of being better or worse off vary systematically by group. This has implications for the poverty risks of particular groups and all the negative consequences that stem from them. Moreover, income differences are compounded by wealth differences. Wealth is highly concentrated and much more unequally distributed. It also matters for life chances and longevity. It is harder to break the cycle of wealth accumulation as it can benefit those starting off in life, helping them to get ahead, as well as being regarded as under the rightful control and transfer of wealth holders.

The next section focuses on the poverty risks of ethnic minority women, an intersection of social groups whose economic well-being has received remarkably little attention, even though income and poverty are clearly of significance to differential life chances and to those of women's families.

Table 7.1 Risks of poverty and percentage of poor, by different family and
household characteristics, UK, 2007/8

	Poverty risk	% of poor
Pensioner couple	19	14
Single male pensioner	21	2
Single female pensioner	30	9
Couple with children	17	32
Couple without children	9	10
Single with children	35	16
Single man without children	18	11
Single woman without children	19	7
Adult man	16	33
Adult woman	18	41
Children	23	26
Disabled individuals	25	25
Non-disabled individuals	17	75
White	17	83
Indian	22	3
Pakistani/Bangladeshi	53	6
Black Caribbean	22	1
Owners	14	56
Rented from council	39	19
All rented privately	20	13
All individuals	18	100

Source: Adapted from DWP (2009), tables 3.1–3.4.

7.3 Ethnic minority women's poverty

Substantial attention and concern is paid to the fact that women on average have lower earnings than men. The pay gap invites angered and embarrassed responses from policy makers, since it is widely regarded as an indication of illegitimate and unjustifiable differential treatment of the sexes. This is despite the fact that it may in part reflect differences in work-relevant experience or a family-oriented approach to income, issues which may lead to explicable differences in pay, even if the underlying structural determinants still remain of concern. (See also the discussion of the pay gap in chapter 3.) There is now extensive information on the inequalities faced by ethnic minorities in the labour market and in earnings and an increasing number of studies of labour market participation among ethnic minority women, with a particular focus on Pakistani and Bangladeshi women (Botcherby 2006; Dale et al. 2002a; Lindley et al. 2006; Tackey et al. 2006), as well as a growing literature on ethnic minority women's pay (Longhi and Platt 2008; Platt 2006).

However, for all women, the extent to which pay gaps translate into access to overall lower resources is complicated, and depends on the other sources of income available to them, including, potentially, resources shared with other household members. An examination of pay tells us nothing about the financial constraints or opportunities faced by the substantial proportion of women who are not economically active, and how these economic constraints also vary with circumstances.

Low pay may be a poor indicator of economic stress for some women and a good one for others, depending on their family circumstances – and other factors such as the hours they work. Some women may receive relatively low pay associated with part-time work because that makes financial sense overall (in dual-earner households). There may still be reasons to be concerned about the valuation of particular forms of work, the impact of working in a low-status job, and the relative bargaining power of women in couples where their financial contribution is much lower. But low pay in itself does not necessarily correspond to low income or financial hardship. Higher pay and longer hours are necessary to maintain single-earner households and to keep them out of poverty, but their relatively higher pay may not translate into relatively more affluent circumstances. The rewards some women might get from work may be insufficient to maintain support in an otherwise jobless household, and may therefore lead to them not participating at all (Platt 2006). The first group may in fact be the 'best off' at the household level, but would reveal the highest pay inequalities; the second group may be struggling financially, but would appear to be less disadvantaged in pay; and the third group would not be considered at all in an analysis of pay, even though they may be the poorest, since they are out of the labour market.

There is some indication that these different scenarios apply differentially to women according to their ethnic group. However, despite this, there has yet to be a single systematic analysis of either ethnic minority women's poverty or their individual incomes. It is hard to avoid framing this apparent analytical neglect in an otherwise richly researched area in terms of the tensions surrounding representations of ethnic minority women. As noted, on one level they are problematized in relation to family structure, labour market participation, religious practice and claimed self-exclusion. On the other hand, analysis which attempts to normalize their experience in terms of an overarching poverty agenda receives little attention. This simultaneous visibility and invisibility of ethnic minority women was raised by Heidi Mirza (2008) with the question: 'Why is it that in 21st century multicultural Britain ethnic minority women are still not part of the race equality picture?' She then goes on to argue that, 'if they are included they are constructed as problematic, but for the most part they are either marginalised or left out when normalised mainstream race or gender issues are discussed', and asserts that

> distinctive differences and disadvantages are not integrated into mainstream British labour market reforms for women. They are dealt with as special case scenarios, in separately commissioned ethnic minority studies. The 'soft' remedial policy implications of these studies are aimed at educating employers about cultural attitudes that lead to discrimination . . . the more fundamental issue of segmented labour markets underscored by structural racism and sexism remains intact. (Ibid., p. 5)

The contention in this chapter is that the poverty of ethnic minority women does not fit easily into gendered discourses focusing on pay, ethnic minority discourses

Table 7.2 Poverty rates across selected ethnic groups, Great Britain, 2004/5–2006/7

Ethnic group	Working-age adults	All persons
White British	13	16
Indian	20	24
Pakistani	48	49
Bangladeshi	54	57
Black Caribbean	22	25
Black African	27	29

Source: Adapted from Platt (2009a).

focusing on employment and participation, and poverty discourses focusing on normative households. By avoiding a direct consideration of ethnic minority women's economic well-being, policy and analysis compounds their inequalities by excluding them from the implied agenda for action that a discussion of poverty brings with it (Walker 1999).

In exploring and attempting to understand inequalities, it is important to be aware of and search for the evidence that demonstrates those inequalities. But it can also be illuminating to look at the absences for what they can tell us. This section is therefore concerned with just such a gap and with providing some preliminary analysis on ethnic minority women's income and poverty, derived from the first systematic intervention into this area (Nandi and Platt 2010).

Table 7.2 shows us the rates of poverty across selected ethnic groups. It demonstrates the exceptionally high rates faced by certain groups and reveals that, for some groups, rates are nearly as high among those of working age as they are among all persons, including children and elderly people. These rates combine both men and women and use a household measure of poverty.

However, turning to figure 7.8, we see the extent to which individual and equivalent income measures tell different stories about economic well-being and how this is much more the case for women than for men. It relates to the point made earlier in the chapter that neither household measures, with implied equal sharing, nor individual income measures, which assume no sharing, are likely to reflect the full economic experience of women. By illustrating both of these together we can see the two opposite assumptions within which 'true' experience probably lies.

Figure 7.9 shows the mean individual income, the mean household income and the proportion in poverty for women from each of the minority groups, compared with the average for majority group men. It therefore allows us to look at women's incomes as a whole and the relationship between their poverty risks and the individual income over which they have control. It demonstrates that equivalent incomes are, on average, higher for most groups of women, since their equivalent income depends also on the incomes of other household members. The difference is particularly large for Chinese, Indian and white British women. However, though black Caribbean and black African women have high average individual incomes, they do not appear to gain under household sharing assumptions, indicating that they share with those with relatively low incomes or that other members of the

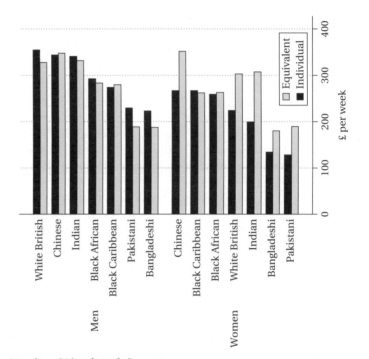

Source: Nandi and Platt (2010), figure 1.

Figure 7.8   Individual and equivalent household income, by sex and ethnic group.

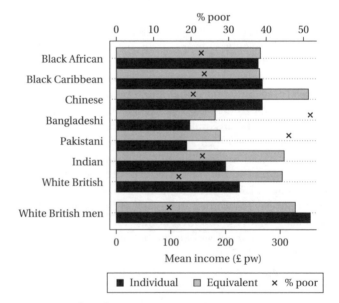

Source: Nandi and Platt (2010), Figure 2.

Figure 7.9   Women's individual and equivalent household income and poverty rates compared with those of majority group men, by ethnic group.

household, such as children, take up the extra available income. Household shar-ing tends to reduce the available income of men relative to their individual income. This suggests that, on average, they contribute more to the household than they gain from sharing.

Figure 7.9 also shows a relatively large gap between the average individual incomes and household incomes of Pakistani and Bangladeshi women, but in this case their overall economic position, even in terms of equivalent income, is strikingly low. This is also reflected in their very high poverty rates. Their low average individual incomes do not appear to be contributing substantially to their average economic well-being; but nor is that a reflection of co-residence with those with much stronger income-generating capacity. Pakistani and Bangladeshi men also tend to have low individual incomes on average (as shown in figure 7.8), and to the extent that Pakistani and Bangladeshi women live predominantly with Pakistani and Bangladeshi men (Platt 2009b), this, alongside their own low average incomes, has the effect of depressing their equivalent net income. Their equivalent income is lower than the individual income of black Caribbean, black African and Chinese women.

We can also see that women from all groups have higher rates of poverty than majority group men, though white British women have the lowest poverty rates among women. Interestingly, Indian and Chinese women have higher poverty rates than white British women despite the fact that their equivalent incomes are higher, suggesting greater polarization in their incomes.

These women vary not simply by ethnicity but also in a large variety of other ways, including the presence of children, which can increase poverty risks, and their demo-graphic profile: there are far fewer single older women among minorities than among the white majority. Figures 7.10 to 7.12 take just one of these factors – age differences – and aim to filter out the impact of age by comparing incomes between women across age bands. Again household incomes and individual incomes are compared. In each case minority groups are compared with majority group women.

Figure 7.10 shows that, age for age, the individual incomes of black African and black Caribbean women tends to be substantially higher than those of white British women. This would appear to reflect their greater earnings at the prime ages. It may therefore also indicate greater control over family income. But that individual con-trol would appear to come at a cost, since their equivalent household incomes, age for age, are substantially below those of white British women, which is true across the span of ages. While the pattern of household income of black Caribbean women mirrors the shape of that of white British women, but at a lower level, that of black African women looks relatively flat. This indicates that there may be less additional income coming into the households in which they live, and may also suggest that there are greater demands on their individual incomes. Of course, these figures represent averages across the age bands and groups, and we should be alert to the fact that the average disguises a lot of variation in the experience across the group (Jenkins 2009b). There is a lot of overlap in incomes across black Caribbean, black African and white women and these income gaps will not apply for all women. Nevertheless the patterns are striking, demonstrating that the overall differences are not being driven by age-related differences in economic activity, fertility and earnings.

The age profiles for individual income and household income shown in figure 7.11

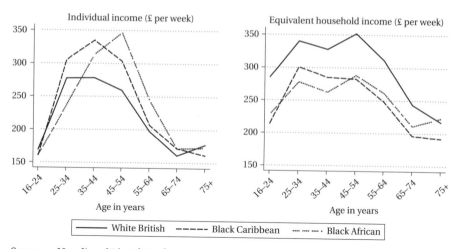

Source: Nandi and Platt (2010), figure 10.

Figure 7.10   Equivalent and individual income of white British, black Caribbean and black African women, by age group, Great Britain, 2002/3–2006/7.

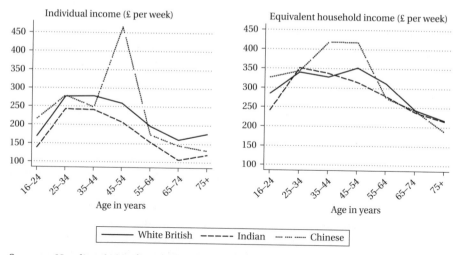

Source: Nandi and Platt (2010), figure 11.

Figure 7.11   Equivalent and individual income of white British, Indian and Chinese women, by age group, Great Britain, 2002/3–2006/7.

are somewhat different. The groups are relatively close in their average individual and household experience, though Indian women seem to have somewhat lower individual income, and Chinese women both higher individual and household income, in the period of middle age. Indian women's lower individual incomes are despite levels of average earnings in comparison with white British women, while their equivalent household income suggests that household sharing compensates to a greater degree for their low individual incomes. It does suggest, if control is related

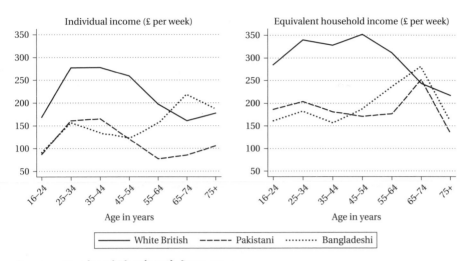

Source: Nandi and Platt (2010), figure 12.

Figure 7.12   Equivalent and individual income of white British, Pakistani and Bangladeshi women, by age group, Great Britain, 2002/3–2006/7.

to income shares, that they may have relatively little command over household resources.

Finally, figure 7.12 provides the comparison for Pakistani and Bangladeshi women. Here there is a different story again. For these women, average individual incomes are low relative to the average for white British women of the same age, but equivalent household incomes are also relatively very low. Pakistani and Bangladeshi women are relatively disadvantaged on both measures. And where for all other groups there was a mid-age increase in average household incomes, though slightly less pronounced and slightly later than that for individual incomes, Bangladeshi and Pakistani women face, if anything, a dip in their average incomes in mid-age, suggesting both different family circumstances and also that the women of these ages may differ in their experiences and earnings and those of their partners from women of younger ages.

For, of course, these figures are comparing different women, and the younger minority group women may differ from older women from the same ethnic group and, on account of faster patterns of change among minority groups, may do so to a greater extent than is the case with white majority women (Georgiadis and Manning forthcoming).

Overall, there would seem to be three income patterns across women from the different groups, and these patterns are roughly consistent with those that were speculated upon above in relation to different pay scenarios, with Chinese women not fitting easily into any of the scenarios but showing high, but also polarized individual and household incomes. Black African and Caribbean women achieve relatively high individual incomes – but they are much more dependent upon them, and not upon other household members, and thus household incomes are relatively low. Their own earnings and other sources of income are therefore essential for their standard of living. For Indian and white British women, individual incomes are not so high, but they do gain some benefit from their households – that is, there is a contribution from other sources of income. For Pakistani and Bangladeshi women, average individual incomes are low, and it is clear that this is not a trade-off with higher levels of household support, since average levels of equivalent household income are also extremely low. Gaining individual income may well be neither practicable nor worthwhile in the face of lack of substantial household income from other family members. They are thus likely to be in a position of both managing on a tight budget and without necessarily very much opportunity to determine how it is spent.

These are of course averages across the groups, but, nevertheless, they form a compelling and intriguing scenario of economic experience at the intersection of ethnicity and gender. They suggest that this intersection is significant for understanding income and poverty and that ethnic gender groups are meaningfully constructed for these purposes.

The analysis also demonstrates how we can use multiple measures to reflect on the intersections between ethnicity and gender and the patterns of multiple disadvantage or of more complex patterns of competing disadvantage and protection that we can infer from these, and how they are clearly distinctive for different groups. Such analyses can introduce particular, previously unremarked inequalities and provide new insights into the ways that group experiences are structured. Diversity in the role and meaning of different forms of inequality at the intersections of different social groups is a theme that has recurred throughout this book, and there is a more general reflection in the final chapter on difference, inequality and the intersection of forms of difference.

Questions for reflection

1 How are income inequality and poverty related?
2 Should we worry about income inequality in the absence of inequalities between groups?
3 Why is the poverty of children considered more important than that of adults?
4 Why are wealth inequalities so much larger than income inequalities?
5 Do they matter more?
6 What can the poverty of ethnic minority women tell us about the structure of inequalities?

Further reading

Hills (2004) is a readable account of income inequalities, poverty trends and dynamics. Jenkins and Micklewright's (2007) edited volume provides a range of perspectives on income inequality and poverty, including international perspectives, while Alcock (2006) has written a comprehensive introductory text. UNICEF (2007) offers a comparative account of child poverty and well-being, and Nandi and Platt (2010) presents a detailed account of income inequalities and poverty at the intersection of gender and ethnicity. The voluminous study of poverty in the UK by Townsend (1979) remains worth reading, while Pantazis et al. (2006) outline a more recent deprivation approach to poverty.

8 Disability and Health

It is very easy if you are a disabled person to get labelled as having a 'chip on your shoulder', even if you haven't, if you are the slightest bit over the top about your needs.

The first time I discovered the social model was when I was researching my dissertation in my final year of the university . . . I just sort of remember reading about the social model and thinking 'yeah, that's how I'd love it, that's me'. You know, it fitted in with everything I'd ever thought about disability, you know, in terms of the fact that if I'm not able to do something and it's other people preventing me from doing that then I've always thought 'well, that's their problem'.

These two quotations come from a study of disabled people and employment, examining what helped them in work and what they found unhelpful (Roulstone et al. 2003). With low average employment rates among disabled people, these respondents – and the rest of the study – highlight the self-consciousness and the energy required in thinking about how to find ways mentally to 'justify' the support they needed to carry out their job and the concern about being seen as 'awkward' or demanding. Disabled people's employment inequalities do not, therefore, cease at the point at which they enter work, even though that can often be the biggest hurdle.

The following quotations come from two respondents to a study of those of working age with long-term health problems in East London (Salway et al. 2007a). The first illustrates the struggle to retain paid work in a context in which employment is the source of validation and meaning, particularly among working-age men. The second reveals how lack of work, when it is no longer possible to participate actively in the labour market, can potentially lead to feelings of anomie.

There was a shop fitting job. I do three or four days maybe, shop fitting job lasted a week and a bit and then I just [pause]. I was swallowing painkillers like nobody's business and I did about a month's worth of painkillers in a week and a half. My doctor went mad at me! And then I said 'no'. I just couldn't do it.

Sometimes I think I haven't got a future, cause what do I do? I just sit here and stare out of the window and that ain't a future. You know, what's the future in that?

The final two quotations, from the same study, indicate the doubts and confusions about what constitutes 'disability' for those who are, for official purposes of law, benefits, and so on, so defined. For these respondents, in contrast with those in the first study, for whom it was an identity to assert in the face of disabling environments and negative attitudes, disability may be a label of convenience or be strongly resisted. For those for whom disability comes later in life or takes the form of the gradual or sudden onset of chronic illness or deterioration of an existing condition, even identifying as a disabled person may prove difficult, differing from young people who have grown up with disability or who, as with the woman in the second quotation (above), have found a model of disability, the social model, which chimes with how they relate to the world.

> Disability, actually I haven't as yet, I am able to walk about to some extent . . . and that's why I haven't applied, because I haven't become disabled as yet.

> Social service people have registered me as a 'registered blind'. I couldn't accept this mentally. I used to say that I'm not blind. I used to think that if they consider me to be a blind person they would stop my treatment and would not see me. And give up. But then the doctor told me that it is not that they would give up. Instead this would help me in getting the services. Then I agreed. But I used to feel very unusual when I used to think that I am a registered blind. I could never accept this. I used to hate this term.

Disability, then, is a complex source of inequality. It has ascriptive elements, like sex, that can bring with them stigma, intolerance or patronizing approaches. But it is something that for the majority of people develops in adulthood rather than being constituted as part of their identity from birth. For some, identification is strong, but, for others, disability can be denied, especially where it conflicts with existing self-perceptions. Disabled people are heterogeneous. Inequalities – in education, employment, income – are typical of their experience. Yet disability or long-term illness itself can be experienced as an inequality by those more vulnerable to it, those who already face inequalities in education, employment or income. This heterogeneity and these issues and contrasts are central to the coverage of this chapter.

8.1 Disability, definitions and scope of chapter

This chapter treats the two distinct but linked areas of inequalities faced by disabled people and health inequalities. First, it discusses approaches to the concept of disability, distinguishing the individual and social models of disability, and goes on to address the inequalities faced by disabled people, in education, employment and life chances. For the purposes of this discussion, disability is conceived of as a particular status, with disabled people forming a social group and with certain consequences stemming from that status, in terms of more limited opportunities, a marginalized social position, and so on. Variation across 'types' of disability is also explored.

Second, the chapter examines disparities in health status and the widening gaps in mortality and health outcomes, where the focus is on the health inequalities faced by people according to their social background, in particular their social class or disposable income. This leads to a discussion of how poor outcomes in health have been explicitly associated with wider inequalities in society.

Health and disability are often distinguished, with disability being seen as a category within which inequalities can occur, and where those who are disabled may or may not have health problems, but without health status being the defining characteristic. Health – or rather ill health – by contrast, is typically regarded as something that is experienced by individuals but which is influenced by the social group to which they belong (ethnicity, class, sex, and so on). However, the distinction is in many ways an artificial one. This is for a number of reasons. First, despite the common understandings, disability is not a fixed state. It is most commonly experienced as a process or a state that is entered. Disability as a condition tends to be defined as long term, but its duration can vary dramatically. Particular conditions may fluctuate and be better and worse at different times. In these ways it is inseparable from what many may think of as ill health. Evidence has pointed to the fluctuating nature of disability, with people not only experiencing moves into disability but also potentially experiencing moves out (Burchardt 2000a). An important consideration when looking at moves into disability is to recognize that they are not equal across social groups. Thus, it is clear that coming from a less advantaged socio-economic background influences disability risks (Jenkins and Rigg 2004). Moreover, the effects of unemployment on psychological health and well-being have been demonstrated since the famous investigation of Marienthal in the early 1930s (Jahoda et al. 1972). Just as with health, inequalities shape the process by which individuals become disabled, and disability then constitutes a source of inequality.

Second, while some people are disabled from birth, the majority of disability is acquired, sometimes abruptly, sometimes gradually. It is clear that there are dramatic increases in the probability of disability with age. Very few young people are disabled and under one-fifth of disabled people are born with a disability. This means that disability, like ageing, can to a large extent can be viewed as part of the life-course experience of a large proportion of men and women (Priestley 2003). Becoming disabled is a transition that takes place within the context of an individual's life. They move from being part of one group to another, even if they may not recognize such a transition or regard themselves as disabled (Salway et al. 2007a). Disability is not, then, discrete, but, like health and ill health, varies in prevalence across the life course and both permeates individuals' lives and potentially alters the ways in which they perceive themselves.

In addition, the extent to which a particular condition is recognized as a disability, by the individual concerned or by society, is liable to be contextually specific and may well vary over time. What is counted as disability is influenced by changing perceptions of disability, and itself influences how we understand the chief contours of disabled people as a group and the extent of variation among them (Shakespeare and Watson 2002). The meaning of, and social response to, disability also changes with age and life stage (Priestley 2003). This parallels some of the ways in which health is re-envisaged over time, and the relationship between health and social background continues to be mediated by social context.

To treat disability as a fixed state rather than as a condition which is itself mediated by other personal characteristics and subject to temporal variation is, therefore, potentially misleading, just as it would be misleading to treat health and ill health as external 'facts' that are not also embedded in social contexts and relations, and most especially in structures of inequality.

The distinction between health and disability cannot, therefore, be maintained on grounds of permanence versus transience or contextual versus decontextualized experiences. In addition, definitions of disability and the way that disability is often measured (which provides us with much of our evidence of the inequalities faced by disabled people) take in chronic health conditions, which vary in severity and which individuals concerned may or may not regard as disabilities. Where illness ends and disability begins is conceptually and, in particular, practically hard to determine. For example, diabetes can be a disabling condition, but those who suffer from the chronic impact of diabetes might not necessarily regard themselves as disabled. Conversely, other diabetes sufferers may regard themselves as disabled by society in its failure adequately to accommodate the specific needs implied to manage the condition effectively. Third, the inequalities faced by disabled people are not incidental but are linked to the greater vulnerability of people who are marginalized in other ways. The relationship between disability and social background works in both directions.

These overlaps between questions of health inequalities and the inequalities of disabled people, and the blurred definitional and measurement boundary between ill health and disability, mean that it makes sense in this chapter to consider both together. The main parts of the chapter are concerned, first, with the inequalities faced by disabled people and, second, with health inequalities.

8.2 Disability and inequality

There is abundant evidence that disabled people have lower incomes on average than the rest of the population. Among working-age disabled people, much of this is due to lack of employment. Berthoud and Lakey (Berthoud et al. 1993) carried out a study of disabled persons' incomes, which revealed the extent of poverty as well as the extra costs they faced through disability. More recently, Burchardt (2003) has demonstrated the disadvantage associated with the onset of disability and its consequences and has argued that poverty rates of disabled people would be even higher if we took the extra costs of disability properly into account (Burchardt and Zaidi 2005). Families with disabled children are particularly susceptible to poverty – and child disability also seems to follow a social class gradient. In what follows we look more closely at the disadvantage associated with disability, with a particular focus on employment.

It is also important to bear in mind the complexity and the diversity of the experiences of disabled people and to recognize the positive aspects of disability. While some people engage positively with their disability and the new ways of looking at the world that it presents (Campbell and Oliver 1996), increasing rates of disability are also in part a consequence of greater levels of survival for major traumas and increasing life expectancy.

Because the chances of disability increase with age, and because occupational disabilities have both reduced and are changing, the nature of the more prevalent disabilities is also changing. The particular profile of the disabled population is testament, in part at least, to achievements in reducing premature mortality, associated with both increasing affluence and redistribution (through the state), the improvement in general health, and the ability of healthcare to maintain people's lives to an extent that was not possible in previous generations. The different ways in which people become disabled, through birth, accident or the onset of (age-related) chronic conditions, may also have implications for the extent to which they identify as disabled and so perceive their connections or interests as bound up with other disabled people.

A further way in which disability has become reconfigured, and which is a major source of heterogeneity in the economic experience of disability, is through the relationship between mental and physical disabilities. While over time mental health problems have increasingly been located within the domain of health, and while physical disabilities and mental health problems can often be found to accompany one another, disability associated with mental illness can be difficult to fit smoothly within models of disability, with popular conceptions of disability as being linked to a particular physical condition or impairment. Yet, at the same time, there is substantial evidence that mental health-related disabilities bring with them the most substantial level of economic disadvantage and stigma. They are thus most closely associated with various forms of exclusion from participation in society – for example, employment and social participation. Disabled people, conceived of as a social group, therefore encompass a range of different perspectives, interests and vulnerabilities.

The concept of disability

There is substantial heterogeneity in the understanding and conception of disability. An important distinction in the way we think about disability has been argued to be that between individual and social models. This is a distinction that has been fundamental to the disability rights movement and was articulated by Oliver in the 1980s, whence it became a core distinction within the sociology of disability and the politics of disablement (Barnes et al. 1999; Oliver 1990, 2009). It has also influenced contemporary legal definitions of disability – and disability discrimination – and there is even now an attempt to use the social model to measure disability (Cuddeford et al. 2010). Oliver argued that society is organized around an able-bodied paradigm that constructs disability as a deficit or lack; and that, rather, it is important to consider the ways in which it is the organization and structure of society which limits the opportunities of individuals because of the way that characteristics, such as certain impairments, are responded to. A crucial distinction then becomes that between the impairment and disability. Rather than the impairment being inherently 'disabling', it is the extent to which social practices and structures fail to respond to it that determines whether or not it is experienced as disability. As Lennard Davis puts it:

> Disability is not so much the lack of a sense or the presence of a physical or mental impairment as it is the reception and construction of that difference. . . . An impairment is a physical fact, but a disability is a social construction. For example, lack of mobility is an impairment, but an environment without ramps turns that impairment into a disability . . . a disability must be socially constructed; there must be an analysis of what it means to have or lack certain functions, appearance and so on. (Quoted in Braddock and Parish 2001, p. 12)

The individual model is often referred to as the medical model, though Oliver argued that the terminology of 'individual' more appropriately reflects the individualized approach to impairment and goes wider than issues of medical intervention or rehabilitation. The contrast between the individual/medical model and the social model is used to reflect on the ways in which disability is treated as well as responded to, opposing a personal tragedy view with a focus on the way that disadvantage is sustained through discrimination. Other illustrative antitheses that Oliver highlighted included individual treatment versus social action, medicalization versus self-help, and control versus choice (2009, p. 45, table 3.1).

However, the distinction between impairment and disability on which the dichotomy between medical and social models rests is not in practice as straightforward as it sounds. The distinction is significant when attempting to address the empowerment of disabled people and to find appropriate responses to enable them to participate. It addresses the ways in which disabled people can be marginalized and patronized and the frequent emphasis on what they cannot do rather than what they can do. It is important from a campaigning perspective and as a means to put disabled people at the centre of considerations of appropriate policy and practice. At the same time, it is less clear to what extent the social model can be effectively maintained at a conceptual level or whether it can fully take account of the variety of circumstances of disabled people indicated above. For an impairment itself requires recognition and definition and is located within a particular context. The assumptions concerning impairment are that it is evident but that its significance is socially constructed. But an impairment often becomes visible or subject to recognition only when required by certain contexts. It is also quite hard to identify what sort of impairment underlies certain disabilities – for example, those associated with mental health problems. In addition, the point at which a health condition becomes an impairment is highly ambiguous, and it is hard to understand at what point we can recognize an impairment unless it is limiting in some way. If disability is socially constructed, it is possible to argue that impairment is too. Thus we might question the distinction between impairment and disability because it depends on a prior socially constructed perspective on what precisely constitutes an impairment, which is likely to vary substantially according to period and local context.

The orthodoxy of the social model of disability for adequately representing the reality of disabled lives has been questioned by a number of disability researchers. Shakespeare and Watson (2002), drawing on feminist analysis, argue that it is important to reinstate the body, which is central to the experience of disability, within understandings of disability, rather than denying its embodied nature. They argue that a new model is needed for the twenty-first century which is more inclusive and acknowledges the diversity of experiences of disabled people, the different social meanings attached to different conditions and the diversity of their identifications. They suggest that a single disability model is not appropriate for the political and personal realities of disability, either in the UK or more widely:

> We would also claim that a modernist theory of disability – seeking to provide an overarching meta-analysis covering all dimensions of every disabled person's experience – is not a useful or attainable goal. For us, disability is the quintessential post-modern concept, because it is so complex, so variable, so contingent, so situated. It sits at the intersection of biology and society and of agency and structure. Disability cannot be reduced to a singular identity: it is a multiplicity, a plurality. (Ibid., p. 19)

The issue of heterogeneity and multiplicity is also argued to be central to the practical issue of appropriate analysis. An overarching model does not allow that different processes may operate in creating or confounding disadvantage for those with different sorts of disability (Berthoud 2008). The insights of the distinction between the social and individual model are important for the definition of disability and in their emphasis on function – what people can do – rather than the condition – what people 'have'. This is also highly pertinent given the variation in impact and experience that can accompany any particular condition. Conditions will also have differentiated impacts depending on the social location of those who experience them. Not only can many conditions vary in severity, but some will be more disabling in some contexts than in others. Chronic arthritis, for example, can limit employment options for a manual labourer much more than for, say, a radio announcer. However, the utility of the social model in adequately capturing the landscape of contemporary disabilities and their relationships to inequality is perhaps limited. As the following discussion illustrates, heterogeneity is core to understanding disabled people's experiences of inequality and the experience of disability and health inequalities across other social groups.

Defining disability

Up until the Disability Discrimination Act 1995 (DDA), there was not in law an authoritative definition of disability. The DDA introduced such a definition, which enabled easier identification of discrimination. According to the Act, disability is 'a physical or mental impairment which has substantial and long-term adverse effects on his ability to carry out normal day-to-day activities'. There were thus two key elements to the definition: that the impairment had to be long term and that it had to limit 'normal' activities. 'Long term' was interpreted as meaning '12 months or more'; and 'normal' day-to-day activities as including 'one or more of: mobility, manual dexterity, physical co-ordination, continence, ability to lift, hearing or eyesight, memory, ability to concentrate or perceive the risk of danger'. Less specifically, it was pointed out that 'substantial' was 'an indication of severity'. This definition has not only clarified in law what constitutes a disability in the UK, it has also enabled the collection of information across the population on who appears to meet these criteria and is thus disabled. It thereby allows disabled people to be enumerated according to a consistent definition, and also helps to evaluate trends and investigate their characteristics. This definition is used in most of the demonstrations of inequalities and disabilities that follow.

Disability has also been defined through state provision. Thus, for example, entitlement to particular disability benefits can be seen as endowing the recipient with disability status and provides estimates of the extent of disability within the population. There are limits, however, to reading back disability from the receipt of disability benefits. First there may be many who are genuinely entitled but who do not receive benefits, either because they do not claim them or because they have had their application turned down. Moreover, there is some evidence that receipt of disability benefits varies by ethnic group across disabled people (Salway et al. 2007b). Thus disability benefits may be subject to inequalities across groups, which render them an unreliable measure of disability.

Counting disabled people

What, then, are rates of disability? Given some variation in past measures, there are inevitably differences in estimates of prevalence. But they all show the numbers of disabled people to be between one and two in ten of the population, with higher rates among older and lower rates among younger people. According to the ONS disability survey of 1996/7, with its detailed measure covering functioning as well as condition and number of conditions, 20 per cent of the population had a disability and 4 per cent had a severe disability. Becker (2003) suggested that 16 per cent of adults have a mental illness, while 14 per cent have at least one disability. Longhi et al. (2009) found that 12 per cent of working-aged men (defined as between twenty-three and sixty-four) were physically disabled, while 2 per cent were mentally disabled. These estimates excluded those with terminal illnesses and learning disabilities. Babb et al. (2004) estimated that, in 2003, over 7 million people of working age were disabled, made up of 4 million men and 3 million women. Comparing results from the two specialist surveys of disability – from the mid-1980s and the mid-1990s – suggested that the numbers suffering from disability had increased from 135 per 1,000 of the population to 198 per 1,000. This was still observed when age standardized rates, which took account of the changing demographic profile of the population, were used. Across all measures and sources there were clear differences in the rate of disability according to socio-economic group.

Disability and paid work

There is clear evidence of lower labour market participation rates among disabled people in the UK (Berthoud 2006). While the rate varies according to the definition used, Berthoud suggests that, in the mid-1990s, only 29 per cent of disabled people were in work of sixteen hours a week or more, while the rate for non-disabled people was 76 per cent. There is also evidence of lower pay for those who are in employment. Disabled people have higher rates of part-time employment (Jones and Dickerson 2007), which tends to attract lower pay than full-time work. But, even among those working full-time, rates of pay for disabled people are lower than those for non-disabled people (Longhi and Platt 2008). Jones and Dickerson (2007) have suggested that part-time work offers a means for disabled people to participate in employment in a way that accommodates them more effectively. Thus, given the major part-time pay deficit, greater access to employment by these means might actually serve to increase the pay gap for disabled people.

The relationship between disability and employment has changed over time. Despite the movement for disabled rights and the development of legislation, Berthoud and Blekesaune (2006) have shown that, if we look at the bigger picture, there have been declining employment rates for disabled people over a long period.

Labour market disadvantage among disabled people can be identified in terms of lower employment rates, higher rates of part-time work and lower pay among those in work. Figure 8.1 shows the distribution of employment across disabled and non-disabled people. Prime factors resulting in these differences in employment and economic activity are related to

- the age structure of the disabled population
- average qualifications levels
- the impact of the disability itself on options for labour market participation and type of participation
- discrimination.

The extent of discrimination and its direct impact on the employment of disabled people is difficult to measure directly, but there is evidence of negative attitudes

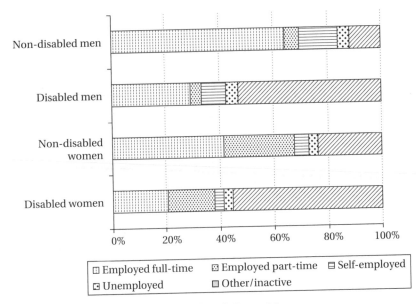

Source: Adapted from Longhi and Platt (2008), figure 2.3.

Figure 8.1   Employment status of men and women, by whether disabled.

towards disabled people and of particularly negative attitudes and great stigma associated with mental health-related disability in particular. These differences in views of disability also correspond to the differences in employment experience according to whether the disability is physical or mental (Berthoud 2006; Schuman and Presser 1996). Specifically, those with serious mental health problems experience substantial labour market disadvantage (Baldwin and Marcus 2007; Jones et al. 2006b; Nielsen-Westergaard et al. 1999). For Britain, Jones et al. (2006b) find that mental health-related disabilities are associated with both employment and pay disadvantage relative to other forms of disability and comparing otherwise similar individuals. This has been associated with both stigma and difficulties with relevant cognitive skills required by employers (Baldwin and Marcus 2007). In the US, mental illness was the most cited disability in employment tribunals, and surveys of employers have also shown that they rate those with mental health-related disabilities at the bottom of the employability scale, considering them less employable than those with physical disabilities (ibid.).

The nature of the impairment itself is likely to be implicated in the extent to which employment options are restricted. Evidence for the impact of 'severity' can be found in the fact that co-morbidities also impact negatively on employment outcomes (Berthoud 2006; Braden et al. 2008; Cook et al. 2007). But the relationship between severity and disability is complex.

Because disabled people are older on average than the population, those of working age are also older than the working population as a whole. This means, on the one hand, that they are likely to have more experience and that, potentially, we might expect higher wages for those in work. But it also means that they may be approaching the end of their working life, and opting for early retirement may be part of the reason for the differences in being in paid work across the groups. There is some evidence that, for older working-age people, becoming disabled can lead to an earlier exit from the labour market. The possibility of work for those with health problems is shaped by what are – or are viewed to be – their options more generally. This can also be seen in the ways in which the majority of disabled people who are not in work regard their disability as preventing their employment, even while there may be those at a similar level of disability but in different circumstances who are in work (Berthoud 2006). Individual characteristics have to be seen to operate within a broader employment context. It is the structure of opportunities that shapes where individuals end up and the extent to which this is associated with social group.

Greater average age also affects the probability of having qualifications, since the rate of qualifications within the population is increasing over time. But, even among those of a similar age, disabled people have lower qualifications than non-disabled people. It has been argued as a consequence that there should be greater attention to increasing educational qualifications among disabled people, though the direction of effects is not clear cut. Do disabled people have restricted opportunities to acquire qualifications (Hollenbeck and Kimmel 2008), or do low qualifications lead to disability (Berthoud 2006)? For some ethnic minority groups, rates of inactivity through ill health are relatively high (Salway et al. 2007a). Disadvantage associated with ethnicity and with disability can thus become conflated. The ways in which particular forms of disadvantage render people more susceptible to other sources of inequality that keep them out of employment is indicated in this association.

Even when taking account of the different characteristics of disabled and non-disabled people, Berthoud (2006) finds that it is hard to explain the large employment differentials among those of working age in these terms. Strong *relative* chances of disadvantage remain, with employment rates of disabled people 40 percentage points lower than those of otherwise similar non-disabled people (29 per cent compared with 69 per cent). That is, on the basis of characteristics associated with being in work, 69 per cent of disabled people could be expected to have jobs. This is lower than for non-disabled people (76 per cent), because non-disabled people have somewhat higher qualifications on average and are more likely to live in high employment areas. But it is still much higher than the actual employment rates of disabled people, which, for his restricted definition of disability, Berthoud puts at 29 per cent.

Yet the problems associated with a particular impairment cannot be seen to be the main driver of the disadvantage for two reasons, according to Berthoud. First, those who do have higher qualifications and who live in high employment areas have strong chances of being in work, even when their disability is severe. This implies that, given the right circumstances or set of opportunities, anyone could work. Second, there is no clear point or set of individual characteristics at which the probability of work dramatically shifts. Even if those with the most severe conditions and the least favourable associated circumstances (such as the demands of caring for children, living in low employment areas, etc.) are very unlikely to be in work, and those with a lower level of severity and more favourable circumstances are likely to be in work, the dividing line between those who can and those who cannot work is not clear cut, despite the assumption of policy that such a line can be drawn. There is therefore a great deal influencing the employment chances of disabled people that concerns the way in which their disability intersects with their characteristics and with their opportunities and wider circumstances.

For disabled people, it has been argued that it is at the point of access to employment that labour market disadvantage is most salient (Baldwin and Johnson 1990; Heath 2001), though others have argued that it is also important to consider in-work barriers (Wilson et al. 2005), and that there is substantial pay disadvantage within employment (Longhi and Platt 2008). The next section considers inequalities within employment in more detail.

In-work inequalities

There is some evidence that disabled people in work cluster in particular occupations or types of job (Longhi et al. 2009); in the US, as well, a high degree of occupational concentration, specifically into less skilled jobs, has been found among disabled people (Kaye 2009). Kaye suggests that there are range of possible reasons for these patterns that might be related to employment expectations as well as to the possession of job-relevant skills and experience and employer discrimination. Others have argued more explicitly that differences in occupational distribution should be understood in relation to differences in the quality or amount of work that disabled people are able to undertake (Schumacher and Baldwin 2000). Differences in ability to carry out the job may seem a plausible explanation for at least part of the differences in pay between disabled and non-disabled people, given the ways in which physical constraints, such as pain and fatigue, are often associated with disability. However, it is hard in practice to distinguish between the limits in a disabled person's ability to complete the job and the extent to which the environment may be disabling, which could also be associated with lower pay through discrimination. Moreover, it is plausible to think that discrimination may increase with the severity as well as the type of impairment, complicating any attempt to distinguish individual capacity to carry out a particular job from the constraints of the working environment.

Related to this point, as we saw from figure 8.1, disabled people are clearly over-represented in part-time work. Part-time work tends to be relatively poorly remunerated and to have long-term consequences on wages (Manning and Petrongolo 2008; Olsen and Walby 2004). Like self-employment, it can be seen as being an available option that allows labour market participation in the absence of full-time possibilities; but there is some evidence that, for disabled people, part-time work facilitates labour market participation, even though its rewards are typically poor (Jones and Dickerson 2007). For disabled people, self-employment has been argued to represent a means to accommodate disability in ways that cannot be achieved in employed work (Pagan 2009).

Over-representation in specific occupational niches and in (poorly paid) part-time work can be interpreted for disabled people as representing a constraint on alternative opportunities for participation, whether full-time work or better paid part-time work. Even if the opportunities are those that best allow accommodation of the health condition or disability, they may not be optimal in terms of making best use of or rewarding the disabled person's skills and experience. These factors indicate that, even in work, disabled people may well face lower pay.

Figure 8.2 translates differences in the pay of disabled men and women and that of non-disabled men into pay gaps, as we did in the discussion of women and pay

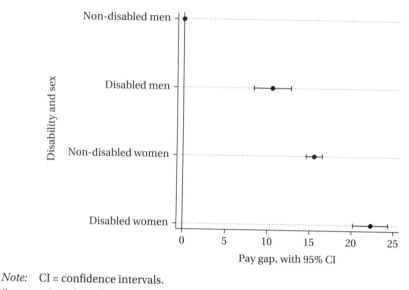

Note: CI = confidence intervals.

Source: Longhi and Platt (2008), figure 3.3.

Figure 8.2   Pay gaps of men and women, by whether disabled.

(see box 3.1, p. 60). The definition of disability is the relatively broad one used in the illustration of employment chances in figure 8.1 and which derives from the DDA. Pay gaps look at the difference between the pay of two groups as the percentage by which one falls short of the other. We can therefore see from figure 8.2 that pay gaps for disabled people are substantial. Disabled men had a pay gap of around 11 per cent, while disabled women had a gap of around 22 per cent. Interestingly, though, in absolute terms the gap for disability was lower among men that it was for non-disabled women. The effect of disability for women appeared to compound the impact of sex on pay.

The potential causes of pay differences are expected to be the same as those implicated in lower employment rates – that is, age, qualifications, discrimination, the limits imposed by the impairment itself, and occupational concentration. The differences in a set of key characteristics of disabled and non-disabled men that are liable to affect pay can be found in table 8.1, broken down by whether the disability was related to a physical or mental health condition. It shows, consistent with previous research, that those with mental disability seem to be slightly better educated than those with physical disability, but that both were less well educated *on average* than non-disabled people in work. However, we do not know the extent to which disability was or was not associated with educational choices and trajectories. As discussed above, we could assume that, in most cases, the onset of disability succeeded the completion of education, so that what we see is that the less-well educated are more susceptible to disability – though Hollenbeck and Kimmel (2008) argue that disability can itself influence education decisions and options.

Qualifications are a very significant determinant of pay, and we have already

Table 8.1 Some characteristics of disabled and non-disabled people in paid work

	Non- disabled	Physical disability	Mental disability
Mean age	41	47	42
Working part-time	3.7	8.4	15.8
Qualifications			
Level 4 or more	33.0	22.4	27.5
Level 3	22.2	20.1	16
Level 2 or less	44.9	57.6	56.5
Occupations			
Managers and senior officials	13.2	11.7	8.5
Professional occupations	9	7.6	8.5
Associate professional and technical	8.9	8.6	7.8
Administrative and secretarial	2.8	4	8.2
Skilled trades occupations	9.1	10.6	9.3
Personal service	1.3	2.5	2.6
Sales and customer service	1.7	2.1	6.1
Process, plant and machine operatives	7.8	12.5	6.4
Elementary occupations	5.7	9.7	15.5
Disability limits amount of work		41.9	51.4
Disability limits kind of work		55.5	65.9

Source: Adapted from Longhi et al. (2009), table 8.

seen their impact on disabled people's employment chances. Qualifications tend to be lower on average among disabled people, though the extent to which they can account for differences in employment outcomes does vary across studies, partly as a result of different definitions of disability and different approaches to the question. They clearly play a role, though, in employment outcomes, and mean that the *relative* employment disadvantage of disabled people is not as great as their *absolute* employment disadvantage, which we find without paying attention to qualifications (Berthoud 2008; Jones et al. 2006a).

Longhi et al. (2009) explored the pay of disabled men and the extent to which inequalities could be accounted for by different characteristics. They also looked at the spread of wages, not simply the average, to ascertain the extent of heterogeneity within the group and whether pay disadvantage was clustered more among the lower paid, indicating the way that those disadvantaged in one area might be more vulnerable to disadvantage in another, or whether there was greater disadvantage among the more highly paid, which would indicate the greater ability to discriminate against those in paid work at higher levels. Table 8.2 shows that, on average, disabled men received lower wages than non-disabled workers. These gaps occur over the whole earnings distribution, from those in low-paid work to those in high-paid work. Workers with mental health-related disability fared much worse, just as they have been shown to do in employment. It is therefore possible that the low pay

Table 8.2 Mean pay and pay at different percentiles of the wage distribution, by disability (majority group men aged 23–64, £ per hour)

Disability group	Mean wage	P10	P25	P50	P75	P90
Non-disabled	12.75	5.87	7.61	10.59	15.34	21.84
Physical disability	11.16	5.21	6.72	9.25	13.36	18.88
Mental disability	9.71	4.69	6.00	7.90	11.38	17.21

Note: Non-disabled excludes all those who have a long-term health condition, even if they consider that it does not affect their daily activities.
Source: Adapted from Longhi et al. (2009), table 4.

prospects form further discouragement to this group in engaging with the labour market.

When attempting to 'explain' the pay gaps – or to look at the relative impact of disability on otherwise similar individuals – those between physically disabled men and non-disabled men appeared to be caused in part by their slight over-representation in low-paid occupations (for example, elementary occupations and process, plant and machine operatives). At the bottom of the distribution, part of the gap was explained by their over-representation in part-time jobs, while at the top it was lack of high-level qualifications. Addressing both the opportunities for qualifications to which (younger) disabled people have access is therefore an important issue for equalizing opportunities at least in pay, as well as for under-standing how less well-qualified people become more vulnerable to disability. We see here that the possibilities of part-time work do additionally bring with them pay penalties.

However, it appeared that the limitations on work associated with disability and as expressed by disabled people themselves were important in explaining differ-ences in pay. That is, those who received lower average pay than their non-disabled counterparts tended to say that they experienced their disability as limiting their work. There are two ways of interpreting this: either that the disability means they are really not able to fulfil the requirements of the job to the same degree or intensity or for the same number of hours as a non-disabled colleague (for example, through fatigue or pain, etc.) or that employers are insufficiently accommodating of their disability such as to make it effectively limit the amount or type of work they can do. The role of disabling environments highlighted by the social model of disability may be pertinent here. Thus the lower pay of those who are 'work-limited' could in fact be partly because they are not being accommodated, and thus feel their condition as work-limiting, rather than they are achieving less at work. Wilkinson (1996) has additionally suggested how discrimination can shape other factors contributing to differences in pay, such as type of occupation.

While the expression of work-related limitations may, as noted, say something about the extent to which environments accommodate disability, they may also say something accurate about the difficulties of disabled people in maintaining paid work at the same level as a non-disabled person, when dealing with a chronic condition and all the additional pressures that can imply. This is reinforced by the evidence that greater severity of condition makes more of a difference to pay. It does seem, though, that, for those with physical disabilities in work, workplace discrimination and constraints on opportunities may be less of an obstacle than obtaining or remaining in paid work in the first place. If pay gaps are to be narrowed, what is at issue is the chance to access better paid occupations and qualifications.

People with mental disabilities, by contrast, do seem to experience worse pay even *relative* to those who are otherwise similar, and this has nothing to do with their own interpretation of the disability limiting their work. The implication is that the stigma of mental illness may persist in the workplace, and that this is a disabled group for whom discrimination may limit their opportunities even when they have overcome substantial obstacles to be in work. There is perhaps good reason for paying attention to this group as encountering very specific and particularly severe inequalities.

Disabled people clearly face labour market inequalities, and they also face educational differentials that compound labour market disadvantage. But they are also a heterogeneous group. The nature and experience of disability can clearly impact directly on their employment options and their opportunities to work full-time. At the same time, differential stigma attaches to different types of disability, with mental health problems being particularly stigmatized. The evidence suggests that this translates into greater difficulty obtaining and sustaining paid work, but also into lower pay once in employment, and indicates that at least some of these labour market inequalities are likely to stem from specifically targeted discrimination.

The next section shifts the focus to health inequalities experienced across groups.

8.3 Health inequalities

It becomes clear that, given the overlap between the ways in which they are both measured and investigated, the distinction between health and disability is difficult to maintain. It can be informative to consider, on the one hand, the inequalities faced by those with different health circumstances and, on the other, the ways in which risks of disability differ across social groups. It can also help us to challenge, or at least to question, implicit assumptions of causation and the relationship between different forms of disadvantage. How is it, for example, that rates of disability are much higher among some ethnic groups, particularly Pakistanis and Bangladeshis, than others (Salway et al. 2007a)? Ignoring inequalities among disabled people may lead us to conflate different forms of disadvantage – for example, ethnic disadvantage and that associated with disability. Ignoring the ways in which those with poor health may face inequalities over and above those associated with health outcomes may cause us to neglect the stratifying impact of health itself. It is therefore relevant both to consider differences across disabled people and to treat health as something which can form a social group, without maintaining such a fixed distinction between the two approaches.

Rather than attempting an exhaustive definition of health or trying to resolve the problems of definition and distinction raised, this discussion takes as its starting point a consideration of the way conditions of ill health *in general* differ across social groups. It therefore focuses on health inequalities between groups. It starts, however, with a consideration of the relationship between inequality and health.

Inequality and health

Wilkinson (1996), in his work *Unhealthy Societies*, argued that inequality is in itself bad for the health of a population. He made the case that, in affluent societies, where basic needs are met, the effect of inequality goes beyond material impacts of low income among the worst off and instead should be understood as stemming from the psychosocial impact of large differentials between different people within the same society. He made this argument at the level of countries or states, comparing those with high and low inequality and finding an association between inequality and poorer health outcomes. Thus, due to the pressure to maintain position, inequality was argued to be bad in highly unequal societies not only for the poor but also for the rich.

The argument provoked substantial debate on the strength of the evidence and on the proposed mechanisms by which income or class inequality translated into poor health, and, with Pickett, Wilkinson attempted to address the evidence supporting his assumptions, concluding that the association between inequality and health was well attested (Wilkinson and Pickett 2007). Although the sweep of the argument was extended to cover a range of 'social ills'(Dorling et al. 2007; Wilkinson and Pickett 2009), the apparent relationship between inequality and adverse outcomes was initiated in an attempt to explain health inequalities and, in particular, the paradox of escalating health inequalities in an increasingly prosperous society.

While Wilkinson and Pickett focused on disparities in income at the society level, a dominant feature of analysis of health inequalities has been the relationship between class and health or mortality (Acheson 1998; Marmot 2010; Townsend and Davidson 1982). Indeed, it has been argued that this relationship has dominated analysis of health inequalities at the expense of the consideration of other dimensions (Bhopal 2007), though there is an extensive literature on wider health inequalities (Graham 2009). This is partly because of the marked differences between outcomes in health between social classes, and because over time they have been straightforward to describe, even if not to explain. There is now a substantial amount of evidence illustrating that social class or poverty has deleterious consequences for health.

This aligns with the recognition that health and healthcare are not the same thing (see box 8.1). Following the creation of the NHS, there had been the optimistic expectation that ill health would effectively be removed from the agenda. As Klein put it:

> Implicit in the consensus about the general aims of policy was a shared, optimistic faith in progress through the application of diagnostic and curative techniques. In turn, this mirrored the belief that medical science had not only triumphed over disease and illness in the past but would continue to do so in future. On this view, the only problem was how best to create an institutional framework which would bring the benefits of medical science more efficiently and equitably to the people of Britain. There might be disagreement about specific policy instruments, but there could be little argument about the desired goal or the eventual rewards. (Klein 1995, p. 25)

While healthcare had helped change the sorts of ill health that dominated the population, it had not resolved the enduring problem of substantial health differences

Box 8.1   Health and healthcare

Health
According to the World Health Organization, health is 'a state of complete physical, mental and social well-being and not merely the absence of disease or infirmity'.

Healthcare
Prevention of disease, infirmity, disability
Cure of the same
Management/amelioration of the same by means of
    medical services, including medical drugs, surgery, pain relief, etc.
    dentistry, ophthalmic services
    sanitation, education, inoculation

across classes. Arguments that there was a selection effect – that is, that those with ill health ended up lower down the social ladder – and that the class relationship was thus somehow independent of socio-economic origins could not be sustained. Bartley and Plewis (1997) used longitudinal data to show the path of causation from lower social class to poorer health rather than the other way round. There has therefore been a shift in policy towards a more comprehensive public approach to health which recognizes that there are wider contextual influences on the major killers in our society (Baggott 1994).

Health differences have been shown to persist, despite the dramatic changes in health and life expectancy of the population as a whole. These changes have been accompanied by changes in the nature of ill health and thus the context of health inequalities (see box 8.2). First, longer life expectancy and better general health has shifted the nature of the primary 'killers'. As early as 1958 it was pointed out that, 'If one is less likely to die of diphtheria as a child, or from pneumonia as an adult, one has a greater chance of succumbing later to coronary disease or cancer . . . by increasing the expectation of life we put greater emphasis on the degenerative and malignant diseases which are characteristic of later years' (Derek Walker Smith, quoted in Klein 1995, p. 28).

Box 8.2   The context of health inequalities

Increased life expectancy
Change in the importance of diseases which kill
Differences in disease according to social group and changes in the nature of those diseases

Second, diseases themselves are socially related. There has been some difference in what constitutes the 'diseases of the poor', and, specifically, there has been a transition to diseases related to overconsumption rather than malnutrition. Complications arising from overweight and obesity are suffered at higher rates among those of the

Table 8.3 Social class inequalities in mortality: cross-class ratios of deaths per 1,000 for women and men, England, 1981–5 and 1986–92

		Women (35–64)	Men (35–64)
Ratio of classes IV/V:I/II	1981–5	1.29	1.53
	1986–92	1.55	1.68

Source: Adapted from Acheson (1998), table 3.

lower social classes. On the other hand, there is some evidence that among the relatively healthy advantaged classes, 'diseases of the rich' may be making a comeback, such as those related to alcohol consumption.

When Acheson (1998) completed his inquiry into inequalities in health, consistent with the concerning findings of earlier studies (Drever and Whitehead 1997; Townsend and Davidson 1982), he came to the worrying conclusion that, despite improvements, social inequalities in health were widening. Table 8.3 illustrates this point by showing the ratio of deaths in the thirty-four to sixty-five age group among those in the lower social classes relative to the higher social classes. In both periods of time, those in the lower social classes had substantially higher risks of death from any cause. But they were greater in the later than the earlier period. There has recently been an apparent decline in health inequalities (see table 8.4, below), but it is too early to say if this is a change in the overall trend. There were also differences in life expectancy at birth and differences in life expectancy at sixty-five by social class. Again, these were shown to have increased rather than reduced.

While a core focus was on socio-economic inequalities in health, the report also considered inequalities across gender and ethnicity. Differences between ethnic groups are substantial and have shown little indication of declining. One issue that has been of persistent concern has been the much higher rates of children of low birth weight born to certain groups of minority ethnic mothers, since low birth weight is a substantial predictor of future outcomes (Dearden et al. 2006; Harding et al. 2004; Kelly et al. 2009). For gender, the picture is more complicated. Women report more illness than men during their lifetime, but have longer life expectancy and are at less risk of dying at all ages. When healthy old age is considered, however, they do not seem to have much advantage over men. Indeed, one of the paradoxes of the analysis is that longer life expectancy does not seem to have been accompanied by commensurate increase in years of *healthy* life for the population as a whole.

In terms of examining the factors that might help to explain inequalities in health, the report explicitly examined trends in

- poverty, income, tax and benefits
- education
- employment
- housing and environment

thus illustrating the interconnectedness of inequalities across dimensions of experience. This demonstrated how little health has to do with healthcare itself compared with other aspects of experience that shape healthy outcomes and that are much more intractable to intervention. Many of the recommendations stressed the importance of reducing inequalities in these areas. However, when scrutinized, the position was rather different from that of Wilkinson. The reduction of inequalities was focused primarily on improving the condition of the most vulnerable or most disadvantaged, whether in income, education, housing or employment, and not specifically on reducing the gap between those at the top and those at the bottom in these areas. Improving the situation of those most disadvantaged is not a necessary way of reducing this gap. It does, then, beg the question, if a clear relationship between socio-economic welfare and health is accepted: At what point is health good enough?

The role of health behaviour has been a vexed one in relation to both understanding and addressing inequalities in health. While some health problems are purely environmental, caused by dangerous work, poor housing, bad air quality, and so on, many are the consequence of the things people do or don't do, in particular their activity in relation to exercise, diet, and smoking and drinking. It has sometimes optimistically been assumed that health education is sufficient to address individual behaviours. But though education may make a difference, it is clear that knowledge is not enough to change behaviour. Health education can also be used as an instrument to locate responsibility for ill health and health inequalities among those who experience them, reducing attention to the wider structural factors that influence or constrain particular patterns of behaviour. This takes us to a more detailed consideration of inequalities across groups.

Inequalities in health

Health inequalities are manifested in the differences between groups in the risks of particular (poor) health outcomes or in mortality. However, there are problems with the interpretive framework implied by a stress on difference between predefined groups. Here we will see how the assumption that health differences between groups are located within those group differences has been open to challenge. When looking at group inequalities there has also been the tendency to focus on illnesses that are group specific – such as those which only women suffer – or where the rates between groups are very different. However, these may not be the diseases that are most prevalent or that lead to most deaths among the disadvantaged groups. The comparison of groups can therefore be potentially misleading. For example, if one group experiences a higher rate of very rare disease, even double the rate – say two in 10,000 among one group compared with one in 10,000 among another group – the condition is not actually affecting very many people in the first group even though it is double the rate of the second group. Conversely, a group may be doing relatively well compared with another group in experience of a major disease, but that does not necessarily make the risk of contracting the disease or suffering the condition negligible. For instance, women have lower rates of coronary heart disease than men, but coronary heart disease still kills a lot of women.

Comparison of groups also introduces the problem of which group is considered to have the 'normal' experience and which is considered exceptional. Explanations of health inequalities are often sought in the specific experience of the group deemed

Box 8.3 Explaining health inequalities: some candidates

Genetic predisposition
Culture
Behaviour (and knowledge/information)
Environment
Healthcare

exceptional. But there is no absolute standard to determine whether doing better or doing worse is the more exceptional situation, or whether either group should be used as reference point.

Finally, a danger of focusing on inequalities *between* groups is that it can tend towards ignoring differences *within* groups. A recurrent theme of this book is the extent of heterogeneity within groups and its implication for how we understand inequalities. In health it is quite possible that differences within groups, however defined, may well warrant more concern than inequalities between groups. This can arise at the points of intersection between, for example, gender and class or with sub-populations such as older and younger people within particular groups.

Explanations of health inequalities have drawn on various points of reference to help understand observed differences (see box 8.3) – genetic, cultural, behavioural and environmental. Despite the earlier caveats about the impact of healthcare on health inequalities, the role of service provision and access can also be pertinent – for example, where screening can capture diseases at an early stage, or where suitable management can reduce the impact of a potentially disabling condition, such as diabetes. These are considered briefly in turn.

Some genetic disorders have unavoidable consequences. Some can be affected, sometimes to a substantial degree, by the type and timing of healthcare provision, while others will interact with context so that they may be revealed in some circumstances, but not in others. Indeed, there is an increasing emphasis on gene environment interaction. Genes on their own typically have little influence on outcomes or on chances of predicting outcomes; they are not deterministic but may interact with certain contexts to result in better or worse outcomes. These ideas can be applied to health as well as to other areas, such as coping and effective psychological functioning.

Culture is often used as a catch-all where group differences cannot be put down to genes but appear to have something to do with longstanding patterns of experience, behaviour or traditions. It is used to represent not innate but strongly instilled characteristics or, more loosely, to reflect the tendency to behave in particular ways or to engage in particular pursuits. In the context of health, working-class 'culture' has been associated with favouring or tolerating particular behaviours, such as smoking, that have health consequences. Such discussions of 'culture' allow a connection to be made between individual behaviours, which are regarded by and large as freely chosen and systematic differences in outcomes.

Behaviour is sometimes linked to 'cultural' factors, but emphasizes individual choice and agency. The expectation is that behaviours can be altered, often by appropriate information. The assumption that knowledge leads directly to behavioural

Table 8.4 Life expectancy by class and sex at birth and age sixty-five, England, 2002–5

		Life expectancy at birth	*Life expectancy at age 65*
Men	Non-manual	79.2	17.9
	Manual	75.9	15.9
Women	Non-manual	83.9	20.5
	Manual	80	18.6

Source: ONS (2009).

change has clearly been challenged, especially as knowledge may only ever be partial or may involve trading off different costs and benefits that have very different time scales: health costs and benefits of current behaviours may only be felt much further down the line. However, it is assumed that adequate knowledge is at least a precondition for behavioural change.

Environmental factors encompass a whole range of contextual factors over which individuals typically have little control but which may have serious implications for health. Air quality, housing conditions (especially damp), proximity of toxic waste, working conditions, drainage, overcrowding and access to outdoor spaces can all vary across social groups and have implications for inequalities in health.

Access to or use of health services may vary systematically across groups and may thus lead to faster or slower treatment or to failure to diagnose serious conditions. Access and use may vary because of inequities within the system itself, as a result of differences in knowledge, or for 'cultural' reasons: groups can have very different expectations of what is an appropriate use of healthcare. Access may also vary simply because some groups have more constrained working patterns or are located far from services, and may simply not be able to access healthcare services within their usual hours of opening. More privileged groups tend to have more flexibility in work patterns.

Though all these frames of reference appear in discussions of health inequalities, a key dichotomy in policy and analysis is that of lifestyle accounts, where the emphasis is on healthy living and healthy choices and a structural account which identifies the constraints on healthy choices (including financial and opportunity constraints).

Class and gender

Table 8.4 illustrates contemporary life expectancies at birth and at age sixty-five by class and gender. It reveals that there are clear differences between aggregated manual and non-manual social classes and that these are found across both men and women. Nevertheless, women who are in manual groups have a longer life expectancy both at birth and at age sixty-five than do men from non-manual groups. The interpretation of class differences is complicated by the fact that gender differences cannot be understood in these terms.

On the other hand, given that there are clear class differences between women, it cannot simply be taken that class does not operate in the same way for women as it does for men. It clearly does. Why is it, then, that, especially given their greater morbidity, women nevertheless live for longer? Answers would appear partly in genetic issues, partly in differential susceptibility to major causes of death, which themselves may be caused by a combination of factors including both genes and behaviour, and partly in the ways in which healthcare is accessed more and more quickly. There are no definitive answers, however.

Turning to morbidity, the difference is reversed. Women are more likely to suffer ill health than men, including mental ill health. It has been 'natural' to look for reasons for these disparities in terms of the distinctions between men and women, specifically in biological accounts based on the physical differences between men's and women's bodies. It has been noted how, in medical terms, women have been clearly defined in terms of their reproductive potential and associated physical manifestations in terms of wombs, ovaries, breasts, menstruation, pregnancy and the menopause. This medicalizing of women's reproductive functions has a long history, which, as some feminist analysis has pointed out, is linked to the construction of women as inferior and the supposed connection between that presumed inferiority in intellectual or rational dimensions and their bodies. Sex differences are not simply explanatory, but, equally, what comes to be defined as illness and health is linked to gendered assumptions. This leads us, then, to be cautious when we approach explanations of sex differences in health in terms of physical difference, even if physical difference may have a part to play.

Substantial attention has now been paid to the contextual and cultural factors that may lead to and maintain women's ill health, but this is a relatively recent development. Brown, Harris and Peto's study from the 1970s on the social context of depression was the first to consider women's greater susceptibility to depression in relation to social context. That is, the authors found that a number of factors could be identified which made *some* women more vulnerable to depression, namely, living alone with small children, being isolated or unemployed, and having lost their own mother at an early age. It was not that these factors were seen as causing the depression – but that they made an individual more likely to suffer from depression if something else acted as a trigger. This was an influential study, as it was the first to examine mental illness directly in relation to social surroundings. This is now an important framework for the way that we think about inequalities in health. They can be approached as variations in susceptibility that are realized or made evident through particular contexts. Both susceptibility and environment may differ across the sexes, but it takes the combination of both to result in distinctive patterns of health and health inequalities.

Ethnicity and class

There is now an extensive and increasing literature on ethnic inequalities in health, though complete explanations for these differences remain elusive. Figure 8.3 illustrates differences in long-term limiting illness by ethnic group. It shows the diversity across groups in terms of poor health, with Pakistani and Bangladeshi men and women, Indian women and 'other black' men reporting particularly high rates of long-term illness. Given the younger demographic profile of many ethnic minority

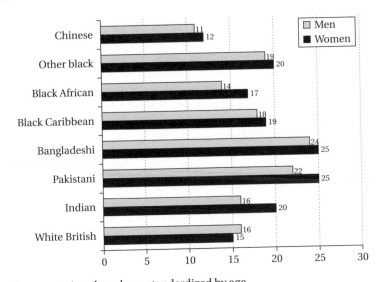

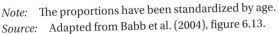

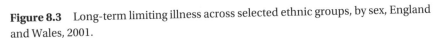

Note: The proportions have been standardized by age.
Source: Adapted from Babb et al. (2004), figure 6.13.

Figure 8.3 Long-term limiting illness across selected ethnic groups, by sex, England and Wales, 2001.

groups, the rates have been standardized by age. This means they reflect poor health net of age effects. Unadjusted rates would not show such clear differences for minority groups, since the white British majority is older, and long-term limiting illness increases with age. Age-standardized rates of long-term illness are below the average for Chinese men and women. Diversity can also be found in the specific conditions faced by groups, with South Asians, particularly Bangladeshis, more susceptible to heart attacks and angina and Caribbeans at greater risk of stroke than the general population. The ethnic health divide is greatest among older people, and there are also differences within groups between men and women and between areas (Parliamentary Office of Science and Technology 2007).

As Nazroo has been at pains to point out (Nazroo 1998, 2003a, 2003b; Nazroo and Williams 2005), accounts of ethnic health differences have tended to take assumptions about underlying biological/cultural differences as their a priori. Comparisons across ethnic groups may serve to prejudge the explanations that are provided for the observed patterns of illness and inhibit the search for alternative accounts (Davey Smith et al. 2000). As Nazroo has claimed, 'postulated cultural and biological differences are assumed rather than directly considered, and assumed on the basis of cultural/biological stereotypes' (Nazroo 1998, p. 83).

Looking for the explanation of ethnic health inequalities 'within' ethnicity can serve to marginalize the role of socio-economic factors. To demonstrate this point, Nazroo set out to test various assumptions about health research into ethnic minorities, analysing differences across white, Caribbean, Indian, African Asian, Pakistani, Bangladeshi and Chinese ethnic groups. By looking at individual groups, he was able to challenge research that started with a South Asian category (as much health-related research has done – and continues to do) and thence assumed some distinctiveness for that overarching group. Rather than assuming that health inequalities lay in the groups as defined, he looked for alternative explanations. He was able to show that, where previous studies had found higher rates of coronary heart disease among what they termed South Asians, his more detailed breakdown provided evidence that all the difference was provided by higher rates among Pakistanis and Bangladeshis. White groups, Indians and African Asians had almost identical rates. Thus, the idea that there was a 'South Asian' 'genetic' effect was unsustainable.

Nazroo went further in questioning traditional explanatory approaches in terms of genetics/culture by looking at breakdowns within the minority groups. Thus he compared migrants with non-migrants – that is, those who came to Britain when they were teenagers or adults with those of the same ethnic group who were born in Britain or who settled here as young children (Nazroo 1998). Here, he found that it was the non-migrants who had the worse health of the two groups.

Nazroo argued that the missing element in the discussion was an examination of socio-economic factors and their connection with health inequalities. In a number of studies, he and others have shown the strong explanatory power that social background – and racism – has in accounting for health differences across groups (Chandola 2001; Karlsen and Nazroo 2002; Nazroo 2003a). While ethnic inequalities in health cannot fully be explained by socio-economic position (Kelly et al. 2009), it clearly has an important role to play. The analysis of ethnic inequalities in health therefore tends to bring us back to class inequalities. However, in demonstrating the relevance of class to 'ethnic' differences, we are left with normalizing or taking as given the relationship between socio-economic background and health, and so many unanswered questions as to how the class relationship operates and why it persists so strongly.

Questions for reflection

1 What is disability?
2 What is the relationship between disability and long-term illness?
3 Are individuals responsible for their health?
4 How can economic inequality lead to health inequalities?
5 If health is improving across the population, should we worry about health inequalities?

Further reading

Graham (2009) provides an account of how health inequalities are shaped by class, gender, ethnicity, geography, etc., and what can be done to tackle them. Barnes et al. (1999) offer an account of the development of the sociology of disability with a particular emphasis on the social model, and explore how disability is researched, represented and constructed. Priestley (2003) provides a life-course approach to disability, which draws out the relevance of age and life stage to the experience of disability. Marmot's review of health inequalities (Marmot 2010) gives an authoritative outline of inequalities across a range of social groups, as well as policy implications. Bhopal's (2007) text on ethnicity and health treats the specific issue of ethnic health inequalities, but the implications of his treatment of measurement, healthcare provision and evidence can be applied more widely.

9 Housing and Geography

One of the rooms is too cold . . . no one can sleep there. We told the council, but they don't do anything about it. We have to use fan heaters and that makes the bills come high. The walls are so damp that you can see the water.

(Phillipson et al. 2003, p. 34)

It is very racist here. My husband was abused yesterday. They called him 'Osama'. I am too scared to go out. I don't let my children go out either. We would like to move out of the area. It has been like this in this area. They take my husband's prayer cap off his head. Once they took it off his head and urinated in it. The English boys go around in big groups. It is very frightening.

(Ibid., p. 38)

I have never liked this area and I still don't and my life has been deeply affected by this area.

(Harries et al. 2008, p. 46)

These quotations, two from a study of Bangladeshi women in the East End of London and the third, the words of a white British woman, taken from a study of women's housing aspirations, capture some of the features of housing and geographic inequality. Thus we find issues of housing quality and of frightening or depressing areas, of fear and psychological impacts and of lack of choice – an inability to move to somewhere preferable. These geographic and housing inequalities are interlinked – poor housing is not only found in poor neighbourhoods, but that is where it clusters. Those who can move may be able to move areas as well as move house, while those who have limited options cannot get out. This chapter looks at inequalities of both housing and geographical area and their interconnection. It also treats the particular question of the residualization of council housing, such that it is the poorest quality housing stock that tends to remain in local authority hands, and explores narratives of 'race' and housing and Rex's development of the idea of housing classes.

People's lives are very different depending on where they live. Inequalities across a range of domains are strongly associated with the areas and the sort of housing in which people live. This is not to say that differences in where people live necessarily cause these inequalities: those who are worse off are more likely to live in poorer areas and in residual housing as a result of their poverty or disadvantage. Nevertheless, there are also some indications that both type of housing and area may have an additional impact on people's life chances. In 2001 the government published *A New Commitment to Neighbourhood Renewal*, outlining its principle that within ten to twenty years no one should be seriously disadvantaged by where they live. This chapter explores the question of whether people are specifically disadvantaged *by where they live*, and how that might be demonstrated.

As well as treating housing and area as a means of defining potentially vulnerable individuals, we can look at inequalities in housing and tenure across groups. We can, for example, consider differences in housing experience, such as living in poor-quality, damp or run-down housing, and differences in areas – whether people find themselves in deprived areas with poor amenities or in well-maintained, affluent areas – as forms of inequality that are experienced across social groups. This chapter therefore pays attention both to area and housing differences as a form of inequality and at residence in deprived circumstances as unequally faced by different social groups.

The chapter starts by considering conceptions of deprived areas, covering issues such as slums and inner cities, and moves on to look at how they are measured. It also treats the overlap between the concept of social exclusion and that of area deprivation. It then examines the concept of 'neighbourhood effects' before investigating differences in area deprivation across the population. The probability of different groups of living in deprived areas is then scrutinized. Despite the ways in which area can be shown to exist as a form of social cleavage, the discussion emphasizes the limitations of using an area-based approach to define disadvantage and the heterogeneity within areas, especially as the size of area on which measurement is based increases. We can see, for example, that areas of deprivation, defined in part as areas of high unemployment, are likely to have higher concentrations of unemployed individuals, even though the majority of unemployed live outside nominated 'deprived areas'. It has often been mentioned that minority groups are more likely to live in deprived areas, but the relationship between relative deprivation of certain groups and their geographical distribution is a complex one.

Area deprivation and housing deprivation are linked, but distinct. It is possible to live in poor housing in an affluent area and in good housing in what is, on average, a deprived area. This also draws attention to the ecological fallacy of inferring individual characteristics from areas. The second part of the chapter looks at differences in housing experience, including housing tenure and the change in local authority provision from quality working-class housing to residual housing. It draws attention to the ways in which housing stress and area characteristics *can* be interlinked by examining Rex's theory of 'housing classes' and the role of housing competition and perceptions of area decline in leading to conflict and disaffection.

9.1 Deprived areas

It has long been recognized that there are vast divergences in the affluence or deprivation of areas. The probability of being poor, unemployed, unhealthy, depressed, and so on, is much greater in some areas than others. Poor and wealthy households have become more geographically segregated from each other and from those that are neither poor nor wealthy (Dorling et al. 2007). In the 10 per cent of areas in England that are most deprived, only just over half of working-age adults were in paid work. This compares with employment rates of over 80 per cent in the best-off areas. Needless to say, it is not assumed that the area necessarily causes the deprivation, but, to the extent that those with different forms of disadvantage become geographically clustered, there may be additional impacts or 'neighbourhood effects' on life chances over and above those associated with an individual's personal circumstances – their health, employment status, income, and so on.

Areas in which disadvantage is intensively clustered have long been of interest to analysts and concern to policy makers for a variety of reasons. From the perspective of analysts and commentators, what has been of enduring interest is the conditions that are created by concentrations of disadvantage, the ways of living attendant on residence in such areas, and their potential to result in particular forms of social relations, whether increasing the probability of lone parenthood (Wilson 1987) or leading to the development of criminal subcultures. In relation to policy interventions, the existence of neighbourhood effects justifies a focus on particular deprived areas rather than on the deprivation of individuals, though only to the extent that such neighbourhood effects can be shown to have a clear cut-off. That is, it has to be clear that highly deprived areas lead to 'neighbourhood effects' that have negative impacts on individuals over and above their personal circumstances, but that such neighbourhood effects do not impact on all those areas that are relatively deprived compared with the most affluent neighbourhoods, so that a focus just on *some* areas makes sense. However, policy makers have also justified intervention in areas where there is a high proportion of deprived people, so that, even if it does not reach all (or even most) of those targeted, the policy directed at them has more chance of being effective.

The logic sounds intuitively reasonable, but it has been strongly questioned. This is for a number of reasons. First, the definition of the most deprived areas is ultimately somewhat arbitrary – a slight difference can count an area in or out of attention, which leaves those on the borders potentially unfairly missed. Second, most people who are disadvantaged, even multiply disadvantaged, do not live in the most deprived areas, however they are defined, so that an area approach misses most of those whom a policy might hope to target. Third, most people who live in what have been classified as deprived areas are not themselves deprived, except through their association with the area, so policies focused on such areas risk targeting those who are not their primary object. And, fourth, there is nothing particular about specific places that can provide an explanation for or account of deprivation, and so focusing attention on the local will not help solve the problems that have led to geographical clusters of disadvantage in the first place. Chris Philo, for example, has argued that

> the roots of poverty are *not* straightforwardly to be found within the places and regions affected (somehow neatly sealed within their geographical boundaries). Rather, the causes of poverty 'in place' derive from many different sources and locations beyond that place, and this must be taken on board in policy formulation and execution. . . . the complexity of the poverty map, with in some places the very poor living alongside the very rich, makes it impossible to devise sound local measures. (Philo 1995)

Moreover, the lack of evidence that the long succession of area-based programmes has been successful in reducing the multiple disadvantages of those living in them further questions the logic of policies based on such an approach.

Nevertheless, area programmes have a long pedigree and are based in a very deep-rooted conception of the significance of disadvantaged areas as a particular phenomenon. It is therefore worth tracing some of these historical formulations of multiply deprived areas and how they have been reconstructed in new versions over time, as well as the policy responses to them, before turning to some issues of measurement and evidence on neighbourhood effects.

The relationship of area disadvantage to urbanization, and the notion of the 'slum' as a site of moral as well as financial deprivation, derives from the era of industrialization. Due in part to this heritage, area deprivation has been associated particularly with cities, even if the poverty of rural areas was often greater and indeed prompted people to move into the city. As Mark Goodwin states:

> Cities have long been synonymous with poverty, and concern about the urban poor has been evident ever since the 'industrial revolution' first ushered in an urbanised society. . . . From the initial half-hearted fumblings of nineteenth-century reform through to the emergence of the post-war welfare state, the introduction of new measures in the fields of housing, planning, sanitation, health education, social security and pensions was partly driven by a desire to alleviate the worst problems of the urban poor. Whether such a desire was underpinned more by moral zeal and by a fear of social unrest than by a true compassion for the poor remains contentious, but the point stands that urban poverty has long been at the forefront of social concern. (Goodwin 1995)

As cities changed their shape, partly because of the shifting of industrial sites from the centre and from processes of deindustrialization more generally, it was 'inner cities' that were regarded as sites of deprivation rather than the city per se. 'Inner city' was a term borrowed from the US, and applied to the UK in the context specifically of industrial decline and the rise of joblessness in previously high-employment working-class areas. Inner cities could also be areas of housing decline and where the dwellings of once prosperous inhabitants, who had subsequently made the move to the suburbs, had been transformed into houses of multiple occupation. 'Inner city', it has been suggested, has the moral connotations attached to it that were previously associated with the idea of the 'slum'.

Certainly, discussions of inner cities and cognate concepts from the 'slums' onwards have been characterized by an anxiety that goes beyond simple regard for the welfare of the inhabitants to express a concern about the threat such areas, or rather those who live there, might present to better-off sections of society. This is despite the fact that the majority of people living in deprived areas are not themselves deprived except through the construction of defining where they live. The anxiety focuses on urban areas because those areas provide sufficient concentration of potentially disaffected people to appear to challenge normative expectations. And anxiety is heightened following disruption or riots, which frequently imply to those investigating them an analysis based on location and neighbourhood, as well as forms of concentration and segregation within that neighbourhood. This can be seen in the Cantle (CCRT 2001) investigation into the riots of 2001 that occurred in Burnley and Bradford. (The racialization of such conflicts is discussed further below.) While it has been recognized that densely populated urban areas are not the only places in which deprivation can occur, the focus remains on those areas, partly for the measurement issues we discuss below. Moreover, it has been shown that poverty is increasingly focused in urban or inner-city areas, while wealthy households are more to be found on the edges of cities (Dorling et al. 2007).

The concept of social exclusion, while having a longer heritage on the continent (Levitas 1998), has become much more dominant in research and analysis in the UK in the last decade or so. While it can be applied to individuals who are marginalized or deprived on a number of counts, and much research has focused on ascertaining the number of *people* who are socially excluded (Burchardt 2002; Gordon et al. 2000; Hills et al. 2002; Pantazis et al. 2006), social exclusion is also used to refer to places. In such usage it relates closely to the definition of particular types of places as warranting specific attention and intervention and shares with the tradition outlined above an anxiety about certain areas representing concentrations of behaviours that place people outside the 'normal' experiences, practices or behaviours in society. The Social Exclusion Unit established by the government in 1999 in order to explore concentration of disadvantages made it clear that it regarded this cumulative experience of deprivation as either an individual or an area issue. Social exclusion was defined as 'a shorthand term for what can happen when *people or areas* suffer from a combination of linked problems such as unemployment, poor skills, low incomes, poor housing, high crime environments, bad health and family breakdown' (Social Exclusion Unit 2001; emphasis added). Areas or individuals could be trapped in cumulating disadvantage, and thus policy response was appropriate at either level. However, at what point social exclusion can definitively be identified is left hazy in light of the qualifier 'such as', and the linked definition immediately raises the question of whether circumstances can and do affect areas and people similarly. As the definition shows, though, particular forms of disadvantage are regarded as associated, and this is seen as the case for both the individual and the area. Moreover, personal circumstances and structural circumstances are linked. It is these aspects, together in part with its lack of clarity, which have connected it to a historically persistent concept of an 'underclass' (Levitas 1998; Welshman 2006).

Social exclusion at the individual level overlaps with the concepts of poverty and multiple deprivation and with the construction of the poor as a class, but it is when applied in relation to area that it is conceptually closer to debates on the underclass which have taken place on both sides of the Atlantic. Ruth Levitas (1998) has identified three models of social exclusion, and what she refers to as the moral underclass strand finds much of its expression in US analysis, where she argues that it is characterized by the features identified in box 9.1.

Those US analysts who are most closely associated – though from rather different positions – with the underclass debate are William Julius Wilson and Charles Murray. Both took as their starting points that:

- poor African American families have distinctive family patterns – that is, large numbers of lone parents – and that there are concentrations of poverty with African American lone parents in receipt of what is known as 'welfare' – that is, means tested benefits;
- there are concentrations of poverty where what might elsewhere be deemed to be normal life is irrelevant;
- the movement of the black middle classes out of black residential areas and into 'white' middle-class suburbs has tended to heighten the extreme disadvantage of the 'underclass' and polarize society still further.

It is worth noting that for both writers the consideration of the underclass was focused on disadvantaged concentrations of African American families specifically,

Box 9.1   Levitas's characterization of the moral underclass

- It presents the underclass or socially excluded as culturally distinct from the 'mainstream'.
- It focuses on the behaviour of the poor rather than the structure of the whole society.
- It implies that benefits are bad, rather than good, for their recipients and encourage 'dependency'.
- Inequalities among the rest of society are ignored.
- It is a gendered discourse, about idle, criminal young men and single mothers.
- Unpaid work is not acknowledged.
- Although dependency on the state is regarded as a problem, personal economic dependency – especially of women and children on men – is not. Indeed, it is seen as a civilising influence on men.

Levitas 1998, p. 21.

though for Wilson the reasons for the concentration were historically based and influenced by major structural changes in US industry. While 'the truly disadvantaged' (Wilson 1987) were predominantly African Americans, recognition of race was not central to an understanding of area-based deprivation (Wilson 1978), which needed to find solutions in structural policy interventions. This did not alter the fact that those most disadvantaged in the US and vulnerable to changes in the economy were African Americans, but it did mean that solutions were not to be sought in racialized accounts. By contrast, Murray (1984) saw race as fundamental to the meaning and position of the underclass and looked for causes in family structure and for behavioural solutions. Murray argued that there was a dysfunctional family form (lone parenthood) which was crucially associated with 'welfare' dependency, which itself was unequivocally problematic. He claimed that the availability of 'welfare' encouraged the creation of lone-parent families through the latter being helped to support children without needing a father. He argued strongly that central government (federal government) should cease to attempt to intervene and leave local areas to work out for themselves how to deal with the problem of families with no earner.

In subsequent work, Murray went on to consider the 'emerging British underclass', arguing that, though small, it existed and was growing (Murray and Lister 1996). He focused his discussion on distinguishing between the 'honest' and the 'dishonest' poor, the worthy thrifty family surviving on a low income and the good-for-nothing 'ne'er do well'. There is a long history of the distinction between the 'deserving' and 'undeserving' poor, and it continues to find expression (Welshman 2006). While, for the UK, he did not regard race as a critical element of the underclass, Murray did emphasize a cultural separation of one group of 'the poor' from the remainder of poor people. In outlining what he believed the underclass to be, he said:

> I am not talking here about an unemployment problem that can be solved by more jobs, nor about a poverty problem that can be solved by higher benefits. Britain has a growing population of working-aged, healthy people who live in a different world from other Britons, who are raising their children to live in it, and whose values are now contaminating the life of entire neighbourhoods – which is one of the most

insidious aspects of the phenomenon, for neighbours who don't share those values cannot isolate themselves. (Murray and Lister 1996)

While the discussion was apparently about individual disadvantage, we can see that it was in fact a discussion about neighbourhoods and clusters of disadvantage at an area level and the effects that this had on others – the 'neighbourhood effects'.

Murray's view has been modified and criticized on a range of fronts in the edited volume in which his account appears (Murray and Lister 1996). One of the commentators, Frank Field, agreed with the idea that there is an 'underclass' but argued that it is not distinguished by a particular 'culture'. Rather, Field argued, there were sections of society who were becoming divorced from the rest of society through increasing inequality and polarization. While the term 'underclass' is commonly used for the idea of a delinquent subsection of society characterized by illegitimate births, welfare dependency and asocial behaviour, social exclusion, as Levitas points out, is also used to characterize the same ideas. Similarly, as we can see from Field's response to Murray, the term 'underclass' can be used to refer to inequalities and a polarized society characterized by extreme pockets of poverty amid general and increasing prosperity. The two terms have thus become effectively interchangeable regardless of the underlying concepts.

The terms can also be used both to describe and simultaneously to provide a framework to account for area-based disadvantage, partly by shifting between area and individual in the process of moving from description to explanation and perpetuating the ecological fallacy.

Responding to neighbourhood disadvantage

Formulations of area disadvantage in the UK have been linked to a series of area-based policy responses to spatially identified problems, despite the ongoing acknowledgement of the ecological fallacy. The late 1960s saw the development of educational priority areas, and these have been followed by a success of programmes, with the New Deal for Communities being one of the most recent. The New Deal for Communities (NDC) identified thirty-nine highly deprived areas subject to substantial investment over a ten-year period. These areas shared very high levels of multiple deprivation but also presented distinctive profiles and characteristics. The NDC was based on a partnership approach in each of the areas in order to address jobs, crime, educational performance, health, and issues relating to housing and the built environment. Unlike many area programmes, the NDC was set up to be long term and to incorporate evaluation of its impact throughout. While there were some positive indications from the evaluations, including in relation to residents' perceptions of their areas, it was not clear how much such a programme can do to address the increasing polarization of rich and poor areas, or the general inequalities faced by those living in different parts of the country.

Different programmes have stressed different underlying understandings of area deprivation and different philosophies and approaches to the perceived 'problem', as Robson (1988) has outlined. For example, during the 1980s there was a strong emphasis on deregulation and removing planning restrictions that were deemed to restrict entrepreneurship and investment, and thus the 'natural' regeneration of marginalized zones. A shift away from local authority control was seen as being nec-essary. This had a parallel in the changes to housing policy, with a major shift from state social housing, which is discussed briefly below.

Other programmes have emphasized the promotion of grassroots activity and the building of local partnerships between state and the private and voluntary sector. 'Joining up' the work of different public-sector organizations (health author-ities, local authorities, and so on) at the local level has also been an aim of much area-based policy. The – perhaps rather optimistic – view of the potential for the local to deliver what seems beyond the power of central government to achieve has driven many small-scale initiatives and can be seen again in recent programmes. However, not only has it been hard to determine the effectiveness of particular initiatives, there have been specific critiques relating to the extent to which they deliver most where most needed or, conversely, whether there is a tendency *within areas* for funding to tend to go to the more advantaged. Moreover, improvements in areas may be the consequence of – or cause – the exodus of the most disadvan-taged, without those people actually being positive beneficiaries. Part of this debate has been the complex role of 'gentrification' in reviving deprived areas, whereby the increasing attractiveness of a place to outsiders may come at the cost of its sustainability for insiders. Similar concerns have been raised in relation to some of the major physical reorganization that has been taking place on the ground in East London as a result of the 2012 Olympics. It is hard, though, to generalize the effect – positive or negative – of area interventions, since deprived areas are extremely heterogeneous across many dimensions, even if they share a low 'score', as work by Ian Cole and others on six deprived neighbourhoods has vividly shown (Crisp et al. 2009).

Moreover, it is not entirely clear that interventions in particular areas are justi-fied. That is, area interventions are based, at least in part, on the assumption that there are additional impacts from living in a deprived area, and the evidence for such 'neighbourhood effects' is equivocal. There have been a number of attempts to investigate to what extent 'neighbourhood' effects can be found. A particular con-cern is whether these effects kick in or are particularly salient at certain high levels of concentration (Buck 2001). This would justify a neighbourhood (as opposed to a purely individual) focus on disadvantage (Clark and Drinkwater 2000; Pagan 2009). However, there are many difficulties in identifying neighbourhood effects (Diez Roux 2001). This is in part because unemployed, sick or otherwise deprived people contribute to the measures which define their area as deprived on these criteria. There is some evidence for the impact of neighbourhood effects on social exclusion (Buck 2001) and some evidence for neighbourhood effects in the UK in influencing social exclusion, while a number of studies from the US have found an association between neighbourhood effects and children's outcomes (Curtis et al. 2004). But the evidence is not decisive, and it would certainly seem insufficiently conclusive to be the focus of policy strategy. Nevertheless, neighbourhood-focused policy retains an intuitive appeal: it appears to make sense that there will be impacts on people living in highly deprived areas that they would not suffer were they living in a more affluent area. On the other hand, the difficulties of being poor in an affluent area have also been debated. Moreover, local organizations can be highly effective in addressing local problems from a bottom-up perspective. Grassroots action also has an intuitive attraction. However, investment in neighbourhood schemes does not always mean that local organizations are funded commensurate with their potential or relative to the composition and needs of constituents. For example, minority ethnic organizations have typically struggled to obtain locally targeted funding on a par with other organizations, despite some perceptions that the opposite is the case (Salway et al. 2007a).

Measuring deprivation

The Indices of Multiple Deprivation 2007 used information on income, employment, health deprivation and disability, education and skills, barriers to housing and services, crime, and living environment to construct a composite score for an area. Scores for the individual components are also constructed individually, so that it is possible to investigate how these compare. The indices allow the ranking of deprivation at a number of geographies, from local authority district (of which there are 354 in England) to super output areas (of which there are 32,482 in England).

The best way of defining a deprived area will depend both on what measures are available to act as proxies for deprivation or poverty and on what the understanding of area deprivation is in the first place. It is clear, though, that scale matters. This raises questions of what is an appropriate level for measuring deprivation – what is the neighbourhood of interest? We can get down to smaller and smaller areas when thinking about 'pockets' of deprivation; and, the smaller the area, the greater the chance of finding specific concentrations of deprivation. For example, one local authority may be more deprived than another but most people living there will not be deprived. A deprived ward or area of a few thousand residents may have a higher proportion of deprived people than a local authority, but even so there will be substantial numbers of non-deprived. However, it is conceivable for everyone in a single street or block to be deprived on some measure, thus resulting in total concentration on that measure in that small area. The New Deal for Communities aimed to identify relatively small 'pockets' of deprivation within districts in order to target the extensive investment of resources. But it was not based on a clear conceptual understanding of what constitutes a relevant area for either measurement or intervention. Of course, if you go small enough you end up with the household, and so are back to individualized rather than area-based conceptions of poverty and disadvantage. By having measures at different spatial levels, and by including measures which adjust for population size, the Indices of Multiple Deprivation resolve some of these problems. But no matter how effective it is at describing variations across and within areas, no measure, particularly a measure that relates areas to one another, can tell us how significant such differences are.

Table 9.1 provides an extract from the Indices of Multiple deprivation for England, illustrating the five most and five least deprived super output areas in the country according to local authority and region. It shows their rank (from 1 = most deprived to 32,482 = least deprived) and the composite score constructed from scores on the various dimensions. It is striking that all but one of the five most deprived areas are in the North West and all but one of the least deprived areas are in the South East, indicating some degree of polarization in relation to intense concentrations of deprivation.

Table 9.1 Sample of the Indices of Multiple Deprivation 2007, England

Local authority containing area	Region containing area	Deprivation score	Deprivation rank
Liverpool	North West	85.46	1
Manchester	North West	84.02	2
Tendring	East of England	82.58	3
Blackpool	North West	82.50	4
Liverpool	North West	82.26	5
Waverley	South East	0.72	32,478
Rushmoor	South East	0.70	32,479
Chiltern	South East	0.70	32,480
South Cambridgeshire	East of England	0.67	32,481
Wokingham	South East	0.37	32,482

Source: Indices of Multiple Deprivation 2007: www.communities.gov.uk/communities/ neighbourhoodrenewal/deprivation/deprivation07/.

Area differences between groups

Table 9.1 gave some indication of the differences between small areas in terms of deprivation, though, while the score enabled a ranking, it was not immediately informative about what the deprivation comprises. There follow now, therefore, some illustrations of inequalities across areas and between groups in their distribution and probability of living in deprived areas. We look at some of the debates relating to the concentration of particular social groups and deprivation.

We start by looking at differences in unemployment rates by area. Opportunity structures clearly make a difference to whether individuals are disadvantaged or advantaged, and the availability of employment is one of the clearest examples of such opportunities. The existence of large differentials in unemployment at the area level affects the probability that individuals will be unemployed according to their location. Of course it is somewhat tautological to say that where there are a lot of people out of work there are reduced individual employment opportunities. Indeed, it has been posited by Meen and his colleagues that 'segregation is not in fact a spatial problem at all. The most deprived and segregated communities are simply the areas in which those with the lowest skills are forced to live' (Meen et al. 2005, p. 2). Lack of jobs can, primarily, be regarded as the cause of high unemployment, though individual employability – for example, the extent to which a person has skills and qualifications relevant to being employed – or the particular labour market in their area is also relevant. Geographical mobility simply cannot be assumed to be an option for all, whether through lack of resources, ties to those who *do* have a job, other family ties, housing constraints, or simply lack of options. Table 9.2 shows the variation in unemployment rates at local authority level in the year ending June 2009. It is clear that there are substantially more opportunities in some areas than in others.

Table 9.2 also shows differences in employment rates. Since non-employment combines those who are long-term sick, looking after home and family, or otherwise unavailable for work with those who are unemployed and looking for work, there is

Table 9.2 Highest and lowest local authority unemployment and employment rates, UK, June 2008 – June 2009

		All	*Men*	*Women*
Unemployment	Highest	17.4	17.4	17.3
	Lowest	1.5	2.1	1.9
Employment	Highest	56.2	61.2	45.8
	Lowest	88.2	93.6	88.0

Source: Local area statistics from NOMIS: https://www.nomisweb.co.uk/.

not a necessary correspondence between employment and unemployment rates. It is conceivable that, if there was no association, for example, between being long-term sick and being in an area with fewer opportunities, there could be relatively low employment without very high rates of unemployment. This is, of course, not the case. Not only is sickness associated with living in a more deprived area, partly because of the factors that cause sickness, but those with chronic ill health in an area of high unemployment can find themselves at the back of the queue for work. They are more likely, therefore, to regard themselves as unemployable rather than unemployed and, not necessarily inaccurately, to see their health problem as preventing their employment (Disney and Webb 1991).

There is no single point at which the severity of disability separates those capable of work from those not capable of work, and it is possible to be in work with severe disabilities if the circumstances are favourable. Conversely, unfavourable circumstances can render the chances of those with even moderate disabilities very unlikely to be in work. Although the relationship between local unemployment rates and long-term ill health is not exact, all but one of the twenty areas with the highest rates of receipt of sickness benefits are in local authority districts with above average unemployment rates. And these recipients are, by definition, not contributing to the unemployment rate, as they will be defined as economically inactive. This does not, however, mean that those who are on disability benefits are not sick or that benefits are simply claimed as an alternative to unemployment benefits (Webster 2000). There is a complex relationship between area, deprivation and sickness, as well as the way that sickness evolves over time, and over time spent out of the labour market and on benefits which provide only a basic level of support, and causal relationships work in multiple directions.

The relationship between ethnicity, area and deprivation is also complicated. There is a tendency for some geographical clustering of minority groups across the country. That is to say, around 75 per cent of the UK's minorities can be found in around 30 per cent of small areas (wards). For example, over three-quarters of black Africans, around three-fifths of black Caribbeans, over half of Bangladeshis and around two-fifths of Indians live in London, compared with around 12 per cent of the population as a whole, while concentrations of Pakistanis are to be found in Yorkshire and the West Midlands as well. Within areas there are also different levels of clustering, with Bangladeshis showing the highest concentration of minority groups at ward level in parts of East London. The smaller the area investigated, the more likely it is that minority group concentrations will be identified. Chinese people are much more geographically dispersed than other minority groups.

We should not forget, however, that it is among the white majority that concentrations are greatest. As a result of numerical preponderance it is possible to find areas that are 100 per cent white, and in the majority of areas, at whatever scale is being used, white people are likely to be in the majority. Of course, as the area of measurement gets larger this is increasingly the case. In some hyperdiverse areas there is a shift in the numerical dominance of the white majority, but those are exceptional situations. Even in London, which is regarded as exceptionally cosmopolitan, around 70 per cent of the population is white.

The different geographical distributions of minority groups and the levels of concentration have been strongly influenced through different histories of migration. The variation in periods of main migration took different groups to different areas, where job opportunities were to be had or where family or 'sponsors' were already settled. Migration patterns were also influenced by the skills the migrants brought with them and the labour markets that were regarded as particularly well suited to those skills (Al-Rasheed 1996; Ballard 1996b; Chance 1996; Cheng 1996; Daley 1996; Eade et al. 1996; Hickman 2005; Modood et al. 1997; Owen 1996a, 1996b; Parekh 2000; Peach 1996; Robinson 1996). The original sequences of migration have intersected with changes in the economy and industry, including the impact of de-industrialization, and with patterns of group mobility to result in particular kinds of settlement among previous and more recent generations of immigrants (Kyambi 2005; Peach and Rossiter 1996) and particular associations with area-level deprivation. These have also been shaped by housing access and tenure, as discussed further below, although there is some evidence of differences in spatial distribution between immigrants.

Although the concentration of ethnic minority groups in Britain is far from the levels associated with those found, say, in the US, the question of whether spatial segregation is increasing has been a source of recent debate, with the implication that the concentration of minorities is a negative phenomenon. In fact, the evidence suggests that, over time, minority groups tend to disperse from (rather than head towards) initial centres of concentration (which are often also areas of high deprivation), in line with expressed desires and with more general moves towards suburbanization (Daley 1998; Simpson 2005). Dorsett (1998) showed how, among Indians, there was a preference for movement into the suburbs and for collocation. The exercise of both preferences was associated with relative prosperity – and therefore the ability to exercise choice. New immigrants, may, however, have little option but to settle initially in areas of concentration – and, indeed, there may be clear benefits associated with doing so (Simpson 2005).

Moreover, it is not clear that the concentration of minorities is an issue for a consideration of inequality in its own right. Dorsett's work also highlighted the fact that, while concentration of deprivation may be a fit issue for policy concern, concentration of groups is not so obviously a subject for intervention. 'Ethnic enclaves' have been credited with being both positive and negative for the future outcomes of group members. Positive advantages accruing from the residential concentration of a group have been argued to be information sharing, informal apprenticeships, social capital formation, and systems for loans; while consequences that have negative impacts on future outcomes (at group or individual level) include greater difficulty making con- nections with 'mainstream' networks, opportunities, services, and so on (Clark and Drinkwater 2002). While Clark and Drinkwater showed that there were few apparent advantages to be gained from concentration, this was strongly associated with the fact that there is a tendency for concentration of minorities to overlap with concen- tration of disadvantage (Dorling 2005; National Audit Office 2008). This is not to say that all deprived areas have an over-representation of minorities, or that all minori- ties live in deprived areas, but that the areas where minorities live have a greater chance of being deprived. It is, then, the association of concentration of minorities with residence in deprived areas that links concentration and inequality, and so may be an issue for groups in the immediate term as well as for subsequent generations (Galster et al. 1999).

Indeed, it has been argued that the racialization of minorities occurs through proc- esses of settlement, which link them to area deprivation. In their study of Sparkbrook in Birmingham, which they called a 'twilight' zone, Rex and Moore (1967) proposed that, where there was housing decline, racialization of the area and of the minority migrant occupations comes to stand for concerns about deterioration, lack of hous- ing in decent repair, and the perceived loss of working-class values and standards of respectability. The authors therefore considered that attitudes developed in this con- text were not straight racial prejudice, which they identified in statements of hatred or contempt not linked to the actual observable deterioration of Sparkbrook. The argument was developed in Rex's discussion of housing classes, which can be used as a way of thinking about the different patterns of tenure and how they are occupied by different ethnic groups. However, it fails to account for the structural processes which result in the specific patterns of migrant settlement in the first place. By regarding racism as highly individualized, it is impossible to recognize it as running through the ways in which deprived areas and minority group concentrations can come to be coterminous. Moreover, if there is no a priori racism, it fails to explain why it is visible minorities who should become subject to these processes. The reasons why perceptions of housing decline are linked to minorities (rather than being located elsewhere) are not fully clarified in this argument.

There have been similar problems in other analyses which take an a priori assump- tion of recognition of difference as a starting point. This was the case with Ted Cantle's investigation into the disturbances in Bradford, Burnley and other towns in the summer of 2001 (CCRT 2001). He argued that separation within small – and deprived – areas led to tension. The apparent naturalness of ethnic divides was rein- forced by this analysis. Cantle took a very different approach from that of Scarman (1981), who had investigated the Brixton riots of twenty years before and had placed inequality at the heart of his interpretation of area tensions.

9.2 Housing

Where a person lives ties them in to the amount of amenity (or lack of it) provided in their neighbourhood and to the composition of the people who live there. Housing choices and options can be important in relation to catchment areas and schooling and thus to enabling or constraining some of the possibilities for future generations. Employment opportunities can also be constrained or enabled in the same way, as an address can play a part in an employer's decision to appoint. Thus housing is in a sense the nexus of issues of life chances more widely, and is clearly linked to discussions of area-based exclusion or disadvantage.

Malpass and Murie would go further and argue that housing provides a way into thinking about a range of other debates: 'Housing has links to and provides a way into a number of contemporary academic debates, including the direction of social change and the notion of an underclass, gender relations and the way they are reflected in housing form and provision systems, and aspects of race and ethnicity' (1999, p. 2). They would thus see housing as heavily implicated in the discussions on area that we have just considered but also to illuminate our understanding of gender relations and race relations. This chapter touches on some of the ways in which housing interconnects with these two areas and also with issues of accumulation and assets.

Housing, and particular forms of housing or housing tenures, is also seen as inextricably linked to unequal outcomes both as cause and as consequence. Those in 'better' housing are there because they are more advantaged, but their opportunities also seem to be shaped by the housing itself, since poorer outcomes associated with growing up in social housing cannot be explained simply by differences in socio-economic circumstances (Lupton et al. 2009). Housing tenure is both an outcome and an indicator of disadvantage and is related to other disadvantage, and this association has become stronger over time as housing tenures have become more sharply distinguished.

Housing is often considered a choice and an opportunity. But the need to find accommodation can act as a constraint on options and have long-term implications. For example, if an area changes over time or job opportunities disappear, but it is hard to sell owner-occupied property, or if housing in an area of greater opportunities is, consequently, very highly priced, possibilities will be restricted.

Housing in the UK has, at least since the period of urbanization in the late eighteenth century, been in high demand and subject to substantial competition. The lack of supply and the tensions that have arisen within and between social groups over access, as well as in policy over an appropriate strategy for provision, have been a feature of housing across the twentieth century, though its nature changed from the early and middle decades of the century, when high-quality council housing was regarded as the most desirable property, and now owner occupation is the tenure of choice. This section starts by outlining patterns of tenure and changes in desirability of particular forms of housing before exploring variations within tenure.

Housing tenure: trends and meaning

Box 9.2 outlines the main ways in which housing can be occupied. The basic distinction is between 'owning' and renting, but there are other variations. There is a critical difference between renting from a public landlord – that is, a local authority – and renting from a private landlord. The terms social housing and council housing have been used to designate rentals from local authorities or councils, though social housing can also incorporate registered social landlords. Council housing is provided as a service and on the principle of need and entitlement, which are evaluated through an application process. Rents are paid to the local authority, and there is greater

> ## Box 9.2   Housing tenures
>
> Owner occupation
> > Owned outright
> > With a mortgage
>
> Private renting
> > Unfurnished
> > Furnished
> > Attached to job
>
> Local authority (LA) housing
>
> Housing association housing/Registered social landlords (RSL)

protection for tenants in this form of tenure than in the private rental sector. Private landlords operate in a market where they aim to make a profit. There is regulation of private landlords, however, both in terms of the guarantees they have to make about the property and the way they handle deposits and in terms of some restrictions on the rents they can charge.

Property owned by housing associations falls somewhere between privately rented and council housing. It is provided by organizations or collectives, usually for particular groups, often those who have particular needs, and may also offer additional services, for example care or support for vulnerable elderly.

Among owner occupiers there is a distinction between owning outright and owning with a mortgage. As the high rates of repossessions in periods of economic crisis have shown, when individuals cannot keep up with their mortgage payments or face a scenario of negative equity – that is, when the value of the mortgage exceeds the current value of the property – taking out a mortgage does not necessarily bring the benefits of ownership that might be anticipated. Nevertheless, this continues to be considered a highly desirable form of housing in general.

The balance of residence across these forms of tenure has shown a dramatic shift over the last century or so, with the 80 per cent of people living in private rented accommodation at the beginning of the twentieth century having now declined to around 10 per cent. Table 9.3 shows the general transition that has taken place since 1938, while figure 9.1 shows in more detail the shift in housing tenure since 1951.

Table 9.3 shows the increase in numbers of dwellings as well as the shifts in tenure over time. While the number of dwellings has more than doubled in the last seventy years, population increase and major changes in the nature of households, with far more people living on their own, mean that there is still high demand for further housing – though this is concentrated particularly in the South East. The number of dwellings needed is predicted to grow by 2021 to 24 million. As the average family size declines, the number of single-person households is predicted to increase to 8.5 million. Of the existing 21 million dwellings, 7.5 percent were deemed unfit for human habitation.

Figure 9.1 shows that, in 1951, privately rented accommodation was still the major form of tenure, but over the next couple of decades there was a major expansion in

Table 9.3 Distribution of housing, by tenure, England, 1938–2003

Stock	1938	1979	2003
All tenures: no. of dwellings	10.6m	17.6m	21.5m
Owner occupied	32%	56%	71%
Privately rented	57%	13%	10%
LA	11%	29%	11%
RSL	n/a	2%	8%

Note: Categories may not be directly comparable over time.

Source: Office of the Deputy Prime Minister, housing statistics 2004, www.odpm.gov.uk.

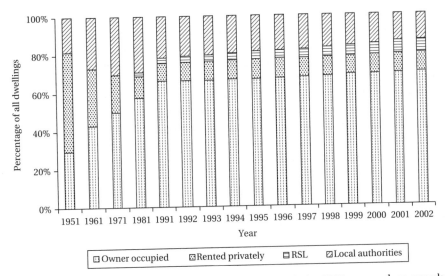

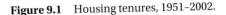

Source: Office of the Deputy Prime Minister, housing statistics 2004, www.odpm.gov.uk.

Figure 9.1   Housing tenures, 1951–2002.

social housing as well as a steady growth in owner occupation. After 1980 and the 'Right to Buy' legislation, which enabled social housing tenants to buy their homes and transferred a large amount of public housing (eventually over 2 million homes) into private stock, there was a dramatic contraction in local authority housing. Its nature also changed, with what was available increasingly becoming accommodation of last resort or 'residual' housing, for particularly needy tenants, rather than the home of choice for working-class families, as it had been in previous decades. Additionally, since people generally chose to buy the best stock, the average quality of the remainder and its location underwent a downward shift.

At the same time, owner occupation came to be seen as a form of investment rather than being predominantly about amenity and use value. Housing capital accumulated and, passed on this way, has contributed to the dramatic differences in and the polarization of the ownership of wealth across the population, as those who are better off are more likely to receive as well as to pass on inheritances. Those who have housing wealth are also more likely to have other forms of wealth, and, conversely, over a third of those with zero or no wealth live in social housing (Hills et al. 2010, p. 212). During the same time period as the substantial sale of council housing, there was a growth in homelessness, and the end of the 1980s saw significant mortgage arrears and repossession of houses bought with loans that could not be paid off. Thus, housing position, which had always been a point of division, indicated some particular cleavages in society and brought into stark relief economic inequalities between the better off and the worse off.

Clapham, Kemp and Smith (1990) have described this transition in housing policy in three ideological and roughly chronological phases. First, they identify environmental management in the nineteenth century and the era of slum clearance. The second period was when state provision of housing came to be seen as a central element of the development of the welfare state. And third was a subsequent emphasis on the market as the best provider of housing, with a particular emphasis on home ownership rather than the private rented sector. These transitions were not inevitable or necessary. For example, owner occupation is much less common in other European countries than in the UK, where it has been driven in part by the constant pressure on housing demand and by the shifting ways in which that demand was met. This has taken place in the context of the wider economic climate and government reluctance or inability to invest at various junctures across the last century. For example, there were substantial differences in the quality of council housing depending on the era in which it was built.

The result of the changes in housing provision, though, has been to create social housing as a stigmatized form of accommodation for the most vulnerable rather than a central element of the British welfare state, such as the health service was enabled to become. The way in which council housing has become increasingly the tenure of the least well off is termed 'residualization'. Explaining this term, Malpass and Murie state that it is 'a process embracing changes in the social composition of council housing as well as the related policy changes. But it is not just to be explained in policy terms; it is a trend influenced by the wider restructuring of the housing market, and is also affected by developments in the labour market' (1999, pp. 17–18). Residualization affects the type of council housing that remains available as well as those who occupy it. For example, Peach and Byron (1994) showed how it was the least desirable council housing which was least likely to have been bought under Right to Buy and that the remainder represented a less desirable stock, which also tended to be inhabited by those with least resources, partly because they could not buy out, and partly as the pressure on existing stock meant that it tended to be allocated to those with the highest needs. They highlighted the ways in which lone parents with high needs and few opportunities for exit could become concentrated in relatively poor-quality housing. They also pointed out that, given that they were more likely to be in less desirable properties, Caribbean tenants were less likely to have bought their properties in absolute terms, but more likely to have bought when taking account of the quality or desirability of the property.

Housing and diversity

Social tenants are a particularly disadvantaged group in their own right, in terms of low employment rates and high poverty risks. But type of tenure is not the only point of difference in housing experience. There are also differences within tenures in terms of their condition, type (e.g. flat versus house), location, and so on. For example, in 2007 around 35 per cent of housing was considered 'non-decent' (DCLG 2009), where decent is defined as 'a) it meets the current minimum standard for housing, b) it is in a reasonable state of repair, c) it has reasonably modern facilities and services' (DCLG 2006). Housing in the social rented sector was more likely to be decent than that held in private hands (DCLG 2009). Vulnerable households – that is, those on low incomes or with disabilities – who were considered in 2007 to be more likely to be living in non-decent accommodation, have been a target of recent housing policy. But all owner occupiers, whether 'vulnerable' or not, were still more likely than those in the private rented sector to be living in decent accommodation.

In terms of variation across groups, we can see distinctions in housing experience according to gender and ethnicity. Female-headed houses have been greater users of local authority housing and have consequently been more affected by the changes in nature and distribution. Moreover, lone parents, who are predominantly women, have increased proportionately in social housing as the stock has diminished. However, they tend to have less opportunity to reject options that arise for accommodation and are more likely to live in poor housing and in poor neighbourhoods. Lone-parent tenancy has thus become a noted feature of residualization, and within council housing lone mothers can often be at a disadvantage in terms of housing quality (Balchin and Rhoden 2002).

Ethnicity and housing inequalities

Ethnic groups reveal distinctive patterns of tenure, which, like their residential patterns discussed above, can be related to specific periods of migration and how those intersect with housing developments and policy.

Ethnic inequalities in housing can be identified in relation to

- differences in tenure patterns for different groups
- differences in the meaning of owner occupation for some groups
- poorer quality of accommodation and greater overcrowding across tenures.

Early migration tended to be into areas of high employment, where there was great demand for workers. These also tended to be areas of high housing demand. Moreover, an ongoing programme of slum clearance heightened the pressure on available housing. During the 1950s and 1960s council housing was seen as the most desirable accommodation among the working class, which at that time formed a substantial majority in the population. Council housing tended to have better amenities and was often more spacious than private rented alternatives. Councils showed a clear reluctance to rehouse people from ethnic minority groups living in situations of extreme overcrowding in what was deemed to be high-quality working-class housing, and length of residence requirements formed one way of avoiding this. Another way was the offer of local authority mortgages to those who had migrated around this

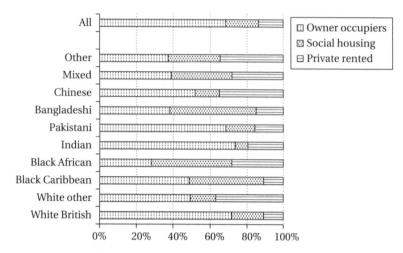

Source: Department of Communities and Local Government, Trends in tenure, table S116: www.communities.gov.uk/housing/housingresearch/housingsurveys/surveyofenglishhousing/sehlivetables/trendstenure/.

Figure 9.2   Housing tenure by ethnic group, England, 2008.

period (Smith 1989). Pooling of capital enabled such families to buy houses in the areas where they were already living, and then rent parts of them out to other migrant workers (Ratcliffe 1997). Buying poor-quality and therefore cheap property became a way of gaining the use value of housing that was otherwise unavailable rather than an investment. Indians and Pakistanis thus became over these decades more likely than the majority to live in owner-occupied housing, but as a matter of constraint rather than necessarily preference. As a result of their being more vulnerable to repossession, there was a decline in owner occupation among all minority groups relative to the majority during the 1990s recession. While Indian rates of owner occupation still exceed the average, Pakistani rates are now somewhat below.

The picture was slightly different for Caribbeans, however. This was partly because their demography was different, with more women immigrants than in the other groups and more families in the earlier years of migration. Caribbean migration also peaked earlier than that of other groups, and so individuals had a greater chance of fulfilling residence requirements earlier and moving into social housing while property was still available. Bangladeshi migration occurred later, and these families are far more heavily concentrated than other groups in social housing, which by this point had become largely a tenure of need. Need could be demonstrated as being high and, with the majority of primary migration into London, local housing costs in the private rented sector could easily be prohibitive. Rates of owner occupation among this group have continued to remain well below the national average.

Thus tenures across ethnic groups have taken on distinctive patterns, as figure 9.2 shows. But these differences do not simply represent inequalities between groups; there are also substantial inequalities within tenures as a result of the ways in which these housing situations arose.

Differences within tenures

The discussion of housing tenures has shown that the observed differences between ethnic groups actually derive from historical constraint rather than reflecting active preference. This can also lead to questioning whether the associations made between status value and types of housing (owner occupied at the top, council housing at the bottom) are consistent across ethnic groups. As Ratcliffe has said: 'One thing is clear from even a cursory reading of the literature: within tenures one would expect minority ethnic populations to be living in very different property types' (1997, p. 139). In fact we find that there are distinct experiences across both owner occupation and council housing.

The variations in council housing are best considered by reference to work on how housing allocations were operated in past decades, since they have had enduring consequences. From the mid-1970s to the early 1980s, issues in the allocation of council housing which seemed to follow ethnic group lines began to be identified. A Political and Economic Planning (PEP) study in 1975 identified three factors that were influential in the different types of housing allocated to different minority groups: the weight given to residential qualifications relative to need; the exclusion of owner occupiers except through slum clearance, which excluded those who had been obliged to buy run-down older property; and bias in allocations, though the study was unable to identify how the bias operated. A seminal study by the Commission for Racial Equality of the London Borough of Hackney's council housing allocations found that there were discriminatory allocation policies. The investigation showed that white applicants were far more likely to be allocated houses and black applicants to be allocated flats. They identified responsibility within the allocation systems and with 'racial' steering by housing managers. Another study, this time in Birmingham, brought together in a clearer form the discussion of housing allocation and issues of expressed preferences than had previously been achieved (Henderson and Karn 1987). It also highlighted the interaction of issues of class with those of ethnicity and the responses of housing managers. The authors' conclusions were that there was extensive racial inequality in allocation, both in area and in type of housing.

The consequences of such allocations, even as they operated a considerable period ago, can be long term. They had implications for the value of the housing when Right to Buy was introduced, on the consequent probability of taking up the Right to Buy (Peach and Byron 1994), and on the extent to which groups were concentrated in less desirable – that is, less advantaged – areas. These could also affect future mobility. The study made clear how the resulting residential patterns had little to do with preference but a lot to do with how allocations were steered. Henderson and Karn concluded that 'The cumulative effect of all these adverse tendencies is to produce an entrenched pattern of racial inequality and growing segregation' (1987, p. 273).

In relation to owner occupation, early patterns of purchase have had long-term effects in similar directions. That is, the purchase of housing in declining areas has had negative impacts on wider experiences and life chances – and made it harder to move. Karn, Kemeny and Williams have pointed out that minorities who purchased within inner-city areas – or twilight zones, in Rex and Moore's formulation (Karn et al. 1985) – enjoyed few of the benefits usually associated with owner occupation.

Ownership patterns also brought increasing segregation, with resulting implications for employment opportunities and increasingly restricted mobility as manufacturing declined and shifted.

Moreover, the quality of the housing that is owner occupied shows distinct variation across ethnic groups. Evidence from censuses and from housing surveys indicates that minority group households are more likely to live in poor quality accommodation (Harrison 2003). Although disamenity for minority groups is found across tenures (Dale et al. 1996; Ratcliffe 1997; Kempson 1999), the differences in owner occupation are important as they belie its advantageous connotations. Pakistanis tended to buy in the older terraces of inner cities. Ballard (1996b) and Bowes and Sim (2002) have drawn attention to the poor quality or lack of amenity in such housing.

The race relations legislation of the late 1960s and mid-1970s was insufficient to counteract the housing and residential patterns that had become established, particularly when they were reinforced by the decline of manufacturing and the processes of de-industrialization, which further limited the mobility of those already living in the inner cities. These inequalities were to have long-term effects on the settlement patterns of minority ethnic groups and for their outcomes (Phillips 1998).

It has been commonplace to regard the housing position of different ethnic groups as reflecting different preferences. However, the evidence suggests that the interaction of historical and current discrimination and class position perhaps provides a better explanation of observed patterns. At the same time these factors tend to be reinforcing, so that, at the level of both asset and amenity and access to other parts of life (e.g. employment, schools, etc.), past housing experience can have a critical role to play in the options or limitations of future generations.

Both area and housing shape the experience of the population and various social groups in very concrete ways. They are a source of inequality and demonstrate the unequal position of many groups within societies. Areas can be a source of support and well-being or of isolation, fear and alienation. Similarly, housing can be a resource and an asset, or it can be associated with health problems, isolation and anxiety. Choice in both is heavily affected by resources and histories, and so area and housing inequalities can compound or stem from inequalities in other aspects of life.

Questions for reflection

1 To reduce inequalities, should policy best focus on individuals or areas (or both)?
2 Does segregation matter?
3 Why does it matter what kind of housing you live in?
4 Does it make sense to understand differences in housing tenure across groups in terms of choice?
5 What processes could explain the existence of neighbourhood effects?
6 To what extent do area concentration and area disadvantage have implications for relations between different social groups?

Further reading

Levitas's (2005) discussion of social exclusion is well worth reading. Dorling et al.'s (2007b) atlas of inequality provides a description of geographical distribution and concentration of inequalities, while Dorling et al. (2005) offer an overview of housing inequality and tenure patterns. Somerville and Steele (2002) treat questions of 'race' and housing in the UK in some detail.

10 Conclusions: Inequality, Intersectionality and Diversity

The preceding chapters have illustrated some of the inequalities that are experienced across social groups. We have seen how inequalities in employment, education, housing, health and wealth play out across groups defined in terms of class position, ethnicity, gender and disability. We have also seen how it is impossible either to illustrate or to begin to explain these inequalities without reference to the points at which social groups intersect. In some cases we have found 'double disadvantage', when being disadvantaged or minoritized in one area compounds that in another. For example, we saw that the pay disadvantages associated with sex and with disability were cumulative: women have lower pay than men, disabled people have lower pay than non-disabled people, and disabled women have pay that reflects both these deficits.

In other cases, however, being part of one social group mediates or complicates the interpretation of disadvantage associated with another. For example, some minority ethnic groups have greater social mobility than the majority. Black Caribbean boys on free school meals do better than white British boys on free school meals in terms of educational outcomes, whereas, overall, black Caribbeans have below average educational attainment.

This raises the issue of the relevance of core distinctions, such as those of class, gender and ethnicity. Given the ways in which they are mediated and modified by other characteristics or allocation to other social groups, we are continually brought back to the consideration of when and how particular differences are relevant and what constitutes a meaningful breakdown by group of the population. If we slice the pie in different ways, as broadly speaking the different chapters of this book have done, we make different claims about inequalities and the groups across which they are salient. We are forced to reflect on the interconnectedness of those points of difference. Such interconnectedness has often been framed in relation to theories of 'intersectionality', and intersectionality has been a recurrent theme throughout the book. It is critical to our understanding of unequal societies to recognize that people are multifaceted and that structures and responses that shape their lives act on them as a whole rather than 'simply' in relation to the different components of their identity or ascribed status. This is not to say that the different elements are not more or less salient in different contexts; rather, that their salience can only be judged through an inspection of the points where different categories meet.

For example, we can see how gender inequalities look very different when class is introduced, and much gender disadvantage is most clearly felt among the working class. Interrogating specific intersections can also lead to highlighting neglected inequalities that might demand attention were they allowed the recognition that an intersectional approach can bring to bear. This was illustrated in the discussion of ethnicity, gender and poverty. Moreover, the complexity of intersections can be important in aiding and revisiting explanation of inequalities. The discussion of educational inequalities at the intersection of ethnicity, class and gender revealed that advantage and disadvantage cannot easily be summed up, as we might think were we to look simply at class and gender in educational attainment, but show distinctive patterns across ethnicity that themselves vary with class position. These intersections clearly have implications as to what is an appropriate way to address such inequalities.

Despite the highlighting of specific intersections and their relevance for both the description and, more so, the interpretation of inequalities, the discussion in this book has made clear that social group membership does not determine an individual's outcomes in one sphere or another. There is great heterogeneity within groups; and the average outcomes, though important in demonstrating the structural processes that suppress or enhance the chances of a particular group, do not necessarily speak for the specific life chances of any individual. The probability of being poor if you are an older woman or disabled is greater than if you are an older man or non-disabled; but not all older men are better off than all older women, nor all non-disabled people than disabled people. The variation is in part on account of variation in other relevant and stratifying characteristics, such as educational level, class background, and so on, but there is simply a degree of difference between individuals that cannot be captured by core observed characteristics.

Not all diversity can be found at the point of intersections of disadvantage. Even where *relative* chances, holding such other factors constant, have been shown to be poorer for a particular group, there remains substantial variation even within groups. Thus, controlling for educational level and social class background, Pakistanis were found to have lower chances of higher occupational class outcomes than the white majority. But this is not to say that this pattern will be true comparing every Pakistani and white person with the same social class background and educational outcomes. The realization of possible life chances depends on so many other things, include chance itself.

This is not to promote an individualistic approach which places all possibilities within the reach of an individual if they can just find the way, nor is it a variant on Beck's formulation of the transformation to a risk society (Beck 1992). It does, though, allow an acknowledgement of the uniqueness of individual trajectories within wider contextual constraints. According to Rubina, a working-class Bengali student in a study by Reay and her colleagues:

> Very soon I think having a degree is going to be a minimum requirement, very soon if you want . . . even just a reasonable job, if you don't have a degree forget it. And for us, first of all we are women, so we are going to be discriminated against, colour of your skin you are going to be discriminated against, so you have to be better than the best if you're trying to get a job. (Reay et al. 2001, p. 869)

Many opportunities will still remain implausible even if not quite impossible for those with particular combinations of characteristics; and structural barriers and gatekeepers will ensure the near, even if not total, closure of many privileged positions in society (Panel on Fair Access to the Professions 2009).

What, then, should constitute the principle of division and when does difference constitute inequality? What are the key intersections that we should consider and where is variation simply 'noise' around those systematic patterns? To put it another way, when does diversity undermine conclusions about inequality? If we took the recognition of diversity to its natural conclusion, we could find ourselves with the individual, and would be unable to say anything about the particular position of people as they are structured by the group or groups with which they are associated. Indeed, this is one criticism which has been levelled against a preoccupation with intersectionality and the multiplication of differences.

Evidence suggests such silencing or rendering invisible of systematic differences cannot be a logical way to proceed. Changes in policy or practice take place on the basis of recognition and, even though they do not do as much as we might hope for them, these would not occur without recognition that there is an inequality and that therefore there is a case to be made to address it (Fraser 2000; McCall 2005). We cannot, for example, have an Equal Pay Act without the recognition of systematic differences in pay between men and women, even if that fails to recognize the complexity of pay differentials among women. There is, then, a case for retaining simple distinctions for the purposes of highlighting inequalities even as we explore the intersections to help us understand them and challenge simplistic associations and inferences.

This is also the reason why the way that groups are measured or constructed matters. This book has shown some of the tensions and contentions around measurement and the establishment of group boundaries. And that is without fully engaging with the extensive literature on the fluidity and permeability of boundaries, including those between ethnic categories and genders. To be within a category can be simultaneously objectifying and politically important. The lobbying around inclusion or exclusion of race or ethnic group categories in both US and UK censuses is one example of that (Burton et al. 2010).

After all, disputes about inequalities or extreme disadvantage are rarely about whether such inequalities are a 'bad thing' so much as whether they are accurate. This denial of the issue has perhaps been most pronounced in discussions about poverty. Those objecting to demands to reduce poverty are more likely to claim that the estimates of poverty are inaccurate or misrepresentations rather than that there is no need to address it. Conversely, acceptance that some groups face disadvantage or that there is inequality between groups has a normative element in that it implies that something should be done about it. It is then worth highlighting inequalities in group terms if there is a chance that they will be addressed. And though some of the results from accounts of the slow decline or even development of inequalities over time make depressing reading, without recognition outcomes could be expected to be far worse.

Difference and Inequality

This brings us to the issue of where difference and structural inequality meet and where they can be distinguished. These are complex questions, and this book does not attempt to offer any final answers. It has treated difference only through the narrow (and partial) conception of social groups (see box 10.1). As noted, these groups are not necessarily owned by those individuals who populate them. But this is to set aside a potentially important site of inequality and difference. Individual expression of difference has often been regarded as an entitlement in its own

Box 10.1   Social groups

The term 'social group' is used to refer to sections of the population across whom inequalities can be identified. I use the term 'social group' rather than the concept of 'social division' that has been employed in other contexts (Payne 2006) for two reasons – first, to emphasize the fact that what are being analysed here are groups or categories, rather than distinctions between groups, which are typically and necessarily indistinct. 'Social group' is also preferred because it is not the intention to make theoretical claims based on conceptual rigour for the groups whose differential outcomes are illustrated. Indeed, as the discussions of measurement make clear, the group categories employed are often at a considerable remove from the conceptual distinctions they are intended to represent.

The groups are not exhaustive. For example, if we compare the list of social groups covered here with those 'equalities strands' that are the concern of the Equalities and Human Rights Commission, it is evident that this book does not pay attention to inequalities relating either to sexual orientation or to religious affiliation. Those considered here are largely immediately recognizable, in the sense that it is possible to allocate individuals to a group with a reasonable degree of precision. How that allocation is carried out is picked up further in the discussions of measurement which are a core element of each chapter.

Being allocated to a particular group does not necessarily imply conscious membership or a sense of belonging, though a sense of membership can derive in part from understanding the ways in which you are perceived by others. Membership also implies recognition by those within the group. However, it is possible to experience the inequalities associated with a particular group membership with no conscious awareness of or identification with that group – a clear example being social class. Throughout, the assumption is that groups are based on allocative rather than identificational criteria. Identity and identification are powerful and important aspects of personal and relational life. And identity and belonging are central areas of sociological research in their own right. However, they have not been a central concern of the discussion of inequality in this book.

right, and as part of what enables individuals to make sense of their lives. It is part of being proactive in one's own life to choose and assert belonging and identity in all its complexity (Tizard and Phoenix 1995). Given the politics of identity, the failure to acknowledge what is personally significant is in itself a form of both misrecognition and inequality. But the extent to which such assertions can operate outside the inequalities that are structurally associated with those identities, even if not personally experienced, remains an open question. Assertion of identity invokes historical processes which are part of the meaning that such identities have acquired (Irwin 2003) and can imply transnational connections. Thus to assert one's womanhood makes connections with the historical and international minoritization of women, even if one is privileged, white and middle class (Brah and Phoenix 2004).

At a basic level, then, it can be argued that difference and inequality are simply different ways of saying the same thing (Bhopal 2007). This is also implied in the measurement or construction of difference by which we reveal inequalities. We would probably not think much of a class schema which failed to distinguish outcomes across its categories in the population. The proposition of this book has been that differences are worth identifying where they can reveal inequality. It is at the point where we can measure inequalities in material, educational or occupational terms that difference perhaps becomes salient. Without measurement, we might remain unaware of and unconcerned by grave differences – inequalities between groups that amounted to serious injustice.

Nevertheless – even in the process of measuring, conceiving of or pondering whether you ought to measure such differences – there is a problematic issue of whether in doing so you essentialize differences that are not fixed (Brah 1992) – that is, you regard as having some inherent meaning differences which are instead historically contingent. We saw in chapter 8 how attempts have been made to understand health differences between ethnic groups. By measuring and identifying differences between groups conceived of a priori, the assumption is that the two types of difference – the ethnic groups and the inequalities of outcomes – must be inherently associated. Even though this may clearly seem analytically misguided, it is nevertheless prevalent in some research areas, as Nazroo points out when he shows how ethnic health inequalities are better understood in terms of class. Class is different from gender or ethnicity in that it is not reducible in the same way to such essentialized interpretations. Moreover, it can make a persistent contribution to illuminating inequalities across other groups, as this book has shown. And, indeed, one of the major contributions of proponents of intersectionality has been to reassert the fundamental importance of class – or income or disadvantage – in developing a better understanding of marginalization of particular women and in particular locations and historical spaces (Brah and Phoenix 2004).

On the basis of recognition that is associated with identifying inequality without equating groups with the causes of such inequalities, categorizing populations into social groups may be defensible and even worthwhile. But is that the only way to address the underlying inequalities in society? This brings us back to the topic, treated in the introduction, of whether an egalitarian focus should have as its target the wider inequalities in society – in income, employment chances, types of occupation, health status, and so on, rather than on the ways in which highly uneven rewards are distributed across groups. Despite the fact that this book has focused on the inequalities between groups and the intersections of these inequalities, the moot point for addressing them effectively may be whether ultimately minority interests are best served by equalizing the distribution of rewards in the population as a whole, rather than by paying attention to the clustering of advantage and disadvantage by ethnicity, sex or class. It is, nevertheless, only by continuing to investigate differences across social groups that we would be able to arrive at an answer to that question.

Moreover, since the social groups we have been considering are, by and large, constructed by social processes within which the recognition of inequality plays a part, it may be that we will know that we have reached equality when we cease to recognize – or recognize in the same way – the social groups considered in this account. But, unfortunately, that prospect remains a long way off.

References

Aassve, A., Iacovou, M., and Mencarini, L. (2006) 'Youth poverty and transition to adulthood in Europe', *Demographic Research*, 15: 21–50.

Abbott, P., Wallace, C., and Tyler, M. (2005) *An Introduction to Sociology: Feminist Perspectives.* London: Routledge.

Abel-Smith, B., and Townsend, P. (1965) *The Poor and the Poorest.* London: Bell & Sons.

Abrams, D. (2010) *Processes of Prejudice: Theory, Evidence and Intervention.* London: Equalities and Human Rights Commission.

Acheson, S. D. C. (1998) *Independent Inquiry into Inequalities in Health.* London: Stationery Office.

Al-Rasheed, M. (1996) 'The other-others: hidden Arabs?', in C. Peach (ed.) *Ethnicity in the 1991 Census*, Vol. 2: *The Ethnic Minority Populations of Great Britain.* London: HMSO, pp. 206–20.

Alam, M. Y., and Husband, C. (2006) *British-Pakistani Men from Bradford: Linking Narratives to Policy.* York: Joseph Rowntree Foundation.

Alcock, P. (2006) *Understanding Poverty.* 3rd edn, Basingstoke: Palgrave.

Aldridge, S. (2004) *Life Chances and Social Mobility: An Overview of the Evidence.* London: Cabinet Office.

Anderson, B. (1991) *Imagined Communities: Reflections on the Origins and Spread of Nationalism.* London: Verso.

Anthias, F. (2001) 'The concept of "social division" and theorising social stratification: looking at ethnicity and class', *Sociology*, 35(4): 835–54.

Arber, S., and Ginn, J. (1995) *Connecting Gender and Ageing: A Sociological Approach.* Buckingham: Open University Press.

Arber, S., Anderssen, L., and Hoff, A. E. (eds) (2007) *Gender, Ageing and Power: Changing Dynamics across Western Societies*, special issue of *Current Sociology*, 55(2): 147–312.

Archer, S. (2003) *Money, Choice and Control: The Financial Circumstances of Early Retirement.* Bristol: Policy Press.

Arnot, M., Gray, J., James, M., Rudduck, J., and Duveen, G. (1998) *Recent Research on Gender and Educational Performance.* London: Stationery Office.

Aspinall, P. (2000) 'The challenges of measuring the ethno-cultural diversity of Britain in the new millennium', *Policy & Politics*, 28(1): 109–18.

Aspinall, P. J. (2002) 'Collective terminology to describe the minority ethnic population: the persistence of confusion and ambiguity in usage', *Sociology*, 36(4): 803–16.

Atkinson, A. B. (1987) 'On the measurement of poverty', *Econometrica*, 55(4): 749–64.

— (1995) *Incomes and the Welfare State: Essays on Britain and Europe.* Cambridge: Cambridge University Press.

— (2000) 'Distribution of income and wealth', in A. H. W. Halsey and J. Webb (eds) *Twentieth-Century British Social Trends.* Basingstoke: Macmillan, pp. 348–81.

— (2006) *Concentration among the Rich.* Oxford: UNU-WIDER Research Paper no. 2006/151.

Atkinson, A. B., Maynard, A. K., and Trinder, C. G. (1983) *Parents and Children: Incomes in Two Generations.* London: Heinemann Educational.

Atkinson, A. B., Cantillon, B., Marlier, E., and Nolan, B. (2002) *Social Indicators: The EU and Social Inclusion.* Oxford: Oxford University Press.

Babb, P., Martin, J., and Haezewindt, P. (eds) (2004) *Focus on Social Inequalities: 2004 Edition.* London: Office for National Statistics.

Baggott, R. (1994) *Health and Health Care in Britain*. Basingstoke: Macmillan.

Bagguley, P., and Hussain, Y. (2007) *The Role of Higher Education in Providing Opportunities for South Asian Women*. Bristol: Policy Press.

Balchin, P., and Rhoden, M. (2002) *Housing Policy*. 4th edn, London: Routledge.

Baldwin, M. L., and Johnson, W. G. (1990) *Labor Market Discrimination against Men with Disabilities in the Year of the ADA*. East Carolina University Department of Economics Working Paper, no. 9715; http://ideas.repec.org/p/wop/eacaec/9715.html.

Baldwin, M. L., and Marcus, S. C. (2007) 'Labor market outcomes of persons with mental disorders', *Industrial Relations*, 46(3): 481–510.

Ball, S. J. (2006) *Education Policy and Social Class*. London: Routledge.

Ball, S. J. (2008) *The Education Debate*. Bristol: Policy Press.

Ball, S. J., Bowe, S. J., and Gewirtz, S. (1995) 'Circuits of schooling: a sociological exploration of parental choice of school in social class contexts', *Sociological Review*, 43(1): 52–78.

Ballard, R. (1996a) 'Negotiating race and ethnicity: exploring the implications of the 1991 census', *Patterns of Prejudice*, 30(3): 3–34.

— (1996b) 'The Pakistanis: stability and introspection', in C. Peach (ed.) *Ethnicity in the 1991 Census*, Vol. 2: *The Ethnic Minority Populations of Great Britain*. London: HMSO, pp. 121–49.

Bamfield, L., and Horton, T. (2009) *Understanding Attitudes to Tackling Economic Inequality*. York: Joseph Rowntree Foundation.

Banton, M. (1998) *Racial Theories*. Cambridge: Cambridge University Press.

Bardasi, E., and Jenkins, S. P. (2002) *Income in Later Life: Work History Matters*. Bristol: Policy Press.

Bardasi, E., Jenkins, S. P., and Rigg, J. A. (2002) 'Retirement and the income of older people: a British perspective', *Ageing and Society*, 22: 131–59.

Barnes, C., Mercer, G., and Shakespeare, T. (1999) *Exploring Disability: A Sociological Introduction*. Cambridge: Polity.

Barth, F. (1969) *Ethnic Groups and Boundaries: The Social Organisation of Culture Difference*. London: Allen & Unwin.

Bartley, M. J., and Plewis, I. (1997) 'Does health-selective mobility account for socioeconomic differences in health? Evidence from England and Wales, 1971 to 1991', *Journal of Health and Social Behavior*, 38(4): 376–86.

Battu, H., and Zenou, Y. (2010) 'Oppositional identities and employment for ethnic minorities: evidence from England', *Economic Journal*, 120(542): F52–F71.

Battu, H., Seaman, P., and Zenou, Y. (2004) *Job Contact Networks and the Ethnic Minorities*. Stockholm: Research Institute of Industrial Economics, Working Paper no. 628.

Bauman, Z. (1973) *Culture as Praxis*. London: Routledge & Kegan Paul.

Beck, U. (1992) *Risk Society: Towards a New Modernity*. London: Sage.

Becker, S. (2003) '"Security for those who cannot": Labour's neglected welfare principle', in J. Millar (ed.) *Understanding Social Security: Issues for Policy and Practice*. Bristol: Policy Press, pp. 103–22.

Bell, B. D. (1997) 'The performance of immigrants in the United Kingdom: evidence from the GHS', *Economic Journal*, 107(441): 333–44.

Beller, E. (2009) 'Bringing intergenerational social mobility research into the twenty-first century: why mothers matter', *American Sociological Review*, 74(4): 507–28.

Beresford, P., Green, D., Lister, R., and Woodard, K. (1999) *Poverty First Hand: Poor People Speak for Themselves*. London: Child Poverty Action Group.

Bernstein, B. (1971) *Class, Codes and Control*. London: Routledge & Kegan Paul.

Bertaux, D., and Thompson, P. (eds) (1997) *Pathways to Social Class: A Qualitative Approach to Social Mobility*. Oxford: Oxford University Press.

Berthoud, R. (1997) 'Income and standards of living', in T. Modood et al. (eds) *Ethnic Minorities in Britain: Diversity and Disadvantage*. London: PSI, pp. 150–83.

— (1998) *The Incomes of Ethnic Minorities*, ISER Working Paper. University of Essex, Institute for Social and Economic Research.

— (1999) *Young Caribbean Men in the Labour Market: A Comparison with Other Ethnic Groups*. York: Joseph Rowntree Foundation.

— (2000) 'Ethnic employment penalties in Britain', *Journal of Ethnic and Migration Studies*, 26(3): 389–416.

— (2005) 'Family formation in multicultural Britain: diversity and change', in G. C. Loury, T. Modood and S. M. Teles (eds) *Ethnicity, Social Mobility and Public Policy*. Cambridge: Cambridge University Press, pp. 222–53.

— (2006) *The Employment Rates of Disabled People*. DWP Research Report no. 298. Leeds: Corporate Document Services.

— (2008) 'Disability employment penalties in Britain', *Work, Employment and Society*, 22(1): 129–48.

— (2010) 'Patterns of non-employment, and of disadvantage, in a recession', *Economic & Labour Market Review*, 12(3): 62–73.

Berthoud, R., and Blekesaune, M. (2006) *Persistent Employment Disadvantage, 1974 to 2003*, ISER Working Paper 2006-9. University of Essex, Institute for Social and Economic Research.

Berthoud, R., Lakey, J., and McKay, S. (1993) *The Economic Problems of Disabled People*. London: Policy Studies Institute.

Bettio, F., Simonazzi, A., and Villa, P. (2006) 'Change in care regimes and female migration: the "care drain" in the Mediterranean', *Journal of European Social Policy*, 16(3): 271–85.

Bhavnani, R., Mirza, H. S., and Meetoo, V. (2005) *Tackling the Roots of Racism: Lessons for Success*. Bristol: Policy Press.

Bhopal, R. S. (2007) *Ethnicity, Race and Health in Multicultural Societies*. Oxford: Oxford University Press.

Blackaby, D. H., Drinkwater, S., Leslie, D. G., and Murphy, P. D. (1997) 'A picture of male and female unemployment among Britain's ethnic minorities', *Scottish Journal of Political Economy*, 44(2): 182–97.

Blackaby, D. H., Leslie, D. G., Murphy, P. D., and O'Leary, N. C. (1999) 'Unemployment among Britain's ethnic minorities', *Manchester School*, 67: 1–20.

— (2002) 'White/ethnic minority earnings and employment differentials in Britain: evidence from the LFS', *Oxford Economic Papers*, 54: 270–97.

— (2005) 'Born in Britain: how are native ethnic minorities faring in the British labour market?', *Economics Letters*, 88: 370–5.

Blackburn, R. M., and Jarman, J. (2006) 'Gendered occupations: exploring the relationship between gender segregation and inequality', *International Sociology*, 21(2): 289–315.

Blackwell, L., and Guinea-Martin, D. (2005) 'Occupational segregation by sex and ethnicity in England and Wales, 1991 to 2001', *Labour Market Trends*, 13(12): 501–11.

Blair, T. (2001) 'The government's agenda for the future', speech, 8 February.

Blanden, J., and Machin, S. (2007) *Recent Changes in Intergenerational Mobility in Britain: Report for Sutton Trust*. London: Sutton Trust.

Bonnett, A., and Carrington, B. (2000) 'Fitting into categories or falling between them? Rethinking ethnic classification', *British Journal of Sociology of Education*, 21(4): 487–500.

Booth, A. L., and van Ours, J. C. (2008) 'Job satisfaction and family happiness: the part-time work puzzle', *Economic Journal*, 118(526): F77–F99.

Botcherby, S. (2006) *Pakistani, Bangladeshi and Black Caribbean Women and Employment Survey: Aspirations, Experiences and Choices*. Manchester: Equal Opportunities Commission.

Bottero, W. (2004) 'Class identities and the identity of class', *Sociology*, 38(5): 985–1003.

— (2005) *Stratification: Social Division and Inequality*. London: Routledge.

Bottero, W., and Irwin, S. (2003) 'Locating difference: class, "race" and gender, and the shaping of social inequalities', *Sociological Review*, 51(4): 463–83.

Bourdieu, P. (1977) *Outline of a Theory of Practice*, trans. R. Nice. Cambridge: Cambridge University Press.

— (1997) 'The forms of capital', in A. Halsey et al. (eds) *Education: Culture, Economy, and Society*. Oxford: Oxford University Press.

Bourdieu, P., and Passeron, J.-C. (1977) *Reproduction in Education, Society and Culture*. London: Sage.

Bowes, A., and Sim, D. (2002) 'Patterns of residential settlement among black and minority ethnic groups', in P. Somerville and A. Steele (eds) *'Race', Housing and Social Exclusion*. London: Jessica Kingsley.

Braddock, D. L., and Parish, S. L. (2001) 'An institutional history of disability', in G. L. Albrecht, K. D. Seelman and M. Bury (eds) *Handbook of Disability Studies*. London: Sage.

Braden, J. B., Zhang, L., Zimmerman, F. J., and Sullivan, M. D. (2008) 'Employment outcomes of persons with a mental disorder and comorbid chronic pain', *Psychiatric Services*, 59(8): 878–85.

Bradley, H. (1995) *Fractured Identities: Changing Patterns of Inequality*. Cambridge: Polity.

Bradley, H., and Devadason, R. (2008) 'Fractured transitions: young adults' pathways into contemporary labour markets', *Sociology*, 42(1): 119–36.

Brah, A. (1992) 'Difference, diversity and differentiation', in J. Donald and A. Rattansi (eds) *'Race', Culture and Difference*. London: Sage.

Brah, A., and Phoenix, A. (2004) 'Ain't I a woman? Revisiting intersectionality', *Journal of International Women's Studies*, 5(3): 75–86.

Breen, R., and Goldthorpe, J. H. (1997) 'Explaining educational differentials: towards a formal rational action theory', *Rationality and Society*, 9(3): 275–305.

Brewer, M., Muriel, A., Phillips, D., and Sibieta, L. (2008) *Poverty and Inequality in the UK: 2008*. London: Institute for Fiscal Studies.

Brewer, M., Muriel, A., and Wren-Lewis, L. (2009) *Accounting for Changes in Inequality since 1968: Decomposition Analyses for Great Britain*. London: National Equality Panel/Institute for Fiscal Studies.

Brown, G. W., Harris, T. O., and Peto, J. (1973) 'Life events and psychiatric disorders, II: Nature of causal link', *Psychological Medicine*, 3: 159–76.

Brown, M. S. (2000) 'Religion and economic activity in the South Asian population', *Ethnic and Racial Studies*, 23(6): 1035–61.

Brynin, M., Longhi, S., and Martínez Pérez, Á. (2009) 'The social significance of homogamy', in M. Brynin and J. Ermisch (eds) *Changing Relationships*. London: Routledge, pp. 73–90.

Buchmann, C., and DiPrete, T. A. (2006) 'The growing female advantage in college completion: the role of parental education, family structure, and academic achievement', *American Sociological Review*, 71: 515–41.

— (2008) 'Gender inequalities in education', *Annual Review of Sociology*, 34: 319–37.

Buck, N. (2001) 'Identifying neighbourhood effects on social exclusion', *Urban Studies*, 38(12): 2251–75.

Bulmer, M. (1996) 'The ethnic group question in the 1991 census of population', in D. Coleman and J. Salt (eds) *Ethnicity in the 1991 Census*, Vol. 1: *Demographic Characteristics of the Ethnic Minority Populations*. London: HMSO, pp. 33–62.

Burchardt, T. (2000a) 'The dynamics of being disabled', *Journal of Social Policy*, 29(4): 645–68.

— (2000b) 'Social exclusion: concepts and evidence', in D. Gordon and P. Townsend (eds) *Breadline Europe: The Measurement of Poverty*. Bristol: Policy Press, pp. 385–405.

— (2002) 'Measuring social exclusion', in J. Hills, J. LeGrand and D. Piachaud (eds) *Understanding Social Exclusion*. Oxford: Oxford University Press.

— (2003) *Being and Becoming: Social Exclusion and the Onset of Disability*. CASEreport 21, London School of Economics, Centre for Analysis of Social Exclusion.

Burchardt, T., and Zaidi, A. (2005) 'Comparing incomes when needs differ: equivalization for the extra costs of disability in the UK', *Review of Income and Wealth*, 51(1): 89–114.

Burgess, S., and Greaves, E. (2009) *Test Scores, Subjective Assessment and Stereotyping of Ethnic Minorities*. Working Paper no. 09/221. Bristol: Centre for Market and Public Organisation.

Burgess, S., Wilson, D., and Worth, J. (2009) *Passing through School: The Evolution of Attainment of England's Ethnic Minorities*. Bristol: Centre for Market and Public Organisation.

Burton, J., Nandi, A., and Platt, L. (2010) 'Measuring ethnicity: challenges and opportunities for survey research', *Ethnic and Racial Studies*, 33(8): 1332–49.

Butler, J. (1990) *Gender Trouble: Feminism and the Subversion of Identity*. London: Routledge.

Butt, J., Gorbach, P., and Ahmad, B. (1991) *Equally Fair? A Report on Social Services Departments'*

Development, Implementation and Monitoring of Services for the Black and Minority Ethnic Community. London: Race Equality Unit.

Byrne, D. (2005) 'Class, culture and identity: a reflection on absences against presences', *Sociology*, 39(5): 807–16.

Callan, T., Nolan, B., and Whelan, C. T. (1993) 'Resources, deprivation and the measurement of poverty', *Journal of Social Policy*, 22(2): 141–72.

Callinicos, A. (2000) *Equality.* Cambridge: Polity.

Campbell, J., and Oliver, M. (1996) *Disability Politics: Understanding our Past, Changing our Future.* London: Routledge.

Cannadine, D. (1998) *Class in Britain.* New Haven, CT, and London: Yale University Press.

Cappellari, L., and Jenkins, S. P. (2007) 'Summarizing multiple deprivation indicators', in S. P. Jenkins and J. Micklewright (eds) *Inequality and Poverty Re-examined.* Oxford: Oxford University Press.

Card, D. (2005) 'Is the new immigration really so bad?', *Economic Journal*, 115(507): F300–F323.

Carter, B., and Fenton, S. (2009) 'Not thinking ethnicity: a critique of the ethnicity paradigm in an over-ethnicised sociology', *Journal for the Theory of Social Behaviour*, 40(1): 1–18.

CCRT (Community Cohesion Review Team) (2001) *Community Cohesion: A Report of the Independent Review Team, Chaired by Ted Cantle.* London: Home Office.

Cemlyn, S., and Clark, C. (2005) 'The social exclusion of gypsy and traveller children', in G. Preston (ed.) *At Greatest Risk: The Children Most Likely to be Poor.* London: Child Poverty Action Group, pp. 150–65.

Chance, J. (1996) 'The Irish: invisible settlers', in C. Peach (ed.) *Ethnicity in the 1991 Census*, Vol. 2: *The Ethnic Minority Populations of Great Britain.* London: HMSO, pp. 221–39.

Chandola, T. (2001) 'Ethnic and class differences in health in relation to British South Asians: using the new national statistics socio-economic classification', *Social Science and Medicine*, 51: 1285–96.

Cheng, Y. (1996) 'The Chinese: upwardly mobile', in C. Peach (ed.) *Ethnicity in the 1991 Census*, Vol. 2: *The Ethnic Minority Populations of Great Britain.* London: HMSO, pp. 161–80.

Cheng, Y., and Heath, A. (1993) 'Ethnic origins and class destinations', *Oxford Review of Education*, 19(2): 151–66.

Cheong, P. H., Edwards, R., Goulbourne, H., and Solomos, J. (2007) 'Immigration, social cohesion and social capital: a critical review', *Critical Social Policy*, 27(1): 24–49.

Chiswick, B. R. (2008) *The Economics of Language: An Introduction and Overview.* IZA Discussion Paper no. 3568. Bonn: IZA.

Clapham, D., Kemp, P., and Smith, S. (1990) *Housing and Social Policy.* Basingstoke: Macmillan.

Clark, K., and Drinkwater, S. (2000) 'Pushed out or pulled in? Self-employment among ethnic minorities in England and Wales', *Labour Economics*, 7: 603–28.

— (2002) 'Enclaves, neighbourhood effects and economic outcomes: ethnic minorities in England and Wales', *Journal of Population Economics*, 15: 5–29.

— (2007) *Ethnic Minorities in the Labour Market: Dynamics and Diversity.* Bristol: Policy Press/Joseph Rowntree Foundation.

Coleman, D., and Salt, J. (1996) 'The ethnic group question in the 1991 census: a new landmark in British social statistics', in D. Coleman and J. Salt (eds) *Ethnicity in the 1991 Census*, Vol. 1: *Demographic Characteristics of the Ethnic Minority Populations.* London: HMSO, pp. 1–32.

Coleman, J. (1988) 'Social capital in the creation of human capital', *American Journal of Sociology*, 94: S95–S120.

Connell, R. W. (2005) *Masculinities.* 2nd edn, Cambridge: Polity.

Connolly, P. (2002) *'Race' and Racism in Northern Ireland: A Review of the Research Evidence.* Belfast: Office of the First Minister and Deputy First Minister.

Cook, J. A., Razzano, L. A., Burke-Miller, J. K., Blyler, C. R., Leff, H. S., Mueser, K. T., Gold, P. B., Goldberg, R. W., Shafer, M. S., Onken, S. J., McFarlane, W. R., Donegan, K., Carey, M. A., Kaufmann, C., and Grey, D. D. (2007) 'Effects of co-occurring disorders on employment outcomes in a multi-site randomized study of supported employment for people with severe mental illness', *Journal of Rehabilitation Research and Development*, 44(6): 837–49.

Cornell, S., and Hartmann, D. (1998) *Ethnicity and Race: Making Identities in a Changing World.* Thousand Oaks, CA: Pine Forge Press.

Crenshawe, K. (1991) 'Mapping the margins: intersectionality, identity politics, and violence against women of color', *Stanford Law Review*, 43(6): 1241–99.

Crisp, R., Batty, E., Cole, I., and Robinson, D. (2009) *Work and Worklessness in Deprived Neighbourhoods: Policy Assumptions and Personal Experiences.* York: Joseph Rowntree Foundation.

Crompton, R. (1998) *Class and Stratification: An Introduction to Current Debates.* 2nd edn, Cambridge: Polity.

— (2008) *Class and Stratification.* 3rd edn, Cambridge: Polity.

Crompton, R., and Harris, F. (1998a) 'Explaining women's employment patterns: "orientations to work" revisited', *British Journal of Sociology*, 49(1): 118.

— (1998b) 'A reply to Hakim', *British Journal of Sociology*, 49(1): 144.

Crompton, R., Devine, F., Savage, M., and Scott, J. (eds) (2000) *Renewing Class Analysis.* Oxford: Blackwell.

Cuddeford, J., Bulman, J., and Glen, F. (2010) *Life Opportunities Survey User Guide.* London: Office for National Statistics.

Curtis, L. J., Dooley, M. D., and Phipps, S. A. (2004) 'Child well-being and neighbourhood quality: evidence from the Canadian National Longitudinal Survey of Children and Youth', *Social Science & Medicine*, 58(10): 1917–27.

Daffin, C. (ed.) (2009) *Wealth in Great Britain: Main Results from the Wealth and Assets Survey 2006/08.* London: Office for National Statistics.

Dale, A. (2002) 'Social exclusion of Pakistani and Bangladeshi women', *Sociological Research Online*, 7(3); www.socresonline.org.uk/7/3/dale.html.

Dale, A., and Holdsworth, C. (1998) 'Why don't minority ethnic women in Britain work part-time?', in J. O'Reilly and C. Fagan (eds) *Part-Time Prospects.* London: Routledge.

Dale, A., Williams, M., and Dodgeon, B. (1996) *Housing Deprivation and Social Change.* London: HMSO.

Dale, A., Shaheen, N., Fieldhouse, E., and Kalra, V. (2002a) 'Labour market prospects for Pakistani and Bangladeshi women', *Work, Employment and Society*, 16(1): 5–25.

— (2002b) 'Routes into education and employment for young Pakistani and Bangladeshi women in the UK', *Ethnic and Racial Studies*, 25(6): 942–68.

Dale, A., Lindley, J., and Dex, S. (2006) 'A life-course perspective on ethnic differences in women's economic activity in Britain', *European Sociological Review*, 22(4): 459–76.

Dale, R. R. (1969) *Mixed or Single-Sex School?*, Vol. 1. London: Routledge & Kegan Paul.

— (1971) *Mixed or Single-Sex School?*, Vol. 2: *Some Social Aspects.* London: Routledge & Kegan Paul.

— (1974) *Mixed or Single-Sex School?*, Vol. 3: *Attainments, Attitudes, and Overview.* London: Routledge & Kegan Paul.

Daley, P. (1996) 'Black-Africans: students who stayed', in C. Peach (ed.) *Ethnicity in the 1991 Census*, Vol. 2: *The Ethnic Minority Populations of Great Britain.* London: HMSO, pp. 44–65.

Daley, P. O. (1998) 'Black Africans in Great Britain: spatial concentration and segregation', *Urban Studies*, 35(10): 1703–24.

Davey Smith, G., Chaturvedi, N., Harding, S., Nazroo, J. Y., and Wiliams, J. (2000) 'Ethnic inequalities in health: a review of UK epidemiological evidence', *Critical Public Health*, 10(4): 375–408.

Davis, K. (2008) 'Intersectionality as buzzword: a sociology of science perspective on what makes a feminist theory successful', *Feminist Theory*, 9(1): 67–85.

DCLG (Department for Communities and Local Government) (2006) *A Decent Home: Definition and Guidance for Implementation.* London: DCLG.

— (2009) *English House Condition Survey 2007: Annual Report.* London: DCLG.

DCSF (Department for Children Schools and Families) (2007) *National Curriculum Assessment, GCSE and Equivalent Attainment and Post-16 Attainment by Pupil Characteristics, in England 2006/07.* Statistical First Release, SFR38/2007. London: DCSF.

— (2008) *Longitudinal Study of Young People in England: The Activities and Experiences of 16 Year Olds: England 2007.* London: DCSF.

— (2009) *Youth Cohort Study & Longitudinal Study of Young People in England: The Activities and Experiences of 17 Year Olds: England 2008*. London: DCSF.

Dearden, L., Mesnard, A., and Shaw, J. (2006) 'Ethnic differences in birth outcomes in England', *Fiscal Studies*, 27(1): 17–46.

Del Bono, E., and Galindo-Rueda, F. (2006) *The Long Term Impacts of Compulsory Schooling: Evidence from a Natural Experiment in School Leaving Dates*, ISER Working Paper 2006-44. University of Essex, Institute for Social and Economic Research.

DES (Department for Education and Skills) (2004) *Youth Cohort Study: The Activities and Experiences of 18 Year Olds: England and Wales 2004*. National Statistics First Release, SFR 43/2004. London: DES.

— (2006a) *Statistics of Education: Trends in Attainment Gaps: 2005*. London: DES.

— (2006b) *Youth Cohort Study: The Activities and Experiences of 18 Year Olds: England and Wales 2006*, SFR 47/2006. London: DES.

— (2007) *Gender and Education: The Evidence on Pupils in England*. London: DES.

Devine, F. (1992) 'Social identities, class identity and political perspectives', *Sociological Review*, 40(2): 229–52.

Devine, F., Savage, M., Scott, J., and Crompton, R. (eds) (2005) *Rethinking Class: Cultures, Identities and Lifestyles*. London: Palgrave Macmillan.

Diez Roux, A. V. (2001) 'Investigating neighborhood and area effects on health', *American Journal of Public Health*, 91(11): 1783–9.

Disney, R., and Webb, S. (1991) 'Why are there so many long term sick in Britain?', *Economic Journal*, 101: 252–62.

Dobbs, J., Green, H., and Zealey, L. (eds) (2006) *Focus on Ethnicity and Religion*. Basingstoke: Palgrave Macmillan.

Dooley, M., Lipman, E., and Stewart, J. (2005) 'Exploring the good mother hypothesis: do child outcomes vary with the mother's share of income?', *Canadian Public Policy*, 31(2): 123–44.

Dorling, D. (2005) *Human Geography of the UK*. London: Sage.

Dorling, D., Ford, J., Holmans, A., C., S., Thomas, B., and Wilcox, S. (2005) *The Great Divide: An Analysis of Housing Inequality*. London: Shelter.

Dorling, D., Rigby, J., Wheeler, B., Ballas, D., Thomas, B., Fahmy, E., Gordon, D., and Lupton, R. (2007) *Poverty, Wealth and Place across Britain, 1968 to 2005*. Bristol: Policy Press.

Dorsett, R. (1998) *Ethnic Minorities in the Inner City*. Bristol: Policy Press/Joseph Rowntree Foundation.

Drever, F., and Whitehead, M. (eds) (1997) *Health Inequalities: Decennial Supplement*. London: Stationery Office.

Drew, D., Gray, J., and Sporton, D. (1997) 'Ethnic differences in the educational participation of 16–19 year olds', in V. Karn (ed.) *Ethnicity in the 1991 Census*, Vol. 4: *Employment, Education and Housing among the Ethnic Minority Populations of Britain*. London: Stationery Office, pp. 17–28.

Drew, E., and Emerek, R. (1998) 'Employment, flexibility and gender', in E. Drew, R. Emerek and E. Mahon (eds) *Women, Work and the Family in Europe*. London: Routledge.

Duncan, G. G., Brooks-Gunn, J., Yeung, W. J., and Smith, J. R. (1998) 'How much does childhood poverty affect the life chances of children?', *American Sociological Review*, 63(3): 406–23.

Dustmann, C., and Fabbri, F. (2003) 'Language proficiency and labour market performance of immigrants in the UK', *Economic Journal*, 113(489): 695–717.

Dustmann, C., and Theodoropoulos, N. (2006) *Ethnic Minority Immigrants and their Children in Britain*, CReAM Working Paper. London: UCL.

DWP (Department for Work and Pensions) (2005) *Department for Work and Pensions Five Year Strategy: Opportunity and Security throughout Life*. London: Stationery Office.

— (2008) *Households below Average Income: An Analysis of the Income Distribution 1994/95–2006/07*. London: DWP.

— (2009) *Households below Average Income: An Analysis of the Income Distribution 1994/9 –2007/08*. London: DWP.

Eade, J., Vamplew, T., and Peach, C. (1996) 'The Bangladeshis: the encapsulated community', in

C. Peach (ed.) *Ethnicity in the 1991 Census*, Vol. 2: *The Ethnic Minority Populations of Great Britain*. London: HMSO, pp. 150–60.

Erikson, R., and Goldthorpe, J. H. (1992) *The Constant Flux: A Study of Class Mobility in Industrial Societies*. Oxford: Clarendon Press.

Ermisch, J., Francesconi, M., and Pevalin, D. J. (2001) *Outcomes for Children of Poverty*. London: Department for Work and Pensions.

— (2004) 'Parental partnership and joblessness in childhood and their influence on young people's outcomes', *Journal of the Royal Statistical Society A*, 167(1): 69–101.

Evandrou, M. (2000) 'Social inequalities in later life', *Population Trends*, 110: 11–18.

Fagnani, J. (1998) 'Recent changes in family policy in France: political trade-offs and economic constraints', in E. Drew, R. Emerek and E. Mahon (ed.) *Women, Work and the Family in Europe*. London: Routledge, pp. 58–65.

Fausto-Sterling, A. (2000) *Sexing the Body: Gender Politics and the Construction of Sexuality*. New York: Basic Books.

Feinstein, L. (2003a) 'Inequality in the early cognitive development of British children in the 1970 cohort', *Economica*, 70(1): 73–97.

— (2003b) 'Not just the early years: the need for a developmental perspective for equality of opportunity', *New Economy*, 10(4): 213–18.

Fenton, S. (2010) *Ethnicity*. 2nd edn, Cambridge: Polity.

Finney, N., and Simpson, L. (2009) 'Population dynamics: the roles of natural change and migration in producing the ethnic mosaic', *Journal of Ethnic and Migration Studies*, 35(9): 1479–96.

Fish, S. (1994) *There's No Such Thing as Free Speech*. New York: Oxford University Press.

Fisher, K., Egerton, M., Gershuny, J. I., and Robinson, A. J. P. (2007) 'Gender convergence in the American Heritage Time Use Study (AHTUS)', *Social Indicators Research*, 82(1): 1–33.

Foucault, M. ([1969] 1972) *The Archaeology of Knowledge*. London: Tavistock.

Francis, B., and Archer, L. (2005) 'British-Chinese pupils' and parents' constructions of the value of education', *British Educational Research Journal*, 31(1): 89–107.

Franklin, J. (ed.) (1997) *Equality*. London: IPPR.

Franzen, A., and Hangartner, D. (2006) 'Social networks and labour market outcomes: the non-monetary benefits of social capital', *European Sociological Review*, 22(4): 353–68.

Fraser, N. (2000) 'Rethinking recognition', *New Left Review*, 3(May–June): 107–20.

Frijters, P., Shields, M. A., and Wheatley Price, S. (2005) 'Job search methods and their success: a comparison of immigrants and natives in the UK', *Economic Journal*, 115(507): F359–F376.

Galster, G. C., Metzger, K., and Waite, R. (1999) 'Neighbourhood opportunity structures and immigrants' socioeconomic advancement', *Journal of Housing Research*, 10(1): 95–127.

Ganzeboom, H. B. G., Treiman, D. J., and Ultee, W. C. (1991) 'Comparative intergenerational stratification research: three generations and beyond', *Annual Review of Sociology*, 17: 277–302.

Gardiner, K. ([1993] 1997) 'A survey of income inequality over the last twenty years: how does the UK compare?', in P. Gottschalk, B. Gustafsson and E. Palmer (eds) *Changing Patterns in the Distribution of Economic Welfare*. Cambridge: Cambridge University Press, pp. 36–59.

Georgiadis, A., and Manning, A. (forthcoming) 'Change and continuity among minority communities in Britain', *Journal of Population Economics*.

Gershuny, J. (2000) *Changing Times: Work and Leisure in Postindustrial Society*. Oxford: Oxford University Press.

— (2004) 'Domestic equipment does not increase domestic work: a response to Bittman, Rice and Wajcman', *British Journal of Sociology*, 55(3): 425–31.

Giddens, A. (1984) *The Constitution of Society: Outline of the Theory of Structuration*. Berkeley: University of California Press.

Gillborn, D., and Mirza, H. S. (2000) *Educational Inequality: Mapping Race, Class and Gender: A Synthesis of Research Evidence*. London: OFSTED.

Gilroy, P. (2000) *Between Camps: Race, Identity and Nationalism at the End of the Colour Line*. Harmondsworth: Penguin.

Ginn, J., and Arber, S. L. (1996) 'Patterns of employment, gender and pensions: the effect of work history on older women's non-state pensions', *Work, Employment and Society*, 10: 469–90.

Glass, D. V. (ed.) (1954) *Social Mobility in Britain*. London: Routledge & Kegan Paul.

Glendinning, C., and Millar, J. (1992) '"It all really starts in the family": gender divisions and poverty', in C. Glendinning and J. Millar (eds) *Women and Poverty in Britain: the 1990s*. Hemel Hempstead: Harvester Wheatsheaf, pp. 3–10.

Glucksmann, M. (1990) *Women Assemble: Women Workers and the 'New Industries' in Inter-War Britain*. London: Routledge.

— (1995) 'Why "work"? Gender and the "total social organization of labour"', *Gender, Work & Organization*, 2(2): 63–75.

— (2000) *Cottons and Casuals: The Gendered Organisation of Labour in Time and Space*. Durham: Sociologypress.

— (2009) 'Formations, connections and divisions of labour', *Sociology*, 43(5): 878–95.

Goldthorpe, J. H., and Marshall, G. (1992) 'The promising future of class analysis', *Sociology*, 26(3): 381–400.

Goldthorpe, J. H., and Mills, C. (2008) 'Trends in intergenerational class mobility in modern Britain: evidence from national surveys, 1972–2005', *National Institute Economic Review*, 205(1): 83–100.

Goldthorpe, J. H., and Payne, C. (1986) 'Trends in intergenerational class mobility in England and Wales 1972–8', *Sociology*, 20: 1–24.

Goldthorpe, J. H., Llewellyn, C., and Payne, C. (1980) *Social Mobility and Class Structure in Modern Britain*. Oxford: Clarendon Press.

— (1987) *Social Mobility and Class Structure in Modern Britain*. 2nd edn, Oxford: Clarendon Press.

Gonzalez, M. J., Jurado, T., and Naldini, N. (2000) *Gender Inequalities in Southern Europe: Women, Work and Welfare in the 1990s*. London: Frank Cass.

Goodman, A., Johnson, P., and Webb, S. (1997) *Inequality in the UK*. Oxford: Oxford University Press.

Goodman, A., Sibieta, L., and Washbrook, E. (2009) *Inequalities in Educational Outcomes among Children Aged 3 to 16*. London: Institute for Fiscal Studies & Centre for Market and Public Organisation.

Goodwin, M. (1995) 'Poverty in the city', in C. Philo (ed.) *Off the Map: The Social Geography of Poverty in the UK*. London: Child Poverty Action Group.

Gordon, D. (2006) 'The concept and measurement of poverty', in C. Pantazis, D. Gordon and R. Levitas (eds) *Poverty and Social Exclusion in Britain: The Millennium Survey*. Bristol: Policy Press, pp. 29–69.

Gordon, D., and Pantazis, C. (1997) *Breadline Britain in the 1990s*. Aldershot: Ashgate.

Gordon, D., Levitas, R., Pantazis, C., Patsios, D., Payne, S., Townsend, P., Adelman, L., Ashworth, K., Middleton, S., Bradshaw, J., and Williams, J. (2000) *Poverty and Social Exclusion in Britain*. York: Joseph Rowntree Foundation.

Goulbourne, H. (1998) *Race Relations in Britain since 1945*. Basingstoke: Macmillan.

Graham, H. (2009) *Understanding Health Inequalities*. Maidenhead: Open University Press.

Gregg, P., and Wadsworth, J. (1996) 'More work in fewer households?', in J. Hills (ed.) *New Inequalities: The Changing Distribution of Income and Wealth in the United Kingdom*. Cambridge: Cambridge University Press, pp. 181–207.

Gregg, P., Harkness, S., and Machin, S. (1999) *Child Development and Family Incomes*. York: York Publishing Services.

Gregg, P., Waldfogel, J., and Washbrook, E. (2005) *Expenditure Patterns Post-Welfare Reform in the UK: Are Low-Income Families Starting to Catch Up?*, CASEpaper 99. London School of Economics, Centre for Analysis of Social Exclusion.

Güveli, A. (2006) 'New social classes within the service class in the Netherlands and Britain: adjusting the EGP class schema for the technocrats and the social and cultural specialists', ICS dissertation, Radboud University, Nijmegen.

Hakim, C. (1991) 'Grateful slaves and self-made women: fact and fantasy in women's work orientations', *European Sociological Review*, 7(2): 101–21.

— (1995) 'Labour mobility and employment stability: rhetoric and reality on the sex differential in labour-market behaviour', *European Sociological Review*, 12(1): 1–31.

— (1998) 'Developing a sociology for the twenty-first century: preference theory', *British Journal of Sociology*, 49(1): 137–43.

— (2000) *Work-Lifestyle Choices in the 21st Century: Preference Theory*. Oxford: Oxford University Press.

Halsey, A. H., Lauder, H., Brown, P., and Wells, A. S. (eds) (1997) *Education: Culture, Economy, and Society*. Oxford: Oxford University Press.

Harding, S., Rosato, M. G., and Cruickshank, J. K. (2004) 'Lack of change in birthweights of infants by generational status among Indian, Pakistani, Bangladeshi, black Caribbean, and black African mothers in a British cohort study', *International Journal of Epidemiology*, 33(6): 1279–85.

Harries, B., Richardson, L., and Soteri-Proctor, A. (2008) *Housing Aspirations for a New Generation: Perspectives from White and South Asian British Women*. Coventry: Joseph Rowntree Foundation/ Chartered Institute of Housing.

Harrison, M. (2003) 'Housing black and minority ethnic communities: diversity and constraint', in D. Mason (ed.) *Explaining Ethnic Differences: Changing Patterns of Disadvantage in Britain*. Bristol: Policy Press, pp. 105–19.

Hatton, T. J., and Bailey, R. E. (2000) 'Seebohm Rowntree and the postwar poverty puzzle', *Economic History Review*, new series, 53(3): 517–43.

Hayek, F. A. (1945) *The Road to Serfdom*. London: Routledge.

Haywood, C., and Mac an Ghaill, M. (2003) *Men and Masculinities*. Buckingham: Open University Press.

Heath, A. (2001) *Ethnic Minorities in the Labour Market*. London: Cabinet Office.

Heath, A., and Cheung, S. Y. (2006) *Ethnic Penalties in the Labour Market: Employers and Discrimination*. Leeds: Department for Work and Pensions.

— (eds) (2007) *Unequal Chances: Ethnic Minorities in Western Labour Markets*. Oxford: Oxford University Press.

Heath, A., and Clifford, P. (1996) 'Class inequalities and educational reform in twentieth century Britain', in D. J. Lee and B. S. Turner (eds) *Conflicts about Class*. London: Longman.

Heath, A., and McMahon, D. (1997) 'Education and occupational attainments: the impact of ethnic origins', in V. Karn (ed.) *Ethnicity in the 1991 Census*, Vol. 4: *Employment, Education and Housing among the Ethnic Minority Populations of Britain*. London: HMSO, pp. 91–113.

— (2005) 'Social mobility of ethnic minorities', in G. C. Loury, T. Modood and S. M. Teles (eds) *Ethnicity, Social Mobility and Public Policy: Comparing the US and the UK*. Cambridge: Cambridge University Press.

Heath, A., and Payne, C. (2000) 'Social mobility', in A. H. Halsey and J. Webb (eds) *Twentieth-Century British Social Trends*. Basingstoke: Macmillan, pp. 254–78.

Heath, A., and Ridge, J. (1983) 'Social mobility of ethnic minorities', *Journal of Biosocial Sciences*, Supplement no. 8: 169–84.

Heath, A., and Yu, S. (2005) 'Explaining ethnic minority disadvantage', in A. F. Heath, J. Ermisch and D. Gallie (eds) *Understanding Social Change*. Oxford: Oxford University Press, pp. 187–225.

Hebson, G. (2009) 'Renewing class analysis in studies of the workplace: a comparison of working-class and middle-class women's aspirations and identities', *Sociology*, 43(1): 27–44.

Henderson, J. W., and Karn, V. A. (1987) *Race, Class, and State Housing: Inequality and the Allocation of Public Housing in Britain*. Aldershot: Gower.

Henderson, S. J., Holland, J., McGrellis, S., Sharpe, S., and Thomson, R. (2007) *Inventing Adulthoods: A Biographical Approach to Youth Transitions*. London: Sage.

Hennock, E. P. (1991) 'Concepts of poverty in the British social surveys from Charles Booth to Arthur Bowley', in M. Bulmer, K. Bales and K. Kish Sklar (eds) *The Social Survey in Historical Perspective*. Cambridge: Cambridge University Press.

Hickman, M. J. (2005) 'Ruling an empire, governing a multinational state: the impact of Britain's historical legacy on the ethno-racial regime', in G. C. Loury, T. Modood and S. M. Teles (eds) *Ethnicity, Social Mobility and Public Policy: Comparing the US and the UK.* Cambridge: Cambridge University Press, pp. 21–49.

Hills, J. (2004) *Inequality and the State.* Oxford: Oxford University Press.

Hills, J., Le Grand, J., and Piachaud, D. (eds) (2002) *Understanding Social Exclusion.* Oxford: Oxford University Press.

Hills, J., Brewer, M., Jenkins, S., Lister, R., Lupton, R., Machin, S., Mills, C., Modood, T., Rees, T., and Riddell, S. (2010) *An Anatomy of Economic Inequality in the UK: Report of the National Equality Panel.* London: Government Equalities Office/Centre for Analysis of Social Exclusion.

Hollenbeck, K., and Kimmel, J. (2008) 'Differences in the returns to education for males by disability status and age of disability onset', *Southern Economic Journal*, 74(3): 707–24.

Hout, M. (2003) 'The inequality-mobility paradox: the lack of correlation between social mobility and equality', *New Economy*, 10(4): 205–7.

Iacovou, M. (2002) 'Regional differences in the transition to adulthood', *Annals of the American Academy of Political and Social Science*, 580: 40–68.

Illich, I. (1982) *Gender.* New York: Pantheon Books.

Irwin, S. (2003) 'Interdependencies, values and the reshaping of difference: gender and generation at the birth of twentieth-century modernity', *British Journal of Sociology*, 54(4): 565–84.

— (2005) *Reshaping Social Life.* London: Routledge.

— (2009) 'Locating where the action is: quantitative and qualitative lenses on families, schooling and structures of social inequality', *Sociology*, 43(6): 1123–40.

Jacobs, S. (1995) 'Changing patterns of sex segregated occupations throughout the life-course', *European Sociological Review*, 11: 157–71.

Jacobson, J. (1997) 'Religion and ethnicity: dual and alternative sources of identity among young British Pakistanis', *Ethnic and Racial Studies*, 20: 238–56.

— (1998) *Islam in Transition: Religion and Identity among British Pakistani Youth.* London: Routledge.

Jahoda, M., Lazarsfeld, P. F., and Zeisel, H. (1972) *Marienthal: The Sociography of an Unemployed Community.* London: Tavistock.

Jenkins, S. (1995) 'Accounting for inequality trends: decomposition analyses for the UK, 1971–86', *Economica*, 62(245): 29–63.

Jenkins, S. P. (2009a) 'Marital splits and income changes over the longer term', in J. F. Ermisch and M. Bryning (eds) *Changing Relationships.* London: Routledge, pp. 217–36.

— (2009b) *Spaghetti Unravelled: A Model-Based Description of Differences in Income-Age Trajectories*, ISER Working Paper 2009-30. University of Essex, Institute for Social and Economic Research.

— (2011) *Changing Fortunes.* Oxford: Oxford University Press.

Jenkins, S. P., and Micklewright, J. (eds) (2007) *Inequality and Poverty Re-examined.* Oxford: Oxford University Press.

Jenkins, S. P., and Rigg, J. A. (2001) *The Dynamics of Poverty in Britain.* London: Department for Work and Pensions.

— (2004) 'Disability and disadvantage: selection, onset, and duration effects', *Journal of Social Policy*, 33(3): 479–501.

Jensen, A.-M. (1999) 'Partners and parents in Europe: a gender divide', *Comparative Social Research*, 18: 1–30.

Jones, M. K., Latreille, P. L., and Sloane, P. J. (2006a) 'Disability, gender and the labour market in Wales', *Regional Studies*, 40(8): 823–45.

— (2006b) 'Disability, gender, and the British labour market', *Oxford Economic Papers*, new series, 58(3): 407–49.

Jones, P., and Dickerson, A. (2007) *Poor Returns: Winners and Losers in the Job Market.* Manchester: Equal Opportunities Commission.

Karlsen, S., and Nazroo, J. (2002) 'Relation between racial discrimination, social class, and health among ethnic minority groups', *American Journal of Public Health*, 92(4): 624–31.

— (2006) 'Defining and measuring ethnicity and "race": theoretical and conceptual issues for health and social care research', in J. Y. Nazroo (ed.) *Health and Social Research in Multiethnic Societies.* Abingdon: Routledge, pp. 20–38.

Karn, V., Kemeny, J., and Williams, P. (1985) *Home Ownership in the Inner City: Salvation or Despair?* Aldershot: Gower.

Karn, V., Dale, A., and Ratcliffe, P. (1997) 'Introduction: using the 1991 census to study ethnicity', in V. Karn (ed.) *Ethnicity in the 1991 Census,* Vol. 4: *Employment, Education and Housing among the Ethnic Minority Populations of Britain.* London: Stationery Office, pp. xi–xxix.

Kaye, H. S. (2009) 'Stuck at the bottom rung: occupational characteristics of workers with disabilities', *Journal of Occupational Rehabilitation,* 19(2): 115–28.

Kelly, Y., Panico, L., Bartley, M., Marmot, M., Nazroo, J., and Sacker, A. (2009) 'Why does birthweight vary among ethnic groups in the UK? Findings from the Millennium Cohort Study', *Journal of Public Health,* 31(1): 131–7.

Kempson, E. (1999) *Overcrowding in Bangladeshi Households: A Case Study of Tower Hamlets.* London: Policy Studies Institute.

Kitchen, S., Michaelson, J., and Wood, N. (2006) *2005 Citizenship Survey: Race and Faith Topic Report.* London: Department for Communities and Local Government.

Klein, R. (1995) *The New Politics of the NHS.* Harlow: Pearson Education.

Korupp, S. E., Ganzeboom, H. B. G., and van der Lippe, T. (2002) 'Do mothers matter? A comparison of models of the influence of mothers' and fathers' educational and occupational status on children's educational attainment', *Quality & Quantity,* 36(1): 17–42.

Kyambi, S. (2005) *Beyond Black and White: Mapping New Immigrant Communities.* London: Institute for Public Policy Research.

Lader, D., Short, S., and Gershuny, J. (2006) *The 2005 Time Use Survey: How We Spend our Time.* London: Office for National Statistics.

Lambert, P., and Bihagen, E. (2007) 'Concepts and measures: empirical evidence on the interpretation of ESeC and their occupation-based social classifications', paper presented at the International Sociological Association Research Committee 28 on Social Stratification and Mobility, Montreal, 14–17 August.

Lambert, P., Prandy, K., and Bottero, W. (2007) 'By slow degrees: two centuries of social reproduction and mobility in Britain', *Sociological Research Online,* 12(1); www.socresonline.org.uk/12/1/prandy.html.

Lauglo, J. (2000) 'Social capital trumping class and cultural capital? Engagement with school among immigrant youth', in S. Baron, J. Field and T. Schuller (eds) *Social Capital: Critical Perspectives.* Oxford: Oxford University Press, pp. 142–67.

Laurie, H., and Gershuny, J. (2000) 'Couples, work and money', in R. Berthoud and J. Gershuny (eds) *Seven Years in the Lives of British Families: Evidence on the Dynamics of Social Change from the British Household Panel Survey.* Bristol: Policy Press.

Law, I. (1996) *Racism, Ethnicity and Social Policy.* New York: Prentice Hall.

Lawler, S. (2005) 'Disgusted subjects: the making of middle-class identities', *Sociological Review,* 53(3): 429–46.

Le Feuvre, N. (1999) 'Gender, occupational feminization, and reflexivity: a cross-national perspective', in R. Crompton (ed.) *Restructuring Gender Relations and Employment: The Decline of the Male Breadwinner.* Oxford: Oxford University Press, pp. 150–78.

Le Roux, B., Rouanet, H., Savage, M., and Warde, A. (2008) 'Class and cultural division in the UK', *Sociology,* 42(6): 1049–71.

Lehmann, W. (2009) 'Becoming middle class: how working-class university students draw and transgress moral class boundaries', *Sociology,* 43(4): 631–47.

Leitner, S. (2003) 'Varieties of familialism: the caring function of the family in comparative perspective', *European Societies,* 5(4): 353–75.

Letki, N. (2008) 'Does diversity erode social cohesion? Social capital and race in British neighbourhoods', *Political Studies,* 56(1): 99–126.

Levey, G. B. (2009) 'Secularism and religion in a multicultural age', in G. B. Levey and T. Modood (eds) *Secularism, Religion and Multicultural Citizenship*. Cambridge: Cambridge University Press, pp. 1–24.

Levitas, R. (1998) *The Inclusive Society: Social Exclusion and New Labour*. Basingstoke: Macmillan.

— (2005) *The Inclusive Society? Social Exclusion and New Labour*. 2nd edn, London: Palgrave Macmillan.

— (2006) 'The concept and measurement of social exclusion', in C. Pantazis, D. Gordon and R. Levitas (eds) *Poverty and Social Exclusion in Britain: The Millennium Survey*. Bristol: Policy Press, pp. 123–60.

Lewis, J. (1984) *Women in England, 1870–1950: Sexual Divisions and Social Change*. Brighton: Wheatsheaf.

— (1992) 'Gender and the development of welfare regimes', *Journal of European Social Policy*, 2(3): 159–73.

— (2000) 'Family policy and the labour market in European welfare states', in J. Jenson, J. Laufer and M. Maruani (eds) *The Gendering of Inequalities: Women, Men and Work*. Aldershot: Ashgate.

— (2001) 'Family change and lone parents as a social problem', in M. May, R. Page and E. Brunsdon (eds) *Understanding Social Problems: Issues in Social Policy*. Oxford: Blackwell, pp. 37–54.

Lindley, J. (2002) 'Race or religion? The impact of religion on the employment and earnings of Britain's ethnic communities', *Journal of Ethnic and Migration Studies*, 28(3): 427–42.

— (2005) 'Explaining ethnic unemployment and activity rates: evidence from the QLFS in the 1990s and 2000s', *Bulletin of Economic Research*, 57(2): 185–203.

Lindley, J., Dale, A., and Dex, S. (2006) 'Ethnic differences in women's employment: the changing role of qualifications ', *Oxford Economic Papers*, 58: 351–78.

Lister, R. (2004) *Poverty*. Oxford: Blackwell.

Longhi, S., and Platt, L. (2008) *Pay Gaps across Equalities Areas*. Manchester: Equalities and Human Rights Commission.

Longhi, S., Nicoletti, C., and Platt, L. (2009) *Decomposing Wage Gaps across the Pay Distribution: Investigating Inequalities of Ethno-Religious Groups and Disabled People*, ISER Working Paper 2009-32. University of Essex, Institute for Social and Economic Research.

Loury, G. C. (2000) 'What's next? Some reflections on the IRP poverty conference, "Understanding poverty in America: progress and problems": poverty and race', *Focus*, 21(2): 59–60.

Lupton, R., Tunstall, R., Sigle-Rushton, W., Obolenskaya, P., Sabates, R., Meschi, E., Kneale, D., and Salter, E. (2009) *Growing Up in Social Housing: A Profile of Four Generations from 1946 to the Present Day*. York: Joseph Rowntree Foundation.

Lyon, D., and Glucksmann, M. (2008) 'Comparative configurations of care work across Europe', *Sociology*, 42(1): 101–18.

McCall, L. (2005) 'The complexity of intersectionality', *Signs: Journal of Women in Culture and Society*, 30(3): 1771–800.

Machin, S., and McNally, S. (2006) *Gender and Student Achievement in English Schools*. London: London School of Economics, Centre for the Economics of Education.

Machin, S., Murphy, R., and Soobedar, Z. (2009) *Differences in Labour Market Gains from Higher Education Participation: Report for the National Equality Panel*. London: Government Equalities Office.

Mack, J., and Lansley, S. (1985) *Poor Britain*. London: Allen & Unwin.

McMahon, W., and Roberts, R. (2008) *Ethnicity, Harm and Crime: A Discussion Paper*. London: Centre for Crime and Justice Studies.

McRae, S. (2003) 'Constraints and choices in mothers' employment careers: a consideration of Hakim's preference theory', *British Journal of Sociology*, 54(3): 317–38.

Malpass, P., and Murie, A. (1999) *Housing Policy and Practice*. 5th edn, Basingstoke: Macmillan.

Manning, A., and Petrongolo, B. (2008) 'The part-time pay penalty for women in Britain', *Economic Journal*, 118(536): F28–F51.

Manning, A., and Roy, S. (2007) *Culture Clash or Culture Club? The Identity and Attitudes of Immigrants in Britain*, CEP Discussion Paper no. 790. London School of Economics, Centre for Economic Performance.

Marini, M. M., and Greenberger, E. (1978) 'Sex-differences in occupational aspirations and expectations', *Sociology of Work and Occupations*, 5: 147–78.

Marmot, M. C. (2010) *Fair Society, Healthy Lives: The Marmot Review*, www.ucl.ac.uk/marmotreview.

Marshall, G., Swift, A., and Roberts, S. (1997) *Against the Odds? Social Class and Social Justice in Industrial Societies*. Oxford: Clarendon Press.

Mason, D. (1995) *Race and Ethnicity in Modern Britain*. Oxford: Oxford University Press.

— (2000) *Race and Ethnicity in Modern Britain*. 2nd edn, Oxford: Oxford University Press.

Mayer, K. U. (2009) 'New directions in life course research', *Annual Review of Sociology*, 35: 413–33.

Meen, G., Gibb, K., Goody, J., McGrath, T., and Mackinnon, J. (2005) *Economic Segregation in England: Causes, Consequences and Policy*. Bristol: Policy Press.

Miller, D. (1997) 'What kind of equality should the left pursue?', in J. Franklin (ed.) *Equality*. London: IPPR, pp.83–100.

Miller, R. (1998) 'Unemployment as a mobility status', *Work, Employment and Society*, 12(4): 695–711.

Mirza, H. S. (2008) 'Ethnic minority women: a prospectus for the future', in Z. Moosa (ed.) *Seeing Double: Race and Gender in Ethnic Minority Women's Lives*. London: Fawcett Society, pp. 5–30.

Modood, T. (1992) *Not Easy Being British: Colour, Culture and Citizenship*. London: Runnymede Trust.

— (1997) 'Employment', in T. Modood et al. (eds) *Ethnic Minorities in Britain: Diversity and Disadvantage*. London: Policy Studies Institute, pp. 83–149.

— (1998) 'Anti-essentialism, multiculturalism and the "recognition" of religious groups', *Journal of Political Philosophy*, 6(4): 378–99.

— (2004) 'Capitals, ethnic identity and educational qualifications', *Cultural Trends*, 12(2): 1–19.

— (2009) 'Muslims, religious equality and secularism', in G. B. Levey and T. Modood (eds) *Secularism, Religion and Multicultural Citizenship*. Cambridge: Cambridge University Press, pp. 164–85.

Modood, T., Berthoud, R., Lakey, J., Nazroo, J., Smith, P., Virdee, S. and Beishon, S. (1997) *Ethnic Minorities in Britain: Diversity and Disadvantage*. London: Policy Studies Institute.

Modood, T., Berthoud, R. and Nazroo, J. (2002) 'Race, racism and ethnicity: a response to Ken Smith', *Sociology*, 36(2): 419–27.

Murray, C. A. (1984) *Losing Ground: American Social Policy, 1950–1980*. New York: Basic Books.

Murray, C. A., and Lister, R. (1996) *Charles Murray and the Underclass: The Developing Debate*. London: IEA Health and Welfare Unit in association with the Sunday Times.

Nandi, A., and Platt, L. (2009) *Developing Ethnic Identity Questions for Understanding Society: The UK Household Longitudinal Study*, ISER Working Paper 2009-03. University of Essex, Institute for Social and Economic Research.

— (2010) *Ethnic Minority Women's Poverty and Economic Well Being*. London: Government Equalities Office.

National Audit Office (2008) *Increasing Employment Rates for Ethnic Minorities*. London: Stationery Office.

Nazroo, J. (1998) *The Health of Britain's Ethnic Minorities*. London: Policy Studies Institute.

— (2003a) 'Patterns of and explanations for ethnic inequalities in health', in D. Mason (ed.) *Explaining Ethnic Differences: Changing Patterns of Disadvantage in Britain*. Bristol: Policy Press, pp. 87–103.

— (2003b) 'The structuring of ethnic inequalities in health: economic position, racial discrimination, and racism', *American Journal of Public Health*, 93(2): 277–84.

Nazroo, J. Y., and Williams, D. R. (2005) 'The social determination of ethnic/racial inequalities in health', in M. Marmot and R. G. Wilkinson (eds) *Social Determinants of Health*. 2nd edn, Oxford: Oxford University Press, pp. 238–66.

Neckerman, K. M., and Torche, F. (2007) 'Inequality: causes and consequences', *American Review of Sociology*, 33: 335–57.

Nickell, S. (2004) 'Poverty and worklessness in Britain', *Economic Journal*, 114: C1–C25.

Nicoletti, C., and Ermisch J. (2007) 'Intergenerational earnings mobility: changes across cohorts in Britain', *B.E. Journal of Economic Analysis and Policy* 7(2): 1–37.

Nielsen-Westergaard, N., Agerbo, E., Eriksson, T., and Mortensen, P. B. (1999) *Mental Illness and*

Labour Market Outcomes: Employment and Earnings, paper no, 99-04. Aarhus, Denmark: Centre for Labour Market and Social Research; http://ideas.repec.org/p/fth/clmsre/99-04.html.

Nolan, B., and Whelan, C. (1996) *Resources, Deprivation and Poverty*. Oxford: Clarendon Press.

Nozick, R. (1974) *Anarchy, State, and Utopia*. New York: Basic Books.

Oakley, A. (1972) *Sex, Gender and Society*. London: Temple Smith.

— (1974a) *Housewife: High Value, Low Cost*. London: Allen Lane.

— (1974b) *The Sociology of Housework*. London: Robertson.

— (2005) *The Ann Oakley Reader: Gender, Women and Social Science*. Bristol: Policy Press.

Oliver, M. (1990) *The Politics of Disablement*. London: MacMillan.

— (2009) *Understanding Disability: From Theory to Practice*. 2nd edn, Basingstoke: Palgrave Macmillan.

Olsen, W., and Walby, S. (2004) *Modelling Gender Pay Gaps*. EOC Working Paper no. 17. Manchester: Equal Opportunities Commission.

ONS (Office for National Statistics) (2008) *Focus on Gender*. London: ONS.

— (2009) 'Life expectancy', www.statistics.gov.uk (accessed January 2010).

Open Society Institute (2004) *Aspirations and Reality: British Muslims and the Labour Market*. Budapest and New York: Open Society Institute.

Orton, M., and Rowlingson, K. (2007) *Public Attitudes to Economic Inequality*. York: Joseph Rowntree Foundation.

Owen, D. (1996a) 'Black-other: the melting pot', in C. Peach (ed.) *Ethnicity in the 1991 Census*, Vol. 2: *The Ethnic Minority Populations of Great Britain*. London: HMSO, pp. 66–94.

— (1996b) 'The other-Asians: the salad bowl', in C. Peach (ed.) *Ethnicity in the 1991 Census*, Vol. 2: *The Ethnic Minority Populations of Great Britain*. London: HMSO, pp. 181–205.

Pagan, R. (2009) 'Self-employment among people with disabilities: evidence for Europe', *Disability & Society*, 24(2): 217–29.

Panel on Fair Access to the Professions (2009) *Unleashing Aspiration: The Final Report of the Panel on Fair Access to the Professions*. London: Cabinet Office.

Pantazis, C., Gordon, D., and Levitas, R. (eds) (2006) *Poverty and Social Exclusion in Britain: The Millennium Survey*. Bristol: Policy Press.

Paoli, P., and Merllié, D. (2001) *Third European Survey on Working Conditions, 2000*. Dublin: European Foundation for the Improvement of Living and Working Conditions.

Parekh, B. (2000) *The Future of Multi-Ethnic Britain*. London: Profile Books [Parekh Report].

Parent-Thirion, A., Fernández Macías, E., Hurley, J., and Vermeylen, G. (2007) *Fourth European Working Conditions Survey*. Dublin: European Foundation for the Improvement of Living and Working Conditions.

Park, A., Curtice, J., Thomson, K., Phillips, M., Clery, E., and Butt, S. (eds) (2010) *British Social Attitudes: 26th Report*. London: Sage.

Parliamentary Office of Science and Technology (2007) *Ethnicity and Health. Postnote*, no. 276.

Passerini, L., Lyon, D., Capussotti, E., and Laliotou, I. (eds) (2007) *Women Migrants from East to West: Gender, Mobility and Belonging in Contemporary Europe*. Oxford: Berghahn Books.

Pateman, C. (1988) *The Sexual Contract*. Stanford, CA: Stanford University Press.

Payne, G. (ed.) (2006) *Social Divisions*. 2nd edn, Basingstoke: Palgrave Macmillan.

Payne, G., and Abbott, P. (eds) (1990) *The Social Mobility of Women: Beyond Male Mobility Models*. Bristol: Falmer Press.

Peach, C. (1996) 'Black-Caribbeans: class, gender and geography', in C. Peach (ed.) *Ethnicity in the 1991 Census*, Vol. 2: *The Ethnic Minority Populations of Great Britain*. London: HMSO, pp. 25–43.

— (2005) 'Social integration and social mobility: segregation and intermarriage of the Caribbean population in Britain', in G. C. Loury, T. Modood and S. M. Teles (eds) *Ethnicity, Social Mobility and Public Policy: Comparing the US and the UK*. Cambridge: Cambridge University Press, pp. 178–203.

Peach, C., and Byron, M. (1994) 'Council house sales, residualisation and Afro-Caribbean tenants', *Journal of Social Policy*, 23: 363–83.

Peach, C., and Rossiter, D. (1996) 'Level and nature of spatial concentration and segregation of minority ethnic populations in Great Britain, 1991', in P. Ratcliffe (ed.) *Ethnicity in the 1991 Census*,

Vol. 3: *Social Geography and Ethnicity in Britain: Geographical Spread, Spatial Concentration and Internal Migration*. London: HMSO, pp. 111–34.

Pfenning, A., and Bahle, T. (2001) *Families and Family Policies in Europe: Comparative Perspectives*. Frankfurt: Peter Lang.

Phillips, D. (1997) 'The housing position of ethnic minority group home owners', in V. Karn (ed.) *Ethnicity in the 1991 Census*, Vol. 4: *Employment, Education and Housing among the Ethnic Minority Populations of Britain*. London: HMSO, pp. 170–88.

— (1998) 'Black minority ethnic concentration, segregation and dispersal in Britain', *Urban Studies*, 35(10): 1681–702.

Phillipson, C., Ahmed, N., and Latimer, J. (2003) *Women in Transition: A Study of the Experiences of Bangladeshi Women Living in Tower Hamlets*. Bristol: Policy Press.

Philo, C. (1995) *Off the Map: The Social Geography of Poverty in the UK*. London: Child Poverty Action Group.

Phinney, J. S. (1990) 'Ethnic identity in adolescents and adults: review of research', *Psychological Bulletin*, 108(3): 499–514.

Phipps, S. A., and Burton, P. S. (1998) 'What's mine is yours? The influence of male and female incomes on patterns of household expenditure', *Economica*, 65(260): 599–613.

Phoenix, A. and Pattynama, P. (2006) 'Intersectionality', *European Journal of Women's Studies*, 13(3): 187–192.

Piachaud, D. (1981) 'Peter Townsend and the Holy Grail', *New Society*, September: 421.

— (1987) 'Problems in the definition and measurement of poverty', *Journal of Social Policy*, 16(2): 147–64.

Platt, L. (2005a) 'The intergenerational social mobility of minority ethnic groups', *Sociology*, 39(3): 445–61.

— (2005b) *Migration and Social Mobility: The Life Chances of Britain's Minority Ethnic Communities*. Bristol: Policy Press.

— (2005c) *Discovering Child Poverty: The Creation of a Policy Agenda*. Bristol: Policy Press.

— (2006) *Pay Gaps: The Position of Ethnic Minority Men and Women*. Manchester: Equal Opportunities Commission.

— (2007a) 'Child poverty and ethnicity in the UK: the role and limitations of policy', *European Societies*, 9(2): 175–99.

— (2007b) 'Making education count: the effects of ethnicity and qualifications on intergenerational social class mobility', *Sociological Review*, 55(3): 485–508.

— (2007c) *Poverty and Ethnicity in the UK*. Bristol: Policy Press.

— (2009a) *Ethnicity and Child Poverty*. Leeds: Department for Work and Pensions.

— (2009b) *Ethnicity and Family: Relationships within and between Ethnic Groups: An Analysis using the Labour Force Survey*. London: Equality and Human Rights Commission; www.equalityhumanrights.com/en/publicationsandresources/Documents/Race/Ethnicity_and_family_report.pdf.

— (2009c) 'Social participation, social isolation and ethnicity', *Sociological Review*, 57(4): 670–702.

Platt, L., and Thompson, P. (2007) 'The role of family background and social capital in the social mobility of migrant ethnic minorities', in R. Edwards, J. Franklin and J. Holland (eds) *Assessing Social Capital: Concept, Policy and Practice*. Newcastle: Cambridge Scholars Press.

Plewis, I. (2009) *Ethnic Group Differences in Educational Attainments and Progress Revisited*, CCSR Working Paper 2009-01. University of Manchester, Centre for Census and Survey Research.

Polavieja, J. G. (2005) 'Task specificity and the gender wage gap', *European Sociological Review*, 21(2): 165–81.

— (2009) 'Domestic supply, job-specialisation and sex-differences in pay', *Social Indicators Research*, 93(3): 587–605.

Polavieja, J. G., and Platt, L. (2010) *Girls Like Pink: Explaining Sex-Typed Occupational Aspirations amongst Young Children*. Madrid: IMDEA.

Portes, A., Fernández-Kelly, P., and Haller, W. (2005) 'Segmented assimilation on the ground: the new second generation in early adulthood', *Ethnic and Racial Studies*, 28(6): 1000–40.

Prandy, K. (1990) 'The revised Cambridge scale of occupations', *Sociology*, 24: 629–55.

— (1999) 'Class, stratification and inequalities in health: a comparison of the Registrar General's Social Classes and the Cambridge Scale', *Sociology of Health & Illness*, 21(4): 466–84.

Prandy, K., and Bottero, W. (1998) 'The use of marriage data to measure the social order in nineteenth century Britain', *Sociological Research Online*, 3(1).

Priestley, M. (2003) *Disability: A Life Course Approach*. Cambridge: Polity.

Purdam, K., Afkhami, R., Crockett, A., and Olsen, W. (2007) 'Religion in the UK: an overview of equality statistics and evidence gaps', *Journal of Contemporary Religion*, 22(2): 147–68.

Putnam, R. D. (1995) 'Bowling alone: America's declining social capital', *Journal of Democracy*, 61(1): 65–78.

— (2000) *Bowling Alone: The Collapse and Revival of American Community*. New York: Simon & Schuster.

Ratcliffe, P. (1996) 'Introduction: social geography and ethnicity: a theoretical, conceptual and substantive overview', in P. Ratcliffe (ed.) *Ethnicity in the 1991 Census*, Vol. 3: *Social Geography and Ethnicity in Britain: Geographical Spread, Spatial Concentration and Internal Migration*. London: HMSO, pp. 1–22.

— (1997) '"Race", ethnicity and housing differentials in Britain', in V. Karn (ed.) *Ethnicity in the 1991 Census*, Vol. 4: *Employment, Education and Housing Among the Ethnic Minority Populations of Britain*. London: HMSO, pp. 130–46.

Rawls, J. (1971) *A Theory of Justice*. Cambridge, MA: Harvard University Press.

Reay, D. (2005) 'Beyond consciousness? The psychic landscape of social class', *Sociology*, 39(5): 911–28.

Reay, D., Davies, J., David, M., and Ball, S. J. (2001) 'Choices of degree or degrees of choice? Class, "race", and the higher education choice process', *Sociology*, 35(4): 855–74.

Reay, D., Crozier, G., and Clayton, J. (2009) '"Strangers in paradise"? Working-class students in elite universities', *Sociology*, 46(3): 1103–21.

Rex, J., and Moore, R. (1967) *Race, Community and Conflict: A Study of Sparkbrook*. Oxford: Oxford University Press.

Reynolds, T. (2005) *Caribbean Mothers: Identity and Experience in the UK*. London: Tufnell Press.

Rigg, J., and Sefton, T. (2006) 'Income dynamics and the life cycle', *Journal of Social Policy*, 35: 411–35.

Ringen, S. (1987) 'Direct and indirect measures of poverty', *Journal of Social Policy*, 17(3): 351–65.

Roberts, K. (2001) *Class in Modern Britain*. Basingstoke: Palgrave.

Robinson, V. (1996) 'The Indians: onward and upward', in C. Peach (ed.) *Ethnicity in the 1991 Census*, Vol. 2: *The Ethnic Minority Populations of Great Britain*. London: HMSO, pp. 95–120.

Robson, B. (1988) *Those Inner Cities: Reconciling the Social and Economic Aims of Urban Policy*. Oxford: Clarendon Press.

Rose, D., and Pevalin, D. J. (2001) *The National Statistics Socio-Economic Classification: Unifying Official and Sociological Approaches to the Conceptualisation and Measurement of Social Class*, ISER Working Paper no. 2001-4. University of Essex, Institute for Social and Economic Research.

Rothon, C., and Heath, A. (2003) 'Trends in racial prejudice', in A. Park et al. (eds) *British Social Attitudes: 20th Report*. London: Sage, pp. 189–214.

Roulstone, A., Gradwell, L., Price, J., and Child, L. (2003) *Thriving and Surviving at Work: Disabled People's Employment Strategies*. Bristol: Policy Press.

Rowlingson, K. (2006) 'Living poor to die rich or spending the kids' inheritance? Attitudes to assets and inheritance in later life', *Journal of Social Policy*, 35(2): 175–92.

Rowntree, B. S. (1902) *Poverty: A Study of Town Life*. 2nd edn, London: Macmillan.

— (1941) *Poverty and Progress: A Second Social Survey of York*. London: Longmans, Green.

Rubery, J. (1998) *Equal Pay in Europe*. Basingstoke: Macmillan.

Runciman, W. G. ([1966] 1972) *Relative Deprivation and Social Justice: A Study of Attitudes to Social Inequality in Twentieth-Century England*. Harmondsworth: Penguin.

Salway, S., Platt, L., Chowbey, P., Harriss, K., and Bayliss, E. (2007a) *Long-Term Ill Health, Poverty and Ethnicity*. Bristol: Policy Press.

Salway, S., Platt, L., Harriss, K., and Chowbey, P. (2007b) 'Chronic illness and sickness-related benefits: exploring ethnic differences and similarities in access', *Sociology of Health & Illness*, 29(6): 907–30.

Saunders, P. (1995) 'Might Britain be a meritocracy?', *Sociology*, 29(1): 23–41.

Savage, M., and Egerton, M. (1997) 'Social mobility, individual ability and the inheritance of class inequality', *Sociology*, 31(4): 645–72.

Savage, M., Bagnall, G., and Longhurst, B. (2001) 'Ordinary, ambivalent and defensive: class identities in the northwest of England', *Sociology*, 35(4): 875–92.

Sayer, A. (2005) 'Class, moral worth and recognition', *Sociology*, 39(5): 947–63.

Scarman, L. (1981) *The Brixton Disorders 10–12 April 1981: Report of an Enquiry*, Cmnd 8427. London: HMSO.

Schermerhorn, R. A. (1978) *Comparative Ethnic Relations: A Framework for Theory and Research*. Chicago: University of Chicago Press.

Schumacher, E. J., and Baldwin, M. L. (2000) *The Americans with Disabilities Act and the Labor Market Experience of Workers with Disabilities: Evidence from the SIPP*, Northwestern University/University of Chicago Joint Center for Poverty Research Working Paper no. 178. Chicago: Harris Graduate School of Public Policy Studies.

Schuman, H., and Presser, S. (1996) *Questions and Answers in Attitude Surveys*. Thousand Oaks, CA: Sage.

Scott, J. (1996) *Stratification and Power: Structures of class, status and command*. Oxford: Blackwell.

Sen, A. (1983) 'Poor, relatively speaking', *Oxford Economic Papers*, 35: 153–69.

— (1987) *The Standard of Living: the Tanner Lectures, Clare Hall, Cambridge, 1985*, ed. G. Hawthorn. Cambridge: Cambridge University Press.

— (1992) *Inequality Re-examined*. Oxford: Oxford University Press.

Shakespeare, T., and Watson, N. (2002) 'The social model of disability: an outdated ideology?', *Research in Social Science and Disability*, 2: 9–28.

Sharpe, S. (1976) *'Just Like a Girl': How Girls Learn to be Women*. Harmondsworth: Penguin.

Shavit, Y., Arum, R., and Gamoran, A. (eds) (2007) *Stratification in Higher Education: A Comparative Study*. Stanford, CA: Stanford University Press.

Shields, M. A., and Wheatley Price, S. (1998) 'The earnings of male immigrants in England: evidence from the quarterly LFS', *Applied Economics*, 30: 1157–68.

— (2001) 'Language fluency and immigrant employment prospects: evidence from Britain's ethnic minorities', *Applied Economics Letters*, 8: 741–5.

Shiner, M., and Modood, T. (2002) 'Help or hindrance? Higher education and the route to ethnic equality', *British Journal of Sociology of Education*, 23(2): 209–32.

Simpson, L. (2005) 'On the measurement and meaning of residential segregation: a reply to Johnston, Poulsen and Forrest', *Urban Studies*, 42(7): 1229–30.

Simpson, L., and Finney, N. (2008) 'Internal migration and ethnic groups: evidence for Britain from the 2001 Census', *Population, Space and Place*, 14: 63–83.

Skeggs, B. (1997) *Formations of Class and Gender: Becoming Respectable*. London: Sage.

Smith, A. ([1776] 1976) *The Wealth of Nations*. Chicago: University of Chicago Press.

Smith, A. D. (1991) *National Identity*. Harmondsworth: Penguin.

Smith, D. E. (2000) 'Schooling for inequality', *Signs*, 25: 1147–51.

Smith, D. J. (1977) *Racial Disadvantage in Britain: The PEP Report*. Harmondsworth: Penguin.

Smith, N., and Middleton, S. (2007) *A Review of Poverty Dynamics Research in the UK*. York: Joseph Rowntree Foundation.

Smith, S. (1989) *The Politics of 'Race' and Residence*. Cambridge: Polity.

Social Exclusion Unit (2001) *Preventing Social Exclusion*. London: TSO.

Somerville, P., and Steele, A. (2002) *'Race', Housing and Social Exclusion*. London: Jessica Kingsley.

Song, M. (2010a) 'Does "race" matter? A study of "mixed race" siblings' identifications', *Sociological Review*, 58(2): 265–85.

— (2010b) 'Is there "a" mixed race group in Britain? The diversity of multiracial identification and experience', *Critical Social Policy*, 30(3): 337–58.

Spender, D. (1982) *Invisible Women: The Schooling Scandal*. London: Women's Press.

Stanworth, M. (1983) *Gender and Schooling: A Study of Sexual Divisions in the Classroom*. London: Hutchinson.

Swift, A. (2003) 'Seizing the opportunity: the influence of preferences and aspirations on social immobility', *New Economy*, 10(4): 208–12.

Szreter, S. (1996) *Fertility, Class and Gender in Britain, 1860–1940*. Cambridge: Cambridge University Press.

Tackey, N. D., Casebourne, J., Aston, J., Ritchie, H., Sinclair, A., Tyers, C., Hurstfield, J., Willison, R., and Page, R. (2006) *Barriers to Employment for Pakistanis and Bangladeshis in Britain*. Leeds: Department for Work and Pensions.

Temkin, L. S. (1993) *Inequality*. Oxford: Oxford University Press.

Thapar-Bjorkert, S., and Sanghera, G. (2010) 'Social capital, educational aspirations and young Pakistani Muslim men and women in Bradford, West Yorkshire', *Sociological Review*, 58(2): 244–64.

Thomas, J. M. (1998) 'Who feels it knows it: work attitudes and excess non-white unemployment in the UK', *Ethnic and Racial Studies*, 21: 138–50.

Tizard, B., and Phoenix, A. (1995) 'The identity of mixed parentage adolescents', *Journal of Child Psychology and Psychiatry*, 36(8): 1399–410.

Townsend, P. (1979) *Poverty in the United Kingdom: A Survey of Household Resources and Standards of Living*. Harmondsworth: Penguin.

Townsend, P. D., and Davidson, N. (eds) (1982) *Inequalities in Health: The Black Report*. Harmondsworth: Penguin.

UNICEF (2000) *A League Table of Child Poverty in Rich Nations*. Florence: UNICEF Innocenti Research Centre.

— (2007) *Child Poverty in Perspective: An Overview of Child Well-Being in Rich Countries*. Florence: UNICEF Innocenti Research Centre.

United Nations Department of Economic and Social Affairs Population Division (2007) *World Population Prospects: The 2006 Revision: Highlights*, Working Paper no. ESA/P/WP.202. New York: United Nations.

Veit-Wilson, J. (1986a) 'Paradigms of poverty: a reply to Peter Townsend and Hugh McLachlan', *Journal of Social Policy*, 15(4): 503–7.

— (1986b) 'Paradigms of poverty: a rehabilitation of B. S. Rowntree', *Journal of Social Policy*, 15(1): 69–99.

— (1987) 'Consensual approaches to poverty lines and social security', *Journal of Social Policy*, 16(2): 183–211.

Walby, S. (1990) *Theorizing Patriarchy*. Oxford: Blackwell.

Walker, R. (1987) 'Consensual approaches to the definition of poverty: towards an alternative methodology', *Journal of Social Policy*, 16(2): 213–26.

— (ed.) (1999) *Ending Child Poverty: Popular Welfare for the 21st Century?* Bristol: Policy Press.

Walker, R., and Ashworth, K. (1994) *Poverty Dynamics: Issues and Examples*. Aldershot: Avebury.

Warren, T., Rowlingson, K., and Whyley, C. (2001) 'Female finances: gender wage gaps and gender asset gaps', *Work, Employment and Society*, 15(3): 465–88.

Weber, M. (1978) *Economy and Society*, ed. G. Roth and C. Wittich. Berkeley: University of California Press.

Webster, D. (2000) 'The geographical concentration of labour-market disadvantage', *Oxford Review of Economic Policy*, 16: 114–28.

Weiner, G., Arnot, M., and David, M. (1997) 'Is the future female? Female success, male disadvantage, and challenging gender patterns in education', in A. H. Halsey, H. Lauder, P. Brown and A. S. Wells (eds) *Education: Culture, Economy, and Society*. Oxford: Oxford University Press, pp. 620–30.

Welshman, J. (2006) *Underclass: A History of the Excluded, 1880–2000*. London: Continuum.

Westergaard, J. (1995) *Who Gets What? The Hardening of Class Inequality in the Late 20th Century*. Cambridge: Polity.

Wilkinson, R. G. (1996) *Unhealthy Societies: The Afflictions of Inequality*. London: Routledge.

Wilkinson, R. G., and Pickett, K. E. (2007) 'The problems of relative deprivation: why some societies do better than others', *Social Science & Medicine*, 65(9): 1965.

— (2009) *The Spirit Level: Why Equality is Better For Everyone*. London: Allen Lane.

Willis, P. (1977) *Learning to Labour: How Working Class Kids Get Working Class Jobs*. Farnborough: Saxon House.

Wilson, D., Burgess, S., and Briggs, A. (2005) *The Dynamics of School Attainment of England's Ethnic Minorities*, CMPO Working Paper no.05/130. University of Bristol, Centre for Market and Public Organization.

Wilson, W. J. (1978) *The Declining Significance of Race: Blacks and Changing American Institutions*. Chicago: University of Chicago Press.

— (1987) *The Truly Disadvantaged: The Inner City, the Underclass, and Public Policy*. Chicago: University of Chicago Press.

Wimmer, A. (2008) 'The making and unmaking of ethnic boundaries: a multilevel process theory', *American Journal of Sociology*, 113(4): 970–1022.

Wollstonecraft, M. ([1792] 1992) *A Vindication of the Rights of Woman*. Harmondsworth: Penguin.

Women and Equality Unit (2005) *Individual Income, 1996/97–2003/04*. London: Department of Trade and Industry.

Wood, M., Hales, J., Purdon, S., Sejersen, T., and Hayllar, O. (2009) *A Test for Racial Discrimination in Recruitment Practice in British Cities*. Department for Work and Pensions Research Report no. 607. Leeds: Corporate Document Services.

Young, M. (1958) *The Rise of the Meritocracy, 1870–2033: An Essay on Education and Equality*. Harmondsworth: Penguin.

Zetter, R., Griffiths, D., Sigona, N., Flynn, D., Pasha, T., and Beynon, R. (2006) *Immigration, Social Cohesion and Social Capital: What Are the Links?* York: Joseph Rowntree Foundation.

Zhou, M. (2005) 'Ethnicity as social capital: community-based institutions and embedded networks of social relations', in G. C. Loury, T. Modood and S. M. Teles (eds) *Ethnicity, Social Mobility and Public Policy: Comparing the US and the UK*. Cambridge: Cambridge University Press, pp. 131–59.

Zhou, M., and Xiong, Y. S. (2005) 'The multifaceted American experiences of Asian immigrants: lessons for segmented assimilation', *Ethnic and Racial Studies*, 28(6): 1119–52.

Index